the terry lectures
EXORCISM AND ENLIGHTENMENT

OTHER VOLUMES IN THE TERRY LECTURE SERIES AVAILABLE FROM YALE UNIVERSITY PRESS

The Courage to Be Paul Tillich
Psychoanalysis and Religion Erich Fromm
Becoming Gordon W. Allport
A Common Faith John Dewey
Education at the Crossroads Jacques Maritain
Psychology and Religion Carl G. Jung
Freud and Philosophy Paul Ricoeur
Freud and the Problem of God Hans Küng
Master Control Genes in Development and Evolution Walter J. Gehring
Belief in God in an Age of Science John Polkinghorne
Israelis and the Jewish Tradition David Hartman
The Empirical Stance Bas C. van Fraassen
One World Peter Singer

H. C. ERIK MIDELFORT

Exorcism *and* Enlightenment

*Johann Joseph Gassner and the Demons of
Eighteenth-Century Germany*

YALE UNIVERSITY PRESS · NEW HAVEN AND LONDON

Published with assistance from the Louis Stern Memorial Fund.

Copyright © 2005 by Yale University. All rights reserved. This book may not be reproduced, in whole or in part, including illustrations, in any form (beyond that copying permitted by Sections 107 and 108 of the U.S. Copyright Law and except by reviewers for the public press), without written permission from the publishers.

Designed by Nancy Ovedovitz and set in Janson OS type by Keystone Typesetting, Inc. Printed in the United States of America by Sheridan Books.

Library of Congress Cataloging-in-Publication Data
Midelfort, H. C. Erik.
Exorcism and Enlightenment : Johann Joseph Gassner and the demons of eighteenth-century Germany / H. C. Erik Midelfort.
    p.   cm. — (The Terry lectures)
Includes bibliographical references (p.) and index.
ISBN 0-300-10669-6 (cloth : alk. paper)
1. Gassner Johann Joseph, 1727–1779. 2. Exorcism—Germany—History—18th century. 3. Faith and reason—Christianity—History of doctrines—18th century. 4. Enlightenment—Germany. I. Title. II. Series.
BX2340.M53 2005
235′.4′094309033—dc22   2004065905

A catalogue record for this book is available from the British Library.

The paper in this book meets the guidelines for permanence and durability of the Committee on Production Guidelines for Book Longevity of the Council on Library Resources.

10 9 8 7 6 5 4 3 2 1

This book is for Anne

**THE DWIGHT HARRINGTON TERRY FOUNDATION LECTURES
ON RELIGION IN THE LIGHT OF SCIENCE AND PHILOSOPHY**

The deed of gift declares that "the object of this foundation is not the promotion of scientific investigation and discovery, but rather the assimilation and interpretation of that which has been or shall be hereafter discovered, and its application to human welfare, especially by the building of the truths of science and philosophy into the structure of a broadened and purified religion. The founder believes that such a religion will greatly stimulate intelligent effort for the improvement of human conditions and the advancement of the race in strength and excellence of character. To this end it is desired that a series of lectures be given by men eminent in their respective departments, on ethics, the history of civilization and religion, biblical research, all sciences and branches of knowledge which have an important bearing on the subject, all the great laws of nature, especially of evolution . . . also such interpretations of literature and sociology as are in accord with the spirit of this foundation, to the end that the Christian spirit may be nurtured in the fullest light of the world's knowledge and that mankind may be helped to attain its highest possible welfare and happiness upon this earth." The present work constitutes the latest volume published on this foundation.

CONTENTS

Acknowledgments   xi

Introduction   1

1 The Experience of Demons   11

2 A Niche in the Incubator: Ecclesiastical Politics and the Empire   32

3 Healing   59

4 Interpretation   87

5 Conversation and Ridicule   118

Epilogue   143

Notes   149

Index   211

ACKNOWLEDGMENTS

This book had its origin in the Dwight H. Terry Lectures delivered at Yale University during the spring semester of 2003 before a lively audience. I should like to express here my profound gratitude for having the chance to live once more at Yale, to use the magnificent library collections, and to enjoy the cordial collegiality that goes with living in a residential college. The Terry Committee served as my introduction to several of the congenial communities of scholars who populate Yale, and I would like to thank specifically committee members Harry Attridge, Michael Della Rocca, Leo Hickey, Dale Martin, Bill Summers, and especially Dianne Witte, who managed the many details of my lectureship with grace and efficiency. My sojourn would also have been much the poorer without the help and constant friendship of Carlos Eire, who commented frequently on my evolving thoughts about Johann Joseph Gassner and reassured me that concentrating on such an apparently minor and largely forgotten figure would prove productive. I would be sadly remiss, too, if I did not acknowledge my debt to the department of history at Yale for granting me an office and administrative support. At Ezra Stiles College, Master Traugott Lawler and his wife Peggy went out of their way to include me in the life of the college and provided me with chances to explain myself to colleagues. They helped make life for my wife, Anne, and me most pleasant. The most extraordinary social experience at Yale, however, came at the hands of Professors Nelson Donegan of neuroscience and Howard Stern of the German department, who together hosted a Friday afternoon "moderately cheerful" *Stammtisch* that surpassed all expectations of affability, learned conversation, and friendship.

This project, however, began ten years ago with the friendship of scholars who helped me find my way into the forbidding world of the late eighteenth century. Wolfgang Behringer was perhaps the first to encourage me to take on Gassner, and I only regret that this book does not settle or even try to settle many of the intriguing questions he posed as I began my research. Elmar Schallert, the diocesan archivist of Feldkirch, was helpful and friendly when I first turned up looking for Gassneriana. He gave me perhaps my first introduction to the surviving manuscript remains of the exorcist and helped me to understand the place and purpose of Gassner's diaries. In Neuenstein I was lucky enough to have the help of Dr. Peter Schiffer, who not only knew what I might be looking for but was willing to photocopy most of it.

In Augsburg I was fortunate to fall in with another remarkable band of congenial scholars, chief of whom were the members of the Thursday Stammtisch comprising scholars and administrators of the local archives and libraries. I should thank by name Hans-Jörg Künast, Marjorie Elizabeth Plummer, and Georg Feuerer. At the Augsburg Staats- und Stadtbibliothek, I was graciously aided by Wolfgang Mayer and Eckehart Nowak, who provided me many courtesies. Without their help, my studies would have taken much longer and would surely have been even more incomplete than they are. This is also the place to thank Klaus Graf for his tireless work for the web list "Hexenforschung," through which I have discovered many researchers in related fields and countless bibliographical leads. Dr. Burkhard Peter kindly allowed me to read several papers on Gassner and psychotherapy before they were published, and Professor Gerhard Ammerer provided me welcome assistance in locating articles he had published in obscure locations. Hermann Ehmer and Martin Brecht were also helpful on specific points of detail. Librarians at the state libraries of Bregenz, Feldkirch, Bamberg, Munich, and Stuttgart have always been willing to help me on short notice. The notes record my specific debts, but I should also like to thank generally the friendly and helpful archivists of state, ecclesiastical, and local archives, who did so much to recover diaries, letters, notes, reactions, and reports concerning Gassner, as well as the postmortem inquest recording his few worldly possessions at the time of his death. These repositories include the diocesan archive of Feldkirch, the princely archive of

ACKNOWLEDGMENTS

Hohenlohe in Neuenstein, the episcopal Ordinariatsarchiv in Regensburg, the Bavarian Hauptstaatsarchiv in Munich, and the episcopal archive of Augsburg.

Near the end of my researches, I spent a semester at Oxford University enjoying the hospitality of Wolfson College. I'm deeply grateful to the many libraries of Oxford for providing a perfect environment in which to read and write. I must specifically thank Lyndal Roper, Robin Briggs, Robert Evans, and Thomas Biskup for their advice and assistance. Various versions of the chapters of this book have been delivered as lectures at the universities of Oxford, Cambridge, and London, as well as at Tübingen University and the Historisches Kolleg in Munich. At Cambridge I learned much in a very short time from Simon Schaffer. At the Institute of Historical Research in London I gained immeasurably from David Wootton. I am grateful to all of these institutions and to my alert listeners, from whom I have learned much. Colleagues at the University of Virginia, moreover, have long had to listen to me go on about an obscure eighteenth-century exorcist. They have done much more than tolerate this tedious behavior, and I owe a great debt to Alon Confino, Ted Lendon, Duane Osheim, and Anne Jacobson Schutte. Sophie Rosenfeld subjected the entire manuscript to a learned and searching critique from which I have gratefully profited. Two anonymous readers for Yale University Press also made several shrewd criticisms, to which I have tried to respond. It was also a proud moment when my daughter Lucy read part of the manuscript and made useful suggestions. Most of all, I am grateful to Anne McKeithen, who has repeatedly rearranged her life and work in order to help me. She has accompanied me to strange towns in strange lands, has cheered me up when I occasionally concluded that this project was going nowhere, and has scrutinized every word of this book more than once, appraising my conclusions and my prose with a humane and critical eye. I might have written a book without her, but it would not have been so good, and the process would not have been so much fun. Thank you, Anne.

INTRODUCTION

In December of 1774 wonders were reported in the little Franconian town of Ellwangen, situated in the broad, pleasant valley of the Jagst River northeast of Stuttgart. The town was the proud seat of the imperial prince provost of Ellwangen and his high noble canons, and a refuge for the embattled former members of the Jesuit Order. Two centuries earlier some of Germany's fiercest witchcraft trials had taken place in Ellwangen, and now the devil seemed to be on the rampage again. Beneath her gray stone walls, in the imposing castle and in a house exempt from the jurisdiction of the bishop of Augsburg, a short, balding, rotund Catholic priest created a sensation by exorcising countless epileptics, the crippled, and even the blind. On the morning of December 21, one supplicant was a sturdy rustic who suffered from "St. Vitus' dance," the strange ailment that caused its afflicted to leap and twitch uncontrollably. We do not know what St. Vitus' dance actually was, and most cases had disappeared by the sixteenth century, but perhaps the condition lingered on in the region around Ellwangen, because the imposing Romanesque church of Ellwangen was dedicated to St. Vitus. An excited crowd had gathered to watch the proceedings, including noblemen and visitors from distant Munich. Astonishingly, the priest did not immediately summon forth the demons afflicting the man; instead, with solemn imprecations he bade demons to do their worst. At his command the demons responded. The farmer began suddenly dancing and snapping his fingers. He hopped round the room three times, making some of the assembled observers giggle. A hostile witness declared that he jigged about as if he were in a tavern. When this had gone on for a time, however, the priest ordered the demons to give the poor man an attack of epilepsy (*fallende Sucht*). Suddenly the fellow collapsed on the floor, flailing and thrashing, hurling himself about and "bellowing like an ox." Then with one Latin word—*cesset*, "let it cease"—the exorcist made it all stop.[1] Only then did the priest proceed to a full canonical exorcism. One skeptical witness from Munich was astonished to see that this piece of religious theater was taken seriously by almost all of those assembled. He laughed at such antics and declared that they were flatly incredible, but he could not deny that the peasant had acted as if possessed by demons and that they seemed to have relaxed their grip on the man as soon as the priest ordered them to do so.

This peasant was not an isolated example. Such episodes were repeated countless times in different places, and the reports by both credulous and hostile witnesses multiplied as southern Germany experienced a full-fledged religious revival surrounding the figure of Father Johann Joseph Gassner, a now little-remembered exorcist from the Vorarlberg in the mountains of far western Austria. His story is full of surprises, not least for those like the incredulous witness in Ellwangen, who refused to recognize that in the controversy between religion and reason in the late eighteenth century most of the best empirical evidence lay on the side of the exorcists.

Slowly, slowly we are learning that the eighteenth century was more than an age of reason. Religious thinkers and believers did not simply evaporate under the brilliant illumination of the self-anointed representatives of Enlightenment; instead they often sturdily resisted the trivializing voices of advanced criticism and crackling anticlericalism. It would also be wrong to assume that religious thinkers merely joined in reaction to the "progressive" forces of the age.[2] In this book we will see that the chief scientific ideas that competed with the religious notion of demonic possession were hardly secure. This is the reason the story of Johann Joseph Gassner (1727–1779) came to fascinate me. I was amazed to discover that he and his enthusiastic supporters often marshaled evidence and arguments that seemed at least as persuasive as those of the Enlightenment. Dr. Franz Anton Mesmer (1734–1815), for example, claimed that he had successfully explained Gassner's exorcisms by invoking his newly discovered force of "animal magnetism," but within a few years such explanations looked even less credible than those that depended upon demons. In five chapters I will explore, first, the reasons why people of the late eighteenth century continued to use demons as a tool with which to understand and explain their experiences. In subsequent chapters I will concentrate on the imperial politics that first guaranteed Gassner a hearing and then shut him down (chapter 2); the cures that Gassner achieved (chapter 3); the learned (and sometimes not so learned) debate over Jesus' exorcisms (chapter 4); and the remarkable contest concerning Gassner that convulsed almost all of Germany, a controversy that helped to define the nature of Enlightened debate (chapter 5).

Critics of Gassner often claimed that his exorcisms achieved their effects by "sympathy" or by suggestion (or what the Germans called *Einbildung*). We may see in this interpretation an early definition of the "placebo response," but unfortunately these critics were usually arguing by unsubstantiated assertion rather than relying on any evidence. Indeed, as we will see in the chapter on healing, Johann Joseph Gassner had bushel baskets of careful eyewitness testimony to the effectiveness of his healing rituals. In accord with the best scientific standards of his day, his sympathetic witnesses included noblemen and sober physicians.

Enlightened biblical commentators tried to show that the stories of Jesus' supposedly powerful exorcisms had been badly misunderstood for centuries and rested on nothing more than Jewish superstition and the errors of translators. But here, too, closer scrutiny shows that the "neologist" biblical critics were usually asserting what they could not easily prove, and in so doing they were imputing to Scripture meanings that we now regard as hopelessly anachronistic. Here again the backers of traditional religion did not slink away in helpless disgrace (see chapter 4). As Jeffrey Freedman has recently pointed out, in their controversies with religious conservatives, Enlightened observers often had such heavy axes to grind, such a priori assumptions that supernatural events were simply impossible, that they could not see that their own prejudices were getting in the way of a more sober evaluation of what evidence they had.[3] Indeed, one could conclude polemically that the Enlightened theologians were trying to perform an exorcism of their own, trying to banish the demons of baroque culture by renaming them as superstition and enthusiasm, thus using their own verbal rituals and gestures of derision.

So when we study the brief period of Father Gassner's celebrity and his final defeat, we are not looking at a simple victory for the Enlightenment. The political forces that ultimately called a halt to Gassner's exorcisms were at least as upset at his evident success and the public tumult he was provoking as they were incensed at his unauthorized extension of exorcism to thousands of cases that the Roman Church would not at that time have approved (see chapter 2).

Even the noisy debate that erupted around Gassner was not a clear-cut victory for the forces of reason over the die-hard partisans of "baroque Catholicism." Participants in the North German Enlightenment and their South German imitators often engaged in raucous, cruel, and demeaning ridicule rather than in the calmer conversation of sweet reason. The Gassner controversy, therefore, polarized without persuading and established a sadly familiar pattern for such arguments that we can observe right down to our own day (see chapter 5).

In all these ways exorcism and this specific exorcist brought out both the worst and the best from the Enlightened opponents of traditional demonology and Catholic ritual. In the struggle over Gassner and his cures we can get to know some of the wrinkled contours of late-eighteenth-century German politics and culture. In the process I think we can also glimpse the origins of problems that have not gone away.

It seems remarkable that an eighteenth-century Catholic exorcist should become the center of religious attention throughout much of southern Germany. Such excitements do not sit comfortably with our schoolbook version of the age. And yet thousands of desperate people, the blind, the halt, and the lame, made their way to visit Father Gassner, hoping that he would heal them of their infirmities by casting out demons. Countless observers came just to gawk. Many others found in Father Gassner welcome proof that traditional religion still had some fight left in it. For us, accustomed to think of the 1770s as the decade of the American Revolution and the flourishing of a trans-

INTRODUCTION

European Enlightenment, the celebrity of a German Catholic exorcist seems distinctly odd. Was this not the age of "the laws of nature and of nature's God"? Was this not the decade when French, German, and British philosophers reached the peak of their influence, an apogee marked by the publication of the last volumes of Diderot and d'Alembert's *Encyclopédie*, by the publication of Joseph Priestley's discovery of oxygen, Adam Smith's *Wealth of Nations*, and the first volumes of Edward Gibbon's *Decline and Fall of the Roman Empire*? Even if we concede that such examples of advanced thought were not to everyone's taste, we may also recall that the 1770s was a time of classic, hard-nosed realpolitik, that in 1772 the kingdoms of Prussia, Austria, and Russia began dismantling Poland by redistributing one-third of her lands and people among themselves. Meanwhile, for Roman Catholics the 1770s are perhaps most memorable for the suppression of the Jesuit Order in 1773, one of the surest signs that the Enlightenment was having a serious impact even on the Catholic Church. What was an exorcist doing attracting thousands of enthusiastic followers in the 1770s?

Gassner does not seem to fit our view of an Enlightened age. But he also seems to defy many other cultural trends of his day. For elite members of the Holy Roman Empire the 1770s marked a time when German culture was finally rejoining the vast concert of European culture and politics. After more than a century of seeming peculiarly backward, German writers and scholars began to celebrate their latest achievements. In 1775, for example, Maria Theresa of Austria abolished the judicial use of torture, thus declaring that her state would no longer inflict deliberate and excruciating pain in order to extract truth from those presumed guilty. The enlightened throughout the Holy Roman Empire applauded noisily. In 1772 Johann Kaspar Lavater of Zurich published the first edition of his remarkably successful *Essay on Physiognomy*, in which he tried to show that a person's character was visible in his facial features. He thus achieved an important new empirical and philosophical synthesis in the study of human nature. In 1774 Johann Wolfgang Goethe published his explosively best-selling *Sorrows of Young Werther*, prompting a wave of proto-Romantic suicides; in the same year Gotthold Ephraim Lessing published anonymously the first of Hermann Samuel Reimarus's sensational *Fragments*, challenging the biblical account of Jesus' resurrection and other miracles. And in 1775 Franz Anton Mesmer began to practice his newly invented healing art ("mesmerism") in southern Germany, well before he moved on to celebrity in Paris. None of these German events suggests the capacity for profound religious renewal coupled with a revival of demonic possession. The people who streamed to visit Father Gassner seem to have lived in a different time and place from the world of Goethe, Lessing, and Lavater, and far from the French Enlightenment and the American Revolution. Perhaps the 1770s were not one decade but several.

When we ignore the awkward realities and contradictions of this or any period, we shortchange the past. We shortchange ourselves as well. If we choose to remember only the "progressive" parts of history, the ones that readily "make sense" to us, we oversimplify the past and our own lives. We cultivate an artificially naive view of the world. I do not mean simply that two hundred years ago a decade could be blandly "the best of times and the worst of times," depending on where you were, but rather that the very act of singling out specific features (and calling them better or worse) always depends on who you are. The 1770s contained unexpected crosscurrents, and the strange fact is that several of the above-mentioned famous events and celebrated authors are connected to each other through Father Johann Joseph Gassner.

This book is far from the first study of Gassner and his movement. He has already found his way into three niches of scholarship, to which I am much indebted. I first learned of Gassner in the inspired pages of Henri Ellenberger, whose *Discovery of the Unconscious* places the dispute between Gassner and Mesmer at the very origins of modern, dynamic psychotherapy.[4] A second vein of scholarship that has discovered and raised Gassner to prominence is the history of witchcraft, a topic with which I have long been concerned. In the brilliant concluding pages of Wolfgang Behringer's history of witch hunting in Bavaria, Gassner appears as a late echo of the 1760s "Bavarian witchcraft war."[5] And thirdly, Father Gassner has not escaped the attentions of local and regional historians, who have combed the archives of South Germany and Austria in an effort to illuminate what one of them called the "regional prism of the past," the way in which local knowledge fleshes out our understanding of the larger historical patterns we learn about in school.[6] In this book I have not subordinated Gassner to some other story or confined him to a region but have concentrated my attention on his healing campaign, the religious revival it sparked, and the heated controversy he provoked. In this way I hope to introduce Father Gassner to a wider public, using him as a vehicle with which to explore the awkward and ungainly transition to secular modernity that was taking shape in those years.

I recognize that I am concentrating on an aspect of Catholic religious culture that was once considered hopelessly superstitious. Demonic possession has long been linked to the darker pages of European history, to the witch hunts of the sixteenth and seventeenth centuries and to the supposed misdiagnosis of hysteria or other psychosomatic conditions. The cardinal fact is, however, that long after witchcraft ceased to trouble the waking and sleeping hours of most Europeans, demons and the devil were thought to be independently active in this world. We live in a day when charismatic healing has revived within the Catholic Church and in certain Protestant churches too. Exorcism is now perhaps more widely and more openly practiced than it was one hundred years ago. And when we inquire into the supposed death of demonic possession in the eighteenth century, we discover that the story is far from straightforward. It was never easy to exclude the *possible* influence of demons unless one simply declared (for whatever reasons) that their effects were imaginary and impossible. Eighteenth-century physicians and commentators, especially in Catholic lands, were often far more cautious in this area than we might suppose. Objections to exorcism were as often rooted in an anti-ritualist Jansenist spirituality or in the fear of "enthusiasm" as in the new science or in a more dogmatic skepticism.[7]

The Gassner scandal was one of the biggest and noisiest of the late eighteenth century in Germany. In consequence we also learn

INTRODUCTION

something substantial about the growth of the "public sphere" during the Enlightenment. In an age when coffee houses, learned societies, and reading clubs were creating a polite space in which literate burghers and aristocrats could gather to discuss the issues of the day without the overt censorship and supervision of an absolute monarch, the cacophony of religious debate strikes an odd note. The historians of the public sphere have too often assumed that the spaces for public discussion were overwhelmingly Protestant, and Enlightened Protestant at that.[8] The Gassner debate was remarkable in part because at least as many partisans as opponents of Gassner took part. A decent respect to the opinions of both sides in this affair yields far greater insight into the world of the eighteenth century and into the peculiarities of the German Enlightenment than we would obtain by listening only to the self-proclaimed members of the "Party of Humanity." Some readers may feel that by paying so much attention to Gassner and the enemies of the Enlightenment, I reveal my own hidden sympathies with critics of that cultural movement. I would maintain, rather, that any Enlightenment worthy of the name should be able and willing to consider the arguments and evidence produced by its opponents without resorting to ridicule and intellectual subterfuge.

For some readers perhaps the biggest surprise will be that Gassner and his supporters could spend so much time and effort on the dangers represented by the devil and not collapse in a paroxysm of witch hunting. Aside from the abortive trial of Maria Anna Schwägelin, Gassner's healing campaign remained free of accusations and remarkably free even of suspicions of witchcraft. In this way the recent surge of scholarly interest in witchcraft actually serves us poorly, for it misleads us into expecting that cases of demonic possession would automatically devolve into accusations of witchcraft. This pattern was indeed common in the sixteenth and seventeenth centuries and did linger on into the eighteenth century. At the Premonstratensian cloister in Würzburg, beginning in 1744, for example, several nuns fell into what appeared to be demonic possession, and the subpriorin, Maria Renata Singer, was accused of being the witch who had provoked these outrages. For over three years exorcisms took place until finally the old woman broke under pressure and confessed that she was indeed guilty.[9] She was beheaded and burned in June of 1749 after a noisy dispute that pitted skeptical administrators of the bishop of Würzburg against the city council of Würzburg along with clerical allies from the Benedictine, Premonstratensian, and Jesuit Orders.[10]

There was, however, no necessary or inevitable connection between cases of demonic possession and witchcraft accusations. Throughout the Middle Ages, in fact, the "discernment of spirits" was a regular exercise in understanding religious experience and in differentiating between fraud and genuine experience, and among divine, angelic, and demonic visitations of various sorts.[11] Until the end of the Middle Ages priests and theologians who tested the spirits did not imagine that witches could induce demonic possession, and this notion represented one of the dangerous cultural inventions that we associate with the sixteenth and seventeenth centuries. Gassner himself was not entirely free of ideas about witches and bewitchment, as we will see, but he reached back to an earlier constellation of ideas by claiming that the devil could cause all manner of disorders. For him, demonic possession was not mainly caused or even prompted by witches (i.e., by human agents) and was not even characterized by supernatural or preternatural (strange) behavior. Indeed, the naturalizing impulse of the Enlightenment may have expressed itself in Gassner's assumption that demons imitated nature so perfectly that only an exorcism could detect them. Ironically, by separating demons and demonic possession from witchcraft, Father Gassner helped ensure their independent survival into the more skeptical nineteenth century and even down to today.

The story that unfolds here is therefore full of ironies and unexpected outcomes. We may not need to decide whether Gassner's healing rituals actually "worked," but two centuries ago it was striking how much empirical and well-attested evidence could be assembled in favor of the view that they did. We may not all accept the force of demons in our world today, but the Gassner debate highlights the difficulties biblical Christians had (and have) when they tried

INTRODUCTION

to reform or deny traditional biblical doctrines concerning the physical effects of unclean spirits and demons. If the Enlightenment as a project has generally advanced across this disputed terrain, it has often done so by mere assertion and self-satisfied ridicule rather than by looking closely at the debates that rattled the comfortable in 1775. Certain elements of this story still seem to me to have an uncanny power of unsettling our familiar assumptions about reason and experience.

one
THE EXPERIENCE OF DEMONS

L[ucius]: "So you're a free thinker and a skeptic. So what? If real and incontrovertible experiences show that Herr Gassner has made many sick persons well, then you just have to believe these experiences."
— [Christoph Heinrich Korn] *Gespräch im Reiche der Lebendigen*

Gassner was not the only one dabbling with the world of demons in the mid-1770s. In the South German, Upper Swabian town of Langenegg a poverty-stricken, guilt-ridden woman, Maria Anna Schwägelin, lay miserably confined in a spital for the poor. Orphaned early in life, she had abandoned her Catholic faith in order to marry a Protestant from Memmingen, but the marriage plans were broken off. She became increasingly convinced that in betraying her faith, she had left herself open to the assaults of the Evil One. Crippled, she began to wonder if her troubles were caused by the devil. A five-year-old child living in the poorhouse now began to seem demon possessed, but a local pastor decided that the child was actually bewitched. Schwägelin was beaten and soon confessed that she was indeed a witch. Transferred to the Imperial Abbey of Kempten for trial, she continued her confessions and was convicted in April of 1775. Historians have long believed that she was the last witch executed on German soil.[1] Recent research has shown that Maria Anna was not executed, however, and perhaps she should stand instead for how little we really understand the Germany of the 1770s.

During the months that Maria Anna Schwägelin was suffering in a poorhouse and confessing to her troubles with the devil, Father Gassner was touring Upper Swabia, demonstrating his abilities to detect and expel the devil with uncanny efficiency. In 1774 he published a pious little book on his methods right in Kempten, probably contributing to the renewed interest in demonic possession and witchcraft that got Maria Anna into such deep trouble. Born in 1727, Johann

Joseph Gassner came from Braz in the Vorarlberg (Austria), and had studied with the Jesuits in Prague and Innsbruck but did not become a member of their Society. Instead, he became a secular priest in 1750 and took up duties in Dalaas (1751–1758) and then in Klösterle, east of Feldkirch (1758–1774), at the foot of the immense Arlberg Mountains. Apparently from early in his pastoral career, Gassner had employed special blessings and cures; but as a result of a series of chronic ailments from 1752 to 1759 he developed a special technique for healing the headaches, fainting spells, and sudden weakness he experienced, especially whenever he was to preach or say Mass. He also sought out doctors and used their prescriptions, he wrote — but to no effect.[2] In the end, Gassner concluded that his illness came from the devil, and accordingly he invoked the Holy Name of Jesus and, in effect, exorcised himself. Using this method of cure, Gassner developed a regional reputation as a healer in the 1760s and learned to tell if the devil was at hand by practicing "test exorcisms," in which he would order the devil, if he was present, to perform certain acts. Sometimes he addressed the devil in Latin, a language that he assumed his parishioners would not understand even though the devil, as a great linguist, would have no trouble. If he found that a demon was in fact present, Gassner took his time, forcing the demon to move around in the patient's body and to manifest himself in various ways, until the patient too became persuaded of this startling truth: that he or she was possessed. This is a good example of how an idea could be mobilized, with practice, to become a full-fledged *experience*. One sometimes reads that Gassner believed all diseases to come from the devil, but this he specifically denied. In fact, his probative exorcisms make sense only if some illnesses and disabilities were of natural origin. By *practicing* on his patients, by helping them to experience their condition as demonic, Gassner was creating the first and crucial precondition for successful exorcism. It was a kind of negative spiritual exercise that paved the way for further experiences.[3] He allows us to see how our concepts and beliefs make certain experiences possible and others almost impossible.

This chapter explores the uses of the devil as a thinking tool, a way of understanding and shaping one's experience and religion. In proceeding in this manner one runs the risk of sounding antiquarian and anachronistic. Few reputable history professors take the devil seriously anymore. What sensible person still thinks that demonic possession might be real or that exorcism might help? "In these Enlightened days," we are told, and we tell ourselves, such ideas are rotting on the compost heap of outmoded and dangerous ideas, displaced by science, psychoanalysis, improved means of understanding Holy Scripture, and by the feeling that if we let the devil back into public discourse, we'll open the door to witchcraft trials and demonically obsessed nursery schools, cloisters, asylums, and hospitals all over again. But here let me make an important clarification. I am not here mounting a defense of the devil, who, if he exists, certainly does not need my defense. Rather, I am suggesting that *how* we talk about such matters matters. How we talk shapes how we think and what we can fully experience. When Gassner and his supplicants spoke of the devil, they were speaking of and simultaneously shaping their own experiences.

Gassner's Healing Career

Hundreds of patients came to Gassner for relief, but he did not treat them all. Only if he first got results with his "praecepta" or admonitions did he feel assured that a full-fledged "benedictio" (blessing) or exorcism would get rid of the devil for good. In a diary ("Diarium") that he kept for 1769 he recorded over two hundred cures and healing miracles, and in chapter 3 we will spend some time looking at these and other cases of healing. It is worth noticing, however, that Gassner did not think that he was dealing with classic instances of full-fledged demonic possession, for which the expected symptoms would have been amazing, supernatural, "wondrous." We find among those who sought him out virtually none of the classic signs of demoniac possession: no supernatural strength, no frothing at the mouth,[4] no unaccountable knowledge of distant events. They showed no mysterious knowledge of foreign languages they had never heard or learned, although Gassner did deploy this last symptom in one of his favorite test exorcisms, addressing the supposed demon in Latin and (often) getting a response that he assumed could only mean that the devil was present. Basically, Gassner employed blessings and exorcisms to treat illnesses that looked natural. It seems that this was one way in which the Enlightenment of the eighteenth century actually affected his practice: the devil no longer looked as if he were separate from the world of normal appearance. Instead, even sickness and chronic crippling that looked ordinary might come from the devil.

In the summer of 1774 Gassner's growing reputation jumped beyond the region of Vorarlberg, Tirol, and eastern Switzerland, where he had gained a sensational but merely regional reputation as a wonder worker. With permission from his bishop in Chur, Gassner made a remarkable tour of Upper Swabia, the region just north of the Lake of Constance.[5] In Wolfegg he healed Countess Maria Bernardina Truchsess von Wolfegg and Friedberg along with many others, then moving on to other tiny counties and abbeys of the region. He spent a month or more with the abbot of Salem and began to cure desperate patients by the score, often treating fifty to eighty a day. Altogether that summer he reckoned that he had treated three hundred nuns and eight thousand persons of all sorts.[6] By the fall of 1774 he was back in his parish of Klösterle, having been gone far longer than his original leave of absence allowed. But now he received a summons to the Princely Provostry (Fürstpropstei) of Ellwangen, where the blind Anton Ignaz von Fugger, bishop of Regensburg (reg. 1769–1787), was also the prince provost of Ellwangen. Although Gassner determined that the bishop's blindness was merely natural and therefore beyond priestly help, his stay in Ellwangen brought him to new levels of success. Thousands of persons seeking help jammed the streets of the little town and overburdened local hostelries. Gassner stayed there from November of 1774 to June of 1775, displaying his techniques to the faithful and to skeptics alike. Members of the higher and lower nobility joined the throngs of commoners in traveling to Ellwangen, hoping for help, but also looking for proof that traditional, unenlightened (perhaps we should call it "Counter-Enlightened") Catholicism still had some fight left in it during the years immediately following the papal dissolution of the Jesuit Order, a move that many German nobles had regarded as a craven concession to the worldly spirit of their age. Bishop Anton Ignaz rewarded Gassner by appointing him his court chaplain and making him a member of his "spiritual council" (*Geistlicher Rat*).

By now Gassner was famous throughout Germany and even in parts of France. But he was also attracting the attention of enlightened skeptics, including especially Don Ferdinand Sterzinger, a reforming Theatine from Munich, prominent member of the Bavarian Academy of Sciences, and one of the leaders of the Bavarian attack on witchcraft in the 1760s; and Johann Salomo Semler, professor of enlightened ("neologist," or cautiously historicizing) theology at Halle in northern (Prussian) Germany. On the other hand, a handful of ex-Jesuits now sprang to his defense and mounted a noisy campaign trumpeting empirical claims based on careful observation and scrupulous reporting. And certain Protestants in Germany and Switzerland were so impressed with these claims that they began to take an intense interest in Gassner. The most famous of these was Johann Kaspar Lavater, the renowned pastor and physiognomist of Zurich, about whom I will have more to say.

In the summer of 1775, Gassner moved with Bishop Anton Ignaz from Ellwangen eastward over one hundred miles to Regensburg, where he worked his wondrous cures until September, when he moved his operations northward to the Upper Palatinate (at Sulzbach and Amberg), but under increasingly intense scrutiny and in apparently decreasing numbers. One reason for moving around like this may have been to bring his healing powers to ever larger groups of sufferers, but these peripatetic missions also firmed up support for Gassner's movement among secular rulers, such as the Upper Palatinate, the court at Sulzbach, or the Bavarian administration in Amberg. As we will see in chapter 2, Gassner seemed for a time to be exploiting the weaknesses or peculiarities of the Holy Roman Empire with great success. Prudent men, however, urged greater caution. In November of 1775 the Emperor Joseph II ordered Gassner to leave

Regensburg; the archbishops of Prague and Salzburg issued pastoral letters warning of the misuse of exorcism; and in April of 1776 ecclesiastical enemies secured a condemnation from Pope Pius VI himself, which settled the matter, at least as far as his actual exorcisms went. Gassner was forced to take up simple parish duties in tiny Pondorf, several hours down the Danube from Regensburg, where he died in 1779. But in his heyday he had exorcised and blessed thousands and tens of thousands.[7]

The Problem of Evil

How shall we understand what Gassner was doing? He was treating a familiar series of miseries with a novel diagnosis, and as we will see, he was using a form of exorcism that was not entirely orthodox either. One way to regard his work is to see it as a response to the question of evil. Susan Neiman has recently pointed out that in the eighteenth century, following the challenge of Pierre Bayle, many European intellectuals had increasing trouble understanding how a gracious God could inflict massive misery on thousands or even millions of innocent sufferers. The Lisbon earthquake of 1 November 1755 had cost perhaps twenty to thirty thousand lives, and it seemed hard or at least hard-hearted to argue the Leibnizian or Wolffian line that this was all part of the "best of all possible worlds."[8] Some, like Voltaire, heaped ridicule upon the claim that the world always worked toward progress and human benefit. Others, like Rousseau, pointed to the human factors that contributed to natural disasters, such as poorly built houses and overcrowding. Following such lines of physical investigation, some began to think that nature was not itself a theater of evil, a place where natural evils existed to punish mankind for its moral evils. For such thinkers natural accidents and natural disasters were merely unfortunate; they concluded that true evil ought to be confined to those events or experiences that were the product of someone's will. This amounted to redefining the distinction between natural evil and moral evil, and thus emphasizing the way evil entered the world as human beings became socially human.[9]

By the middle of the eighteenth century it was beginning to seem that efforts to explain evil might be doomed to blasphemy if they seemed to blame God for flaws He might have avoided. But as Neiman stresses, the refusal to deal with evil as a problem provided no solution. People still demanded (and reason still demands) an explanation, even if the wrongs we suffer and the wrongs others suffer do not come as divine punishments anymore. From this perspective, it makes historical sense that Johann Joseph Gassner was emphasizing the role of the devil in causing a large share of the miseries to which humankind is subject. It was Gassner's way of saying that misery was in fact intelligible; it was not accidental and not merely natural but rather the product of a cunning and depraved will. Banishing the devil was his therapeutic solution, but Gassner did not proceed in the manner that a naturalizing Enlightenment did. For most Enlightened intellectuals did more than banish the devil: they read him out of reality. The trouble was that declaring the death of the devil became a prelude to the death of God and signaled an early defeat on the field of meaning. Without the devil, it seemed, certain evils simply could not be understood.[10] It will appear, therefore, that demonology was actually a practical means of doing theology, a negative theology to be sure, but one connected closely to the human quest for meaning. So instead of flatly forgetting the devil, Gassner was trying on a massive scale to retain and yet banish (but not to annihilate) the devil. That was an unstable effort, one doomed to condemnation by both the church and the state in his day. But it was not so foolish as the Enlightened thought then and frankly have ever since.

Franz Anton Mesmer as Rival

At just the moment that Gassner's fame was at its peak and was attracting the skeptical attentions of churchmen and enlightened rulers such as Emperor Joseph II and Elector Maximilian III Joseph of Bavaria, another healer came out of Austria to fascinate his own throngs of enthusiastic followers. Inspired by the work of Viennese Jesuit court astronomer Maximilian Hell (1720–1792), Franz Anton

Mesmer (1734–1815) had discovered in 1774 that he could manipulate strange forces in some of his patients, forces that he called magnetic. Following Hell's example, he had begun working with "real magnets" made of metal, glass, and stone, but subsequently found that he could achieve the same amazing effects on patients by mere touch and concentration; and so he distinguished this new magnetism from the magnetism found in inanimate nature and called it "animal magnetism," a term he probably picked up from the seventeenth-century Jesuit savant Athanasius Kircher.[11] With this new therapeutic weapon and with the elaborate theory that went with it, he became a celebrity in Vienna, entertaining the young Mozart and healing the rich and famous. After a frustrating therapeutic setback at the Slovakian castle of a Hungarian nobleman, however, Mesmer decided to return to his homeland, just north of the Lake of Constance.

It was July 1775, exactly one year since Gassner had spent three successful months in the region. Like Gassner, Mesmer began to attract crowds of hopeful patients, and his fame built to such an extent that the electoral court of Maximilian III Joseph in Munich called Mesmer to consult in the matter of Father Johann Joseph Gassner, who was still conducting his own healing operations in Regensburg, an exempt imperial city surrounded by Bavarian territory. In November of 1775 Mesmer gave the Munich commissioners and the Bavarian Academy of Sciences extraordinary demonstrations of his "magnetic" powers, prompting patients to display and then to suppress symptoms with little more than the touch of a finger. His "cures" seemed to be just like those of Gassner, except that they did not involve the use of exorcisms, blessings, or the name of Jesus. He even claimed to have cured Peter von Osterwald, one of the chief members of the academy and a leading figure of the Bavarian Enlightenment. Dr. Mesmer, indeed, declared that Father Gassner was actually using "animal magnetism" without knowing it; after all, he too held the patient's head between his hands and sometimes stroked affected parts of the body, much as Mesmer stroked patients with his magnetic fingers. All of Gassner's talk about the devil as a cause of human ills seemed to Mesmer like nothing more than superstitious window dressing. Henri Ellenberger has pointed to this collision of religious and scientistic therapies as the dramatic hour when dynamic psychiatry was born. For Ellenberger this was when a psychiatric paradigm of healing through natural means was first substituted for the world of spirits and exorcism. The Bavarian Academy of Sciences voted Mesmer into membership, the first and only such official recognition of his new science and an indication that at that point he looked like a major figure of the Enlightenment.[12]

Mesmer and Gassner

Mesmer did not long confine himself to South German backwaters, but this is not the place to trace again his roller-coaster ride through Parisian society in the years 1778–1785 and his enthusiastic adoption by radical social reformers in France.[13] I wish to call attention instead to several formal parallels between the cures of the exorcist Gassner and the therapeutic methods of the naturalizing, self-proclaimedly scientific Mesmer.

First and most importantly, both men invoked invisible qualities or forces as the root cause of physical ailments. Father Gassner regularly admitted that the devil was not at the root of all human ills,[14] but when he was, it only made sense (to him) to employ blessings and probative exorcisms. Neither the magnetic fluid nor the devil, however, was strictly visible or palpable, even though popular images of Gassner's exorcisms often include a picture of a small, black creature flying up out of a patient's mouth or out a window. Reputable observers, and Gassner himself, gave no credence to such visible demons, and Mesmer, too, never claimed that one could see the forces of animal magnetism. One could only see the results of these entities, in either case, and some invisible force seemed a reasonable inference. Remember that researchers into electricity and magnetism had only recently, with the work of Aepinus (1759), established the connection between electricity and magnetism, and on into the 1790s (in the work of Galvani) scientists studied what they called "animal electricity." During the 1770s and early 1780s natural philosophers in

England and France were eagerly pursuing a program of research into the therapeutic benefits of magnets.[15]

Careful observers were well aware that swindlers and tricksters could appear to provoke preternatural or even supernatural effects. The new forms of electricity and magnetism had been exploited for their entertainment value for over fifty years, and careful scholars were skeptical of all that was claimed for these wondrous forces.[16] That is why commissions of inquiry looked so carefully at both Gassner's and Mesmer's methods. In 1784 it was a French royal commission including Antoine de Lavoisier, Benjamin Franklin, and Dr. J. I. Guillotin (inventor of the "guillotine") that condemned Mesmer's claims to have discovered an occult magnetic fluid.[17] Ironically, Gassner withstood scrutiny more often than the supposedly more scientific Mesmer. While Gassner, for example, passed the tests set for him by four professors from the University of Ingolstadt in 1775, Mesmer stood officially condemned by both royal commissions that examined his theories in 1784. It was not until 1826 that a committee of the medical section of the French Royal Academy of Sciences reopened the question of Mesmer and this time concluded far more favorably.[18] But my point is that demonologists were just as eager as naturalists to prove their claims in a public arena. Gassner's diaries recording his therapeutic victories mentioned often that the cures were permanent (rather than merely transitory) and listed distinguished (and therefore supposedly credible) witnesses. He was certainly not claiming that one must take such religious phenomena on faith. Unfortunately, as

---

(*opposite page*) Johann Joseph Gassner (1727–1779) casting out a demon, 1775. It is worth noting that none of the eyewitness accounts of Gassner's healings ever claimed to have seen what this engraving depicts: a visible demon in the shape of a black, flying, lizardlike creature. But the scene also illustrates the mixed and crowded company that often gathered to witness Gassner's exorcisms. *Source: Gespräch über die heilsamen Beschwörungen und Wunderkuren des Herrn Gassners,* 1775, title engraving; reprinted by the kind permission of the Bayerische Staatsbibliothek, Munich.

THE EXPERIENCE OF DEMONS

we shall see, the Enlightened did not respond well to Gassner's requests for empirical investigations into these healings.

Indeed, that is what fueled the truly extraordinary literary battle over Gassner. Partisan tracts flew about Germany with an intensity that we otherwise associate with revolutions. The most complete bibliography of the so-called Gassner-Streit lists twelve editions of Gassner's own little treatise, *Weise fromm und gesund zu leben, auch ruhig und gottselig zu sterben, oder nützlicher Unterricht wider den Teufel zu streiten* (The Way to Live Piously and Healthily, And how to Die Peacefully and in God's Grace; Or, Useful Instruction on How to Fight against the Devil). That bibliography goes on to list 55 separate books and pamphlets in favor of Gassner, 31 works opposing him, and 25 works that were neutral or interested in special aspects of the controversy. In my researches, I have been able to add numerous titles and editions to this list as well. Counting second and third editions, translations, and all the newly discovered titles, it now appears that close to 150 works appeared, the overwhelming majority published in 1775 and 1776.[19] All of Germany, North and South, Protestant and Catholic, took part in this controversy, which depended not just on general principles (for and against the testimony of Scripture, or for and against the existence of the devil) but on what supposedly reliable witnesses claimed to have seen. This means that the Gassner controversy has a good claim to being one of the largest and noisiest arguments of the whole German Enlightenment. It certainly illustrates the fact that the German Enlightenment was much more concerned with religious matters than was the case in France.

Understanding the German Enlightenment

How shall we understand this strange controversy? For one thing, this religious and scientific controversy erupted at a moment when publicity was becoming something like what it is today. Germany was experiencing its second media revolution, if we count the invention of printing and the pamphlets of the Reformation period as constituting the first. Newspapers and journals, books and pamphlets flew off the presses at a rate that no one had previously experienced, and new rules had to be developed to cope with this novel situation.[20] But this vehement exchange of tirade and polemic was also extraordinary because it involved both Protestants and Catholics. To a degree that we may find hard to believe, Lutheran theologians and public commentators generally left South German and Catholic affairs out of account, as if such predictably superstitious and ignorant regions could present nothing of permanent importance to the cultivated Protestant reader. Similarly Catholics in the South often paid closer attention to events and books in Italy or France than to what their German brethren were doing and writing in the Protestant North. But in Gassner's case, this was not true. Careful observers and connoisseurs of experimental method revealed that Gassner's cures apparently withstood scrupulous investigation. Enlightened Catholics and Protestants took this as a serious provocation. Ordinary Protestants too took notice of Gassner, flocking in disturbing numbers to Ellwangen in order to be healed from ailments that their doctors and pastors could not alleviate. And Pastor Lavater in Reformed Zurich remained positively obsessed for several months with the possibility that in Gassner he might find a carefully attested case of God's direct intervention into earthly affairs, just the sort of miraculous wonder that he had been looking for and emphasizing since the late 1760s.[21] On this point, Gassner was perhaps not so different from Mesmer as has often been assumed. Mesmer too believed that animal magnetism was the "demonstrated presence of God" in the world.[22] But most importantly, Gassner's cures involved the devil, and the 1770s were not so far removed from the age of witch hunting that this circumstance could be ignored. Enlightened commentators were swift to charge that Gassner threatened to unleash a new wave of witchcraft trials, and with Maria Anna Schwägelin suffering in the poor house of Langenegg, accused of witchcraft in the jurisdiction of the prince abbey of Kempten, they seemed to have a serious point. Recall that Schwägelin was in fact convicted of witchcraft in the spring of 1775, and that she only barely escaped execution.

The official *Roman Ritual* of 1614 itself proclaimed that certain cases of demonic possession were the result of bewitchment, so that belief in exorcism could reasonably lead some to look for the human agents who had facilitated or willed a fall into demonic possession.[23] That accounts for the fact that some of Gassner's fiercest critics concentrated on the supposed revival of witchcraft accusations and witchcraft trials that Gassner's exorcisms seemed sure to provoke, even though Gassner himself did not promote or underwrite such accusations. It was, of course, difficult for Gassner's supporters to deny that witchcraft was at least theoretically a possibility even if its prosecution had recently become hopelessly entangled in judicial uncertainties and moral dilemmas.[24] So one of the tacit and sometimes explicit issues in the Gassner controversy was witchcraft, whose conquest had seemed to be the very symbol of the Enlightened age.

Thinking with Demons: The Grounds of Experience

Recent work on the history of witchcraft has shown that this crime depended on a specific worldview, one in which most people (but not all) were accustomed to "thinking with demons," as a way to think and converse about reality.[25] Many early modern Europeans found witchcraft and demons a reasonable vehicle with which to wonder about the nature of political and social authority, the limits of natural causation, the origins of sin, the coming apocalypse, and the problems of mental disorder. For centuries demonology comprised a set of rational and coherent beliefs that helped many thinkers to integrate the scholarly fields of history, medicine, law, politics, and theology. At no time, however, did everyone agree about demons (or anything else). We sometimes simplify the past by imagining that in bygone days everyone thought alike, but that's a modern conceit that rests on pride combined with naiveté about the past. There were as many disputes about demons as about almost any other topic two or three or four hundred years ago, and many models of the world competed for attention. And that takes only the discourse of the learned into account. Among the poorly educated and illiterate, we sometimes catch glimpses of assumptions and beliefs that the better educated and better disciplined, the more orthodox in short, were appalled (or sometimes titillated) to contemplate. Demons were often part of their world too, but not always in the well-ordered and systematically connected manner favored by intellectuals.[26]

In our own day it is still common enough among evangelical and charismatic groups to see the work of the devil in the troubles of this world, in sickness, "accidents," and in the supposed infidelity, immorality, and godlessness of our times. But the urge for witch hunting has died out in the modern West, even though the cry is easily audible in many parts of Africa and Asia.[27]

Once witchcraft trials were dead, as they were in most corners of the West by 1750, we may wonder how certain contemporaries of Thomas Jefferson and Benjamin Franklin, of Edward Gibbon and David Hume, could still bring themselves to see the devil in so many unsuspected places. One answer is that we have often vastly overestimated the supposed powers of the Hegelian Zeitgeist or the Foucaultian *epistème* to shape the thoughts or undergird the assumptions of all who happen to be living in the same time and place. Postmodernist reflections have sometimes run the risk of suggesting that anything is true if you think it is, that our concepts and beliefs are so powerful a constituent of experience that we are usually unable to see "around" them, to experience anything objectively. This has been part of the postmodern condition with its attack upon "the language of reference," the notion that our words and ideas actually refer to realities outside ourselves. Taken literally, the thought can paralyze scholarship. But the interesting truth seems to be that most of us live simultaneously in various worlds of thought and words. Most of us are not trapped in one verbal game. So, to arrive at provisional conclusions amidst such confusions, it may help to recognize that groups of early modern people (what we may recognize as early modern subcultures) could entertain worldviews that diverged radically from one another, paradigmatic attitudes toward the world that structured radically different early modern experiences even in the late eighteenth century and made it difficult or even impossible for some people to speak to others of what they knew. I think that these worlds were more than just conceptually distinct, for it is also true that many conceptual forms, many religious ideas, carry with them distinctive practices, specific habits that are cultivated either in order that specific experiences might come more easily and more predictably, or so that one might, on the contrary, be readier to cope with them, suppress them, or suffer them with greater equanimity.

It is, however, also true that our outlooks and our mental furniture literally prefigure what we are able to experience. Although we probably can have some form of an experience even if we do not have the verbal or mental categories with which to think and talk about it, usually if we do not have the concepts and the words that go with the concepts, we cannot well express or communicate what we experience. But without the words and the ideas, we essentially do not have the full experience. In this way the concepts we think with, the words we use, prefigure our possible experiences.

"Thinking with demons," as Europeans had done for centuries, made so much sense in so many areas that the devil and his minions were very hard to give up, even for those who had, often for practical reasons, abolished witchcraft trials. And where the devil survived as a concept and hence as a lived reality, there one continued to find numbers of the demonically possessed. In eighteenth-century Germany, this insight itself became controversial in the form that Ludovico Antonio Muratori (1672–1750) posed it. The learned and Enlightened Italian scholar noted that "it is strange that there are only bewitched and possessed where there are exorcists." The remedy, therefore, seemed clear to Muratori's enlightened readers. Get rid of the exorcists, throw out their mental furniture, and the devil and his effects would find somewhere else to reside.[28] To religious conservatives, such a conclusion did not follow at all. If Muratori was right, it merely showed that where there were no detection devices, no exorcists, there no devils could be detected. And so Gassner's cures seemed to raise fundamental issues about the existence of spirits, the continuation of miracles, the efficaciousness of the Roman Catholic sacramentals and especially of exorcism, and the hitherto untested powers of the human imagination.

Catholics and Protestants for whom the devil was still a biblical and (therefore) a living reality did not have to stretch far to experience the devil's effects both outside their own bodies and even within. Belief in the devil helped to activate him as a possible experience, and helped make it easier for him to leave behind the telltale traces of specifically demonic activity. Indeed, we may agree that where people have learned to get along without demons and the devil, the devil could indeed still be at work. How would we know? But under such modern conditions the devil rarely leaves behind the sulphurous odors and frantic convulsions found in explicit cases of demonic possession.

The Enchanted World

Thus for some believers the world was "enchanted," in the famous image of Max Weber. It contained spirits of various sorts, occult forces, and hidden dangers. Ordinary believers often held the view (and acted on the view) that miracles regularly occurred in this world. By this they meant that God or His saints intervened to rescue certain favorites and that unexpected but happy outcomes were common enough to be hoped for. To put oneself in this frame of mind and simultaneously to put God in a giving frame of mind, one might go on pilgrimage, say a specific round of prayers, or involve oneself in other devotional exercises. From this premodern point of view it made little sense to ask whether a miracle represented a breach in the otherwise immutable laws of nature. Who had time to care about that when the real point was that relief from mortal dangers might be only moments away? And if an Enlightened critic objected that the ideas involved here were unsubstantiated or unproved, many a person could retort that he or she had *experienced* the demon, and had seen the wondrous effects of exorcism with his or her own eyes. Then as now, that was a nearly irrefutable argument.

Such an enchanted worldview describes pretty well the humble Lutheran and Catholic supplicants who thronged to visit Gassner in Klösterle, Ellwangen, Regensburg, and Sulzbach, and who hoped that he might grant them just a gesture, a word of miraculous healing, a compassionate glance. Sharing part of this worldview were many of the learned but disgruntled ex-Jesuits after 1773, who hoped that Gassner's amazing and numerous exorcisms would serve to reveal a world that was so full of evil spirits that only a traditional Catholic priest, armed with the sacramentals of his church, had any chance at all of effectively countering their attack. For the former Jesuits, relief of immediate suffering was not the main point, but restoration of the Jesuit Order was. This was certainly not the main concern of ordinary Christians, but it can be seen that both Jesuits and ordinary believers inhabited an "enchanted" world. In Gassner's day, the chief stronghold of the ex-Jesuits was Augsburg, an imperial city with strong, mutually distrustful populations of both Catholics and Lutherans. The magistrates of Augsburg and the bishop of Augsburg were so eager to suppress religious vituperation that long after 1773 the papal decree dissolving the Jesuit Order was not even recognized. Ex-Jesuits found a welcoming refuge there, and many of Gassner's strongest supporters lived, preached, or published in Augsburg.[29]

On the other side of the magical line, there were several sorts of disenchanted. Among Lutherans and Reformed, for example, theologians had agreed for two hundred years that the age of miracles was over. Yes, miracles had occurred in the years of the early church. Yes, of course Jesus had worked real miracles and had cast out demons. But those acts of Spirit and Power, those "signs," "wonders," and "mighty works," had served the purpose of establishing Christ's identity, and of building up the early church. They did not compete with God's Word, could not confirm new truths, and were, in the view of Protestant theologians, no longer necessary now that Christians had the benefit of Holy Scripture.[30] Of course, for most Protestants God might continue to govern and steer his creation through the exercise of his Providence, but the subtle point was usually that He did so by mobilizing the ordinary forces of nature, not by breaking the natural rules He had established for all time.[31]

For traditional Roman Catholics, this was nonsense. On every side they counted dramatic miracles of healing and rescue that had no imaginable natural explanation. For many Catholic polemicists the survival of miracles within the Roman Communion was all the proof they needed that their church was true and that the various Protestant "sects" were bankrupt. By the end of the sixteenth century, however, even Roman Catholics, at least the careful and scholarly among them, had grown weary of Protestant charges that their priests were tricksters and that the Catholic laity were simply gullible. Too often what had seemed like a miracle had turned out on closer inspection to be fraud, deception, or simple mistake. And to prevent their position from being ridiculed by hostile Protestants, they tightened up their criteria for the truly miraculous. By the end of the sixteenth century they had come to accept Thomas Aquinas's strict view, which held that "a miracle is defined as an event that happens outside the ordinary processes of the whole of created nature." And increasingly that meant that miracles had to be tested carefully against all the possible powers of nature. If a possible natural explanation could be found for some amazing event, it was difficult to affirm with certainty that it was nonetheless a miracle.[32]

Along with these stricter notions of miracles, demonic possession now came under much more stringent regulation; the *Roman Ritual* of 1614 essentially defined it as a condition that could have no natural explanation. Demonic possession had become a sort of negative miracle. This is a point that will occupy us more fully in a later chapter, but here the point is simply that learned Protestants and Catholics of the seventeenth and eighteenth centuries came to regard miracles not as wonders (things that make us wonder) but as events that could have no natural explanation. Then the only question remained whether they still occurred at all, and on that score learned Catholics triumphantly insisted that God did still intervene to break the "laws of nature." They were His to break, after all. But, logically enough, the proof of any supposed miracle now required a profound knowledge of nature and of experimental method.

During the eighteenth century still another position took shape among the self-proclaimed partisans of Enlightenment: that miracles, being breaches of the natural order, simply *could* not happen, or just as tellingly, that our human resources are so feeble or so easily deceived that we cannot tell if an amazing event actually breaches the rules of nature.[33] Do we in fact know all the rules of the natural order? How could we ever be sure that an event was thoroughly miraculous? Notice what had happened. As miracles became more amazing, more wondrous, ever more impossible to explain, they also became less common until they were virtually impossible. These were the results of theological speculation and disagreement on a level that scarcely concerned those people who saw the whole world as "enchanted." But the strongly empirical claims of Hume, Voltaire, and Diderot forced their Catholic opponents to become scrupulous scientists in order to defend essentially empirical claims for the survival of miracles. And all of that applies as well to what we have labeled "negative miracles," instances of demoniac possession.

There was yet another Enlightened view that gained ground in the eighteenth century, one that did not pronounce upon miracles or demoniac possession directly (or theoretically) but which declared all events suspect if they promoted social disorder. As we will see in the next chapter, these were the grounds on which Emperor Joseph II ruled against Gassner's healing campaigns. He needed no proof that Gassner's cures were false or that the demon possessed were in fact naturally ill, for he had learned of the thousands of common people who flocked to see Gassner to be healed by him. Thousands of commoners converging anywhere represented a frightening spectacle for any absolute ruler. On grounds of good order alone, certain Enlightened political thinkers and rulers decided that Gassner and his exorcisms simply had to stop.

The Meanings of Experience

These various views expressed in the late eighteenth century created the basis for strikingly various experiences. For some, Gassner's test exorcisms served to prove to the suffering supplicant that he or she harbored one or more demons; and onlookers often drew the same conclusion. But for others this was a flatly impossible conclusion. For some petitioners, any relief from daily misery was miraculous, although Gassner himself was careful not to claim the power of working proper miracles. For ordinary Germans this was not an obvious distinction since the word *Wunder* could mean either miracle or marvel. For some Catholics the promiscuous use of exorcism gave Protestants and the Enlightened a broad brush they could use to tar the Catholic faith with charges of superstition and ignorance, but for other Catholics the enthusiastic throngs of supplicants constituted a major social problem.

From the other side of the confessional divide, Pastor Johann Kaspar Lavater frankly hoped that demonic possession could be proved, for that would constitute for him proof of the unseen world, proof that the desiccated, materialistic world presented by the followers of Spinoza was hopelessly inadequate to the task of accounting for life as we live it. Lavater and some other Protestants hoped that Gassner would be the proof of God's continuing interventions that would put the Enlightenment to flight.

For still other Protestants, as we have seen, Gassner represented the very incarnation of dangerous folly, the revival of bewitchings and the spark in a powder keg that might lead to renewed witchcraft trials. For them, Gassner represented the risks that emerged when one did not truly understand Scripture and took literally what God had intended as beautiful parables.

These are matters that will occupy our attention in the coming chapters, but it should now be clear why certain believers in the 1770s could find themselves convinced that they were themselves possessed by the devil, and why that claim seemed ludicrous to others. The stage was set for a gigantic and perhaps irresolvable dispute, one that bears a striking similarity to many of the disputes of our own day, in which an initial problem often is the failure to attend with any care to what our interlocutors are actually saying. To grasp how and why Gassner's religious revival erupted where it did, however, we must also attend to the politics of the ecclesiastical states within the Holy Roman Empire, states that provided, at least for a time, a cultural niche for his ideas and practices.

two
A NICHE IN THE INCUBATOR: ECCLESIASTICAL POLITICS AND THE EMPIRE

> Gassner and the movements that erupted around him are more important and more instructive matters for the ecclesiastical history of our times than most of my readers will have suspected.
> —Christian Wilhelm Franz Walch, *Neueste Religionsgeschichte*

Johann Joseph Gassner found himself and his religious movement embroiled in a web of tense relations involving many of the most powerful Catholic forces in the Holy Roman Empire. He was originally doubted and expelled by the cardinal prince bishop of Constance, Franz Konrad von Rodt; favored and supported by the prince bishop of Regensburg, Anton Ignaz von Fugger; blocked by the elector of Bavaria, Maximilian III Joseph, but supported by the counts of Hohenlohe and by Duke Ludwig Eugen of Württemberg, brother of reigning Duke Karl Eugen; criticized by the archbishops of Salzburg and Prague; and finally stopped by Emperor Joseph II and by Pope Pius VI. To understand this constellation of conflicting forces, we must grasp the complex nature of the Holy Roman Empire and of German Catholicism in the late eighteenth century.

The Holy Roman Empire has seemed both weak and ridiculous to those who expected it to perform like a nation-state. In the last generation, however, inasmuch as nations appear to cause at least as many problems as they solve, historians have studied afresh the hidden strengths and discreet charms of the empire, virtues that allowed it to survive and even flourish, in a sense, throughout the "age of absolutism."[1] With a vibrant image, Mack Walker once described the Holy Roman Empire of the eighteenth century as an incubator, a loose federation of extremely diverse members that served to shelter and protect each constituent part from the designs of more powerful or more numerous neighbors.[2] So long as most members found living in this cocoon more secure than taking their chances as the clients of one or another powerful patron-state, the empire functioned to keep cities and states of various strengths in rough balance. Walker's image helps the modern reader understand why the empire, although it did not fit neatly into the Aristotelian political categories, actually functioned and won the loyalty of many. Until the late eighteenth century it seemed to protect the interests of the numerous smaller principalities and cities from the ambitions of the overmighty. By the middle of the eighteenth century, however, it was becoming clear that Prussia represented one such threat, but others were not far behind, especially Bavaria and Austria. Meanwhile the Saxon dukes had converted to Catholicism and become the kings of Poland while the dukes of Braunschweig had assumed the throne of Britain. All of these powers seemed increasingly willing to sacrifice imperial institutions in order to strengthen their own territorial or international power. Napoleonic armies dealt the final blow to the empire, seizing territories on the left bank of the Rhine and forcing the secularization of hundreds of church lands and the consolidation of secular principalities in the famous final decree of the imperial deputation of 1803, the *Reichsdeputationshauptschluss*. Although secularizations of church lands had been in process ever since the late Middle Ages and had accelerated during the Reformation, and although further secularizations had been discussed among the German Catholic powers ever since the 1740s, even keen observers often failed to recognize just how fundamental the ecclesiastical states were to the functioning of the Holy Roman Empire. With their disappearance in 1803 the empire was no longer governable, at least by a Catholic emperor, and so it was no wonder that the Holy Roman Empire of the German Nation collapsed entirely just three years later, after an existence of about a thousand years.[3]

Although the empire survived as an incubator or cocoon for the myriad small and smaller members, those images do not do full justice to the tangled tensions within the web, conflicting interests that pulled in different directions. Nowhere was this more evident than among the ecclesiastical states of Germany. The modern reader, especially the American reader, may have difficulty understanding just how important and peculiar the prelates of the Holy Roman Empire were. We have perhaps grown so used to the separation of church and state, or perhaps so accustomed to think that the English, French, and Spanish monarchies provided the norm for all of Europe, that we badly underestimate the role of ecclesiastical princes in the odd confederation that constituted the empire.

The chief peculiarity of the Catholic Church in the Holy Roman Empire was that its hierarchy (its bishops and archbishops) were simultaneously heads of their dioceses or provinces but also major princes of the empire with extensive lands and secular rights of rule (including taxation, military conscription, legislation, jurisdiction both civil and criminal, and responsibility for all manner of local administration). This mixture of ecclesiastical and secular roles had characterized the medieval German monarchy along with much of the rest of Western Europe, but the western monarchies had long since curbed and curtailed the secular powers of their clergy, while in the German lands these glorious and vainglorious potentates had retained their strength.[4] It has been estimated that at the time of the Reformation roughly one-third of the German lands were under the secular control of ecclesiastical princes. That percentage had been reduced in the century after Luther, but the grand baroque palaces and gold-encrusted chapels of even minor prelates in South Germany reveal how powerful and self-confident they still were.[5] In southern and western Germany they numbered twenty bishoprics and about forty imperial abbeys or other sorts of ecclesiastical foundations with a population of perhaps 2,650,000, a number that includes something

---

(*opposite page*) Map 1. Catholic Ecclesiastical Administration of Central Europe in the Late 18th Century. Before a series of reforms of the 1780s, the administrative districts of the Catholic Church in German-speaking Europe did not correspond at all to the political constituents of the Holy Roman Empire. There was, for example, no diocese or archdiocese of Bavaria or Austria. Similarly, the provinces of Cologne, Mainz, and Trier did not correspond to any one principality.

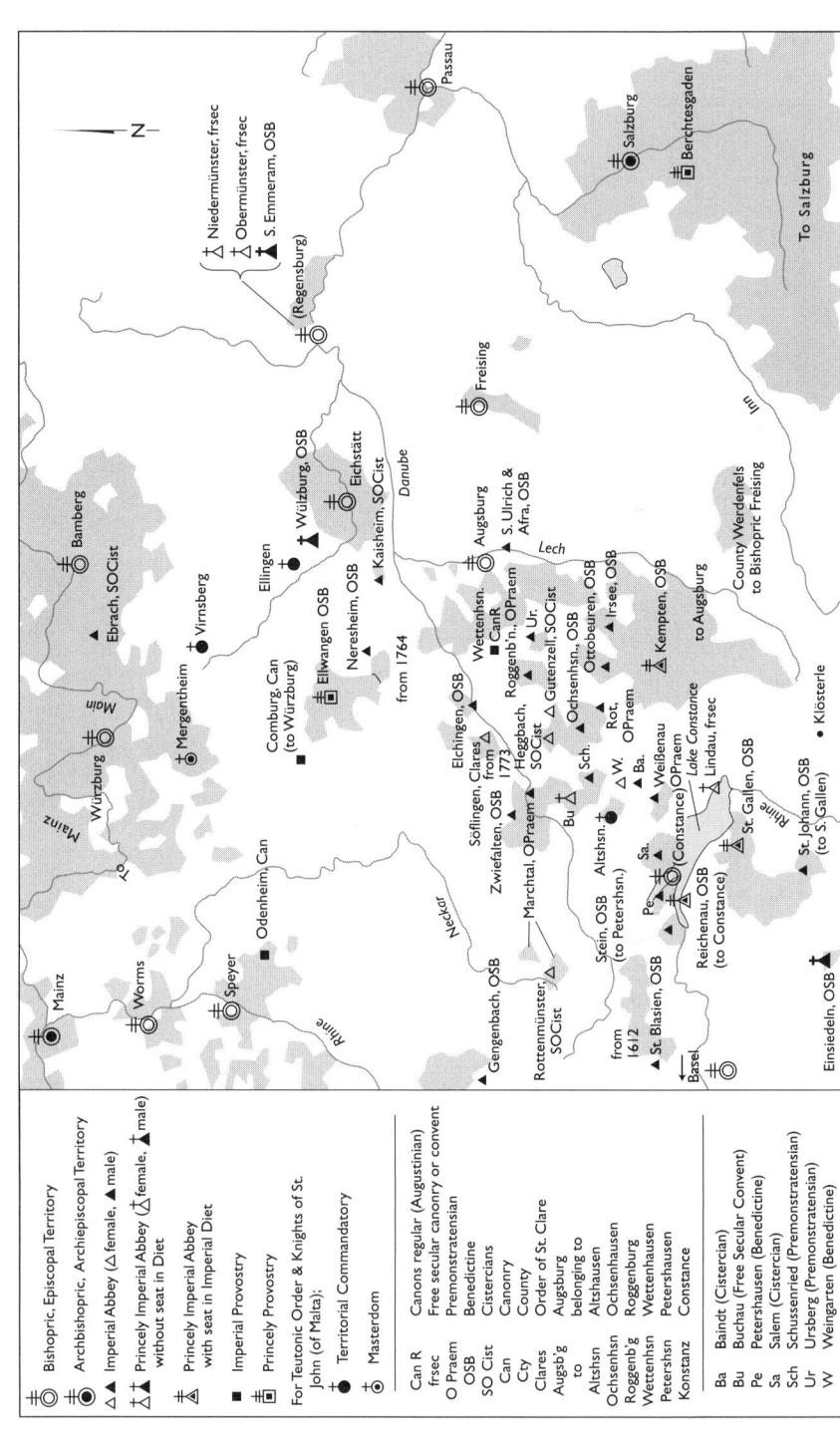

like 70,000 regular and secular clergy.⁶ These were the lands in which Gassner's healing campaign and religious movement took root. In fact, he moved easily from one ecclesiastical state to another, almost never residing long in any secular principality. He depended on favorable prelates, who give him shelter, advertised his successes, and in the case of the prince bishop of Regensburg, raised him to the rank of councillor.

The lands of an imperial princely prelate never corresponded to his diocese or archiepiscopal province, moreover, so that the same man might rule ecclesiastically over one district (his diocese) but as a secular prince over quite a different principality. At the end of the eighteenth century, for example, the bishop of Passau personally controlled a little territory of only 134 square kilometers (about 52 square miles), squeezed between Bavaria and Austria, but he oversaw a diocese of 42,000 square kilometers (about 16,400 square miles) that reached from northern Bavaria to the borders of Hungary. Because of these dual roles, the German bishops and archbishops were almost always members of the high nobility and often enough the brothers of ruling dukes or counts. Although they were elected to their offices by cathedral chapters or other corporate bodies, the most powerful families established ecclesiastical dynasties, such as the Wittelsbachs of Bavaria (who for generations had a lock on the electoral archbishopric of Cologne), but this is true also of smaller families such as the Schönborns of electoral Mainz and Franconia (who for a century dominated the bishoprics of Würzburg and Bamberg, among others). This arrangement, often simply referred to as the *Reichskirche* (the imperial church) guaranteed that the German Catholic bishops would be far more sensitive to secular political considerations than most of their

---

(*Opposite page*) Map 2. Ecclesiastical Principalities in the Southern Holy Roman Empire. The map shows how dense were the ecclesiastical principalities in the South (prince bishops, imperial abbeys, and the lands of various other ecclesiastical bodies). The heads of these lands ruled not as ecclesiastical administrators but as secular princes.

fellow prelates in France, Italy, or Spain. Many were grand secular princes first and only secondarily churchmen, and so many of them appointed suffragan bishops to attend to spiritual matters in their dioceses. The most distinguished of these potentates were the archbishops of Cologne, Mainz, Trier, Prague, Vienna, and Salzburg. The first three of these were so emphatically charged with secular responsibilities that they were imperial electors, who shared (along with the princes of Saxony, Brandenburg, Prussia, the Rhine Palatinate, Bavaria, and Hanover) the task of electing each Holy Roman emperor and of constituting the first chamber of the "perpetual" imperial diet, which had been meeting as a standing committee in Regensburg on the Danube since 1663.[7]

The archbishop of Mainz was also the chancellor (or "archchancellor") of the empire, second only to the emperor in importance and (through a deputy) head of the imperial diet meeting in Regensburg. The huge province of Mainz, the most extensive of all the German provinces, extended from Hamburg in the north to Chur on the Upper Rhine in the South, in a central swath about two hundred miles wide. It included the dioceses of Chur, Constance, Augsburg, Würzburg, Bamberg, and Strasbourg in the south (along with others in the north) and was, therefore, nominally in charge of most of the territory in which Gassner was active. The diocese of Regensburg, however, was subordinate to the archbishop of Salzburg, whose extensive province included the bishoprics of Freising, Passau, Brixen (Bressanone), and even (until 1722) Vienna.

In addition to this territorial hierarchy governing the secular clergy of the empire and overseeing the thousands of parishes to which most Catholic laity belonged, the Catholic Church in the German lands included a wide array of imperial abbeys, imperial convents, and military orders (the Teutonic Knights and the Knights of St. John, or of Malta), and "princely provostries" (*Fürstpropsteien*) of Ellwangen and Berchtesgaden. Many of these ecclesiastical lands had secured exemptions from the jurisdiction of their bishops and made up a series of jurisdictionally autonomous islands, ultimately under the control of Rome but often free to run their own affairs, at least so long as they did not call too much attention to themselves. A good example was the imperial abbey of Salem, where Gassner had achieved some of his first major successes outside his own parish. Eight miles north of the Lake of Constance and just east of the small imperial city of Überlingen, the abbey had survived the Reformation as a Cistercian monastery but had to struggle with the secular counts of Heiligenberg and with the electors of Bavaria to retain its scattered lands and then with the bishops of Constance regarding Salem's jurisdictional exemptions and ceremonial pretensions.[8] To strengthen Salem's hand against local rivals, the abbey sometimes flirted with joining the scattered Swabian lands of "Anterior Austria" (Vorderösterreich), but in the 1760s and 1770s Prince Abbot Anselm Schwab (reg. 1746–1778) appealed directly to Pope Clement XIII, who sent the head of his papal archive to investigate trumped-up claims of misconduct and mismanagement. Despite a victory in 1761 for Abbot Anselm, the prince bishop of Constance, Cardinal Franz Konrad von Rodt (reg. 1751–1775) continued his efforts to depose the abbot and to annul Salem's liberties.[9] Such tensions were common in Catholic Germany, where exemptions and overlapping claims made controversy almost unavoidable.[10] When some of Gassner's first German successes were recorded in Salem, it should not surprise us to learn, the cardinal prince bishop of Constance immediately intervened, demanded an investigation, and determined to expel Gassner from his diocese, an order that Gassner was slow to obey.

Another source of difficulty for the Reichskirche and its bishops was the steady exploitation by seventeenth- and eighteenth-century popes of permanent nunciatures. Although these offices began as diplomatic representatives of the Holy See, by the eighteenth century nuncios often had powers that went well beyond simple representation. They had wide administrative powers and were charged with granting dispensations, undertaking visitations, and clarifying doctrine, thus competing directly with the German archbishops. No wonder the archbishops of the empire reacted bitterly to what they regarded as an invasion of their proper rights and duties.[11] A focal point for this resentment exploded in 1763 in the work of a certain

"Justinus Febronius," the pseudonym of Johann Nikolaus von Hontheim (1701–1790), the suffragan bishop of Trier. In his vehemently anti-papal book, *De statu ecclesiæ et legitima potestate Romani Pontificis Liber singularis ad reuniendos dissidentes in religione christianos compositus* (On the State of the Church and the Legitimate Power of the Roman Pontiff, Written for the Purpose of Reuniting the Dissidents of the Christian Religion), Hontheim urged a conciliarism that would allow the creation of a German Catholic national church and the reconciliation of differences with the Protestant churches. The pope would be reduced to nothing more than a benign administrator and, primus inter pares, charged with guaranteeing the unity of the church but not seen as the final arbiter of matters of faith. So radical a conclusion, urged by a suffragan bishop, did not spring to life without parents. Indeed, it has become common to place Hontheim in a movement that has been called the "Catholic revolution of ideas" in the eighteenth century.[12] Building upon the recent historical recovery and study of fifteenth-century ecclesiastical documents (especially from the Council of Basel of 1438, the Viennese Concordat of 1448, and the regular lists of complaints or *Gravamina*, ca. 1450–1521, of the German nation against the papacy), a coalition of German canon lawyers, Jansenists, and Catholic reformers hoped to duplicate the successes of the French kings, whose Pragmatic Sanction of Bourges (1438) and Concordat of 1516 had established the French monarch's right to appoint all French bishops.[13] In this way, as Peter Hersche, Volker Pitzer, and Karl Otmar von Aretin have emphasized, Catholic reformers hoped to create a national Catholic Church.[14] Of course these hopes depended upon regarding the confessional divide in Germany as purely political and did not adequately take either the theological differences of the learned or the deeply ingrained mutual religious aversions of ordinary people into account. As a practical matter, ideas of confessional reconciliation were premature at best, but among high councils of state, Febronian ideas continued to ferment for decades after Hontheim's forced recantation of 1778.

During the 1770s and 1780s the German archbishops applied their

A Niche in the Incubator

Gallican or episcopalist ideas to the task of curbing the papal nunciatures, not only those already in existence (especially the nunciature of Cologne) but the special office in Munich, planned by Prince Elector Karl Theodor in order to produce a centralized church for Bavaria in the mid-1780s. We have already noted that dioceses rarely coincided with territorial borders in the empire, and this was especially true in Bavaria, whose various parts were subject to several bishops, most of them with seats outside Bavaria. To establish his own Bavarian national church, the elector appealed to Pope Pius VI and received a nunciature to act as a sort of archbishop for all the Wittelsbach lands. He also enlisted the support of Emperor Joseph II, who had just reformed and rationalized the diocesan borders of Austria (creating two new bishoprics in Linz and St. Pölten while decisively enlarging the diocesan boundaries of Vienna, Gurk, and Seckau), but these measures threatened to disrupt the whole Reichskirche by bringing the Catholic Church firmly within the orbit of territorial politics.[15]

It is a measure of the complexity of the German ecclesiastical scene that the bitter opposition of the archbishops to the Bavarian nunciature and their passionate support for Febronian politics met with little support among the German bishops. Even though Febronius-Hontheim had argued for an episcopalism that seemed to promise more independence and authority for the German bishops, they were as a group far more worried about the power of the archbishops than about the pope in Rome. Such proposed reforms were even less popular among the imperial abbeys, which depended upon papal exemptions for their autonomy and dignity.[16] Gassner's movement reflects and illuminates these tensions too, for he succeeded best among those Catholic territories least closely controlled by the archbishops: the tiny county of Wolfegg (where Gassner had healed Maria Bernardina, Countess Truchsess von Wolfegg und Friedberg) and especially imperial abbeys and convents (notably the princely abbeys of Kempten and Salem), the imperial provostry of Ellwangen, along with the proud bishoprics of Regensburg, Freising, and Eichstätt. The bishop of Constance was skeptical from the start, and in the end, both

Archbishop Hieronymus Colloredo of Salzburg and Antonín Petr Prichovic of Prague issued pastoral letters warning about Gassner's superstitious and disorderly excesses.

Catholic reform touched not only the location of political power in the church. In addition to the diocesan reforms mentioned, both Joseph II and his mother Maria Theresa (reg. 1740–1780) had issued orders as early as the 1750s sharply curbing the influence of the Jesuits over education and censorship (1759), limiting the number of feast days and the wealth of the monasteries. In the late 1760s Joseph raised the minimum age at which one could join religious orders, dissolved small and "useless" monasteries, taxed the clergy, abolished monastic and episcopal prisons, limited the gift of lands to the church, curbed pilgrimages and processions, improved the education of and increased the numbers of the parish clergy, while generally subordinating the church to the state.[17] It appeared to an earlier generation that Joseph was following a thoroughly secular or even a rationalist Enlightenment program, but the recent work of Beales and others has made it crystal clear that Joseph saw himself as a deeply religious Catholic reformer. His zeal for the state and for limiting the power of both the pope and the monasteries was matched by an almost evangelical zeal for improving the education and effectiveness of the priesthood.

What these revisions show is that Reform Catholicism had deep roots in Austria and elsewhere in the empire.[18] Some statesmen were moved by late Jansenism to promote a strict moralism, an intensely inward religious worship, and a theology of grace at the expense of works (even at the expense of church rituals and ceremonies). Those inspired by Febronius urged a dramatic expansion of the rights of bishops and strict limits on the papacy in order to create a German national church that might even reconcile the dissenting Protestant churches. Others agreed with Joseph II that force should play no role in religion and that therefore the toleration of Protestants and even of Jews would have benefits for true religion (Catholicism in their view) as well as for the state (by tolerating rather than expelling industrious workers).

It was, of course, one thing to decree changes from above and quite another to realize them on the ground. As Marc Forster has emphasized, Catholicism was not uniform throughout the German lands, and the territorially splintered German Southwest was perhaps peculiarly resistant to orders from above. Ordinary villagers and townspeople were usually devoted to their parish priests, to their local pilgrimage shrines, and to their local abbeys. In this world the thorough reforms ordered by the Emperor Joseph II and his ministers met with widespread popular opposition, except for Joseph's plans to provide new parishes. Otherwise, ordinary Catholics in this region resisted the closure of their shrines, convents, monasteries, and confraternities, and they worked with surprising tenacity and success to retain feast days, processions, and pilgrimages.[19] Especially where a mixture of Protestants was found among the population, as in many parts of the German Southwest, humble Catholic parishioners found themselves feeling ever more profoundly Catholic. Often these villagers were enthusiastic backers of both the Jesuits and the even more numerous Capuchins, from whom they received religious instruction and preaching. In Upper Swabia this was a piety that did not respond well to orders from bishops or secular princes; instead these ordinary Catholics were bound up in a dense sacral landscape and often felt closer to the imperial abbeys of their region than to diocesan administrators, perhaps precisely because they were not so bound up in a centralized hierarchy, not fully obedient to the reforms of Trent and the episcopal decrees that tried to impose them.[20] It makes sense that Gassner's first extramural successes should have come in the German Southwest, even though the cardinal bishop of Constance did what he could to curb and discredit his healing campaign.

Even more decisive steps were taken by other Catholic authorities. After Sterzinger received Gassner's little book in October of 1774, he brought it to the attention of Count von Sprezzi (Spretti), head of the Bavarian ecclesiastical council (*geistlicher Rat*), who immediately forbade its sale in Bavaria.[21] The authorities in the diocese of Augsburg also forbade Gassner to work there, for Sterzinger noted that even in Ellwangen Gassner had had to work his "operations" in a special

A Niche in the Incubator

house that was exempt from the jurisdiction of the bishop of Augsburg.[22] Indeed, in a letter dated 1 December 1774 the cathedral provost of Augsburg notified the authorities in Ellwangen that Elector Klemens Wenzeslaus, archbishop of Trier but also bishop of Augsburg, had forbidden Gassner to enter the diocese of Augsburg.[23] The skeptical elector was clearly annoyed that Gassner was exploiting exempt properties in Ellwangen to evade his general obligation to abstain from exorcizing until he had the permission of the appropriate diocesan bishop. He explicitly warned his sister-in-law, the electress of Saxony, against seeking the help of Gassner for herself or for her depressed son, Prince Karl of Saxony.[24]

Opinion was sharply divided at the electoral court in Munich, however, and in particular the "Protomedicus" and privy councillor Johann Anton von Wolter was eager to see if Gassner might heal his daughter, the Baroness von Erdt, who suffered from epilepsy and dizziness. Believers also included the court physician Johann Nepomuk Anton Leuthner. As a result of these bitterly contentious opinions, the elector of Bavaria issued a decree dated 13 February 1775 forbidding noisy religious discussions and threatening punishment for those who ridiculed the Catholic faith or its personnel.[25] At about the same time, however, Max Joseph forbade Gassner to enter Bavarian territory because he was eager to forestall unrest and religious excitement. He therefore became enraged when four professors at "his" university in Ingolstadt undertook on their own initiative to investigate and confirm Gassner's claims (27 August 1775). One professor from each of the then accepted academic disciplines (philosophy, medicine, theology, and law) had traveled to Regensburg and observed Gassner's "operations" for two days, and had come away fully persuaded.[26] Elector Max Joseph sent a stiff letter in December demanding an explanation and warning that the reputation of the university was at stake. With obedient alacrity the four professors retreated and meekly claimed that they had not intended to publish their views, and certainly had not meant to involve the university in their claims. The elector sternly directed the professors to give up their interference in the "all too exciting" Gassner affair.

Gassner had encountered skeptical lay administrators before, starting as early as 1767 in the Vorarlberg, where the local governor, Landvogt Baron von Sternbach, had complained to the bishop of Chur about Gassner's "superstitious" dealings; but after an investigation the bishop had taken Gassner under his protection.[27] The autonomy and exemptions of the bishop of Regensburg also sheltered Gassner from civil disapproval in that city. In vain the city magistrates tried in July of 1775 to stem the tide of poor, sick, and "suspicious" persons who were sneaking into the city without official permission.[28] Indeed, bishop Anton Ignaz delighted in showing off his wonder worker to the assembled Catholic delegates to the imperial diet, which sat in permanent session in Regensburg. The constitution of the Holy Roman Empire guaranteed that if Gassner remained in good odor with his immediate ecclesiastical superior, he was safe enough, at least so long as the highest authorities were content to ignore him.

From the beginning of 1775 storm flags were beginning to fly from the towers of the Austrian administration, but by the time the Freiburg authorities of Anterior Austria (Vorderösterreich, the disconnected Habsburg lands mainly in southwestern Germany) began to make the necessary inquiries, Gassner was no longer in their territory, and so it was no longer up to them to pursue the matter.[29] Therefore the imperial government in Vienna took over the investigation. In March of 1775 Chancellor Wenzel Anton von Kaunitz asked for a "thorough report" on Gassner from Freiherr von Ried, the imperial delegate to the Swabian-Franconian circle in Offenburg. But Ried was too far distant to have had any personal contact with the healer, and could only report that from what he had been able to learn, opinions were divided about him. From accounts concerning those whom Gassner had healed, Ried could report that many seemed to have reverted to their former conditions. By the time Gassner moved on to Regensburg at the beginning of summer 1775, the Empress Maria Theresa was ready to demand her own investigation; she ordered a commission sent to Regensburg including the emperor's personal physician, Anton de Haen, and Freiherr Gottfried van Swieten, the son of a previous imperial physician, Gerhard van Swieten. The empress was stacking the deck, for both Anton de Haen and Gottfried van Swieten were well known for their opposition to ideas of witchcraft.

Probably as a result of his investigative visit to Regensburg, imperial physician de Haen (1704–1776) worked an analysis of the operations of Gassner into his elaborate inquiry into miracles, which was published just as he lay dying in 1776. In general the Jansenist physician believed in the possibility of miracles and magic, but Gasssner was another matter.[30] He conceded that many troubled patients probably benefited simply from the change of climate and of diet involved in traveling to the exorcist, and that some just needed a break from domestic worries. It also seemed entirely possible that Gassner possessed secret knowledge of occult natural forces, of "sympathy," and magnetism. It was entirely conceivable that the wonder worker achieved beneficial effects on certain hypersensitive individuals by means of strange manipulations. It also seemed to Dr. de Haen that most of the "healed" had suffered from chronic but periodic ailments, and so a real test required ample time to determine whether a supposed cure was permanent rather than merely a calm interval in a natural disorder. "If Gassner's defenders stubbornly maintain that Gassner's cures are indisputable, achieved by no natural forces and not by deceit, then I would have to attribute Gassner's wonderworks (portenta opera) to the devil for they cannot be attributed to God or to natural powers."[31] In the enlightened and Jansenist atmosphere of Vienna it did little good to make the theologically accurate but overly subtle point that Gassner had never claimed to be working miracles, even if the effects he achieved were supernatural. The exorcist claimed he was only using the ordinary powers granted to every priest, but the point was pointless.

Demonic possession was under general assault among the intellectuals of the Habsburg capital. Even though Christoph Anton Cardinal Migazzi, the prince archbishop of Vienna, was a vehement enemy of Enlightenment theology, a supporter of the Jesuits, and an opponent of most of the Emperor Joseph II's ecclesiastical reforms, he also opposed what he saw as "superstition." In June of 1758 he had published a decree condemning the treatment of natural illnesses as if they were bewitchments or demonic possessions. Henceforward there were to be no exorcisms and no investigations to determine if an illness was the result of witchcraft or possession without his own written permission.[32] Obviously Bishop Anton Ignaz and Gassner could not expect a warm reception even from such a thorough opponent of the Enlightenment as Cardinal Migazzi.

Considering the expressed attitudes of both Maria Theresa and Joseph as well as the intellectual climate in the Viennese court, it is not surprising that in November of 1775 Emperor Joseph II ordered Bishop Anton Ignaz to banish Gassner from Regensburg and to stop "all of his exorcistic treatments that have excited such a sensation."[33] We obtain another glimpse of the emperor's personal view from a letter that Gassner sent to a clerical friend in Vienna on 12 December 1775, in which Gassner expressed his disappointment that despite his friend's efforts to represent his controversial exorcisms favorably to the highest personages at court, a critical article had just appeared in the newspaper, the *Wiener Diarium* (2 December 1775), to the effect that the cardinal archbishop, acting on the command of the emperor, had just ordered Gassner to be exiled from Regensburg. Secretly Gassner admitted to his friend that he knew the emperor had personally ordered his bishop to dismiss him "because my 'operations' in Regensburg have caused unrest among the councillors, and in my [new] parish I won't cause any more trouble."[34] By early December the bishop, after dragging his feet, had finally bowed to the will of the emperor, finding in the inconspicuous parish of Pondorf a suitable refuge for his embattled exorcist. He insisted, however, that one could not prevent Gassner from continuing to perform occasional exorcisms.

Despite the emperor's order, Gassner was still residing in Regensburg more than two months later when his bishop petitioned Cardinal Migazzi in Vienna on his behalf. On 9 February 1776 Bishop Anton Ignaz wrote requesting that Migazzi try to convey a more favorable view of the Gassner affair to the imperial court in Vienna.

In support of his petition, he claimed that he (Fugger) and four other bishops who had witnessed Gassner's amazing cures could testify to the exorcist's sterling character, to the orthodoxy of his rituals, and to the total absence of fraud. He might have added the prince abbot of Kempten as well.[35] "I therefore as bishop regard Gassner's system as most valuable because it confounds the blind wisdom of the world, puts free thought to shame, revives the dying faith of many, strengthens the reputation and power of the Church, and spreads the healing force of the most holy name of Jesus (which is so abundantly commended to us by Holy Scripture) ever more to the honor of God and to the welfare of our neighbor, as we do really see from daily experience." No better statement could have summarized the sense in which Gassner's movement represented a genuine religious revival, but these were hard times for revivals. Migazzi replied with coolness that in this matter he could do nothing, but that the bishop of Regensburg should send Gassner to Rome, where he might persuade the pope of his methods, which were, he said, "causing quite a stir" in Vienna. In a separate note, Migazzi recorded that he had personally taken the matter up with the emperor, but that "His Majesty had told me such unpleasant things" that he did not wish to depress the bishop of Regensburg by telling him all the details. It would be better to go to Rome with a view to persuading the Holy See of Gassner's orthodoxy.[36] Before sending this sensitive letter to Regensburg, Migazzi showed it to Maria Theresa, who remarked that "there was much to criticize in the bishop's letter, but nothing in your answer, which is fine." Obviously Maria Theresa and her son Joseph were of one mind concerning Gassner. The continuing efforts of Count Karl Albert von Hohenlohe-Schillingsfürst on Gassner's behalf also came to nothing, even though they attest to the attraction Gassner had for some of the high nobility of southern Germany.[37]

What we have here looks almost like a game of chess, in which various religious and political authorities used whatever specific rights, powers, and exemptions they enjoyed to counter the moves of their opponents. At first Gassner won the backing of the bishop of Chur and used his protection to counter scattered clerical complaints about

A NICHE IN THE INCUBATOR

his practice in Klösterle and to beat back skeptics in the secular administrative district of Vorarlberg (the Landvogt von Bludenz, Baron von Sternbach) and in the Anterior Austrian administration in Freiburg.[38] Later Gassner exploited the rights of the tiny counties and the various exemptions provided the imperial abbeys of Upper Swabia, despite the displeasure of the cardinal bishop of Constance, in order to unfold his arsenal of spiritual cures.[39] The bishopric of Augsburg set up a barrier to the east, and the elector of Bavaria kept him out of Bavaria, but Gassner found in the bishop of Regensburg and in the exemptions provided the princely provostry of Ellwangen a second major theater of operations. The bishops of Eichstätt and Freising firmed up Gassner's political strength in that region. Initial inquiries of the Austrian authorities came too slowly to catch Gassner in their lands, but by the time Gassner moved with his bishop to Regensburg, Emperor Joseph II and Empress Maria Theresa were ready to act decisively to investigate and to condemn Gassner's tumultuous procedures. They were in no position to condemn him theologically, but they could order the bishop of Regensburg to banish the priest to a quiet little parish, where he would no longer disturb the peace of the empire.

In the months after the emperor had moved against Gassner, mighty ecclesiastical lords issued their own warnings and prohibitions. The problem was not only one of stopping Gassner but of stopping his growing band of disciples and imitators. Nowhere was this more evident than in the archdiocese of Prague, where several priests had begun to heal the sick by publicly employing the name of Jesus. On 6 December 1775 Archbishop Antonín Petr Prichovic issued a pastoral letter, one in which Ferdinand Sterzinger was deeply involved. For that reason the letter was full of characteristically sharp theological objections to the methods and theories of Gassner. In addition to the normal admonitions against exorcizing in public, ignoring the exact guidelines of the *Rituale Romanum*, and acting without the permission of the bishop, therefore, this official warning claimed that it was truly an insult to the honor of Christ to suggest that his holy name could cure only "unnatural" illnesses but not natural disorders. Such a distinction might call into question the very miracles Christ had performed in his lifetime and would spread an unjustified fear among ordinary Christians that they were possessed (or perhaps "circumsessed") by devils, when in fact their ailments were thoroughly natural. Even worse was Gassner's conclusion that those who could not be helped were lacking in faith. The archbishop also argued that it was nothing more than an excuse and a subterfuge when Gassner and his followers taught that those "who tended to depression, anger, or other natural passions either could not be healed or else easily fell back into their prior disabilities."[40] It was, moreover, a harsh affliction for suffering patients to tell them that their relapses were due to their own sinful attitudes. A truly God-given act of healing would be permanent. This pastoral letter left little doubt that Gassner and his followers or imitators were not to be tolerated throughout the province of Prague.[41]

In the province of Salzburg the ruling archbishop was a Jansenist Febronian, Hieronymus Joseph Franz de Paula von Colloredo, a man who had already made a reputation for himself as a vehement reformer in the mold of Joseph II, a steady opponent of popular exorcisms and blessings.[42] Already in 1774 and 1775 he had issued orders to his diocesan priests to dissuade parishioners from seeking help from Gassner. On 5 January 1776 Colloredo followed the lead of the archbishop of Prague and issued his own pastoral letter against "certain exorcists" (without naming Gassner) in his archdiocese. For him Gassner's system was pure and dangerous nonsense. The use of "probative exorcisms" had been often and rightly condemned, for they only added needless tortures to those who were already suffering. Moreover, such a usage was a serious abuse of Jesus' name. Those supposedly healed by such exorcisms regularly fell back into their former conditions, no better than before. So priests and teachers should persuade ordinary people that the devil did not actually have the enlarged powers that Gassner and his imitators ascribed to him. "In the light of our times, it was no longer acceptable," the archbishop declared, to ascribe whatever one cannot explain to demons or miracles.[43]

Of course Rome represented the last word in such matters, and both Gassner's supporters and his opponents appealed to the curia to settle things once and for all. At first, in the summer of 1775, Pope Pius VI took notice of the Gassner affair but did not decide anything. Without analyzing the diplomatic jockeying for position and advantage in Rome, we can merely note that on 20 April 1776 the pope finally wrote to the bishop of Regensburg in answer to his appeal for Gassner. He conceded, of course, that exorcisms in and of themselves were laudable, so long as the guidelines of the *Roman Ritual* were carefully followed, "but we can in no way approve the procedures Gassner uses in his exorcisms." His operations were too public, too sensational, and were above all based upon the false idea that most illnesses and disabilities are either simply caused by the devil or exacerbated by him. To prevent giving even greater offense, therefore, Pope Pius declared that the usages invented by Gassner had to be completely abolished and swept away ("omnino inductum ab ipso hunc exorcismorum morem tollendum abolendumque"). Henceforward Gassner was to desist from his healings and was never to exorcize again, except in secret, rarely, and only if it was clear after the most careful investigation that someone really was possessed by the devil; and then he was to proceed only in the strictest accord with the *Roman Ritual*. Despite continuing efforts to extract something favorable for Gassner's healing methods, Joseph Hanauer is right in concluding that the pope's language represented a clear and total defeat for the priest from Klösterle.[44]

Here the political maneuvers might have reasonably ended, but two diehard princes of the empire continued to assail the pope's decision and urged him to reconsider. Neither Count Karl Albert von Hohenlohe-Schillingsfürst nor Duke Ludwig Eugen realized how little chance they had, but together with Prince Abbot Martin Gerbert of St. Blasien they kept up their efforts until Gassner's death in 1779.[45]

The ecclesiastical politics of the Holy Roman Empire had allowed a remarkable religious revival in the form of a wave of exorcistic healings to spread and flourish, but the empire's constitution also saw to it that once the pope and the emperor were adequately notified and motivated, Gassner's movement had to stop. We are perhaps used to reading that after 1648 the structures of the empire were so stiff and unwieldy that this strange polity could no longer function. But we have found that the empire worked rather well, first permitting and then forbidding an enthusiastic anti-Enlightenment healing movement.

One matter deserves more attention. We have noticed that Gassner's healings raised a host of serious questions for fervent Catholics of the 1770s. It may be surprising that the secular authorities cracked down before the system of bishops, archbishops, and finally the pope stepped in. But it is also clear that the Catholic leaders of the empire did not condemn Gassner on theological grounds. Instead, many writers esteemed him as a person and recognized the value of his religious claims but still registered what they called political objections. A Catholic admirer of Frederick the Great's Prussia, for example, asked whether a wise ruler could remain indifferent to Gassner's style of healing. Scoffers could be heard from as far away as London and Florence, he claimed, and engravers were exploiting the credulous with images of Gassner. Worthless little books were selling in editions of five to six thousand copies, and at higher prices than usual. Pharmacies were selling "eye lotions, olive oil, universal powders, and teas for incense," all blessed by Father Gassner; Ellwangen had attracted two thousand strangers a day, including both the disabled and the merely curious.[46] These cures and the false hopes of cure were harming simple people and the territories from which they came. Making a rough calculation, one author claimed that already twenty thousand invalids had gone to Ellwangen or Regensburg, taking with them at least one million gulden, money that was desperately needed closer to home. Continuing his political arithmetic, he estimated that every invalid needed at least two healthy assistants, which made for another forty thousand persons on the road to Ellwangen or Regensburg. But for every disabled person one could guess that there were five or six gawkers willing to pay two to three hundred gulden (surely an outrageous exaggeration — such a sum represented the cost of a small house). Developing a sort of mini-mercantilist protectionism aimed at defending each imperial territory's fiscal base, the author waxed indignant at the amount of specie being exported to Ellwangen or Regensburg and then wasted there. At the end of July 1775, he calculated, there were some three thousand invalids in Regensburg waiting and hoping for Gassner's help, most of them from Bohemia, even though Gassner could not treat more than fifteen to twenty a day. Assuming that these disabled were accompanied by six thousand able-bodied assistants, and assuming that each person on average spent three to six weeks waiting, spending perhaps ten gulden during their visit, one could easily estimate the travel costs alone at 600,000 gulden, and that did not count extra expenses for books, pious engravings, cartoons, anti-papal images (directed at Pope Clement XIV, probably for dissolving the Jesuit Order), prayer books, drugs, drink, indulgence pennies, and for the soldiers to keep order; one could easily chalk up Gassner's cost to surrounding territories at one million gulden.[47]

To make matters worse, the author claimed that it was not even clear that Gassner provided real help to those who temporarily felt better. A careful investigation was needed to determine if he was doing any good at all. The writer also worried that by overemphasizing the agency of the devil, Gassner ran the risk of devaluing all the good that physicians did and of reviving the age of witch trials, an age that Empress Maria Theresa had only recently closed off with her Edict of 1766 prohibiting witchcraft prosecutions. It would make more sense to seek out Dr. Mesmer, whose cures, he thought, were better attested.[48] Note that this Catholic writer did not try to score any theological points against Gassner and his system but criticized the social and fiscal effects of Gassner's popularity. For some observers this was just the sort of "unrest" that prudent rulers suppressed.

Another Catholic writer, political adviser to the princes of Öttingen-Wallerstein and privy councillor to the prince provost of Ellwangen, was at first a fervent supporter of Gassner and a scurrilous opponent of Sterzinger; over time he came to have his own political reservations about Gassner.[49] Known to modern historians as the rather colorless winner of a journalistic essay contest in 1785 concerning ecclesiastical states of the empire, Joseph Edler von Sartori was far from colorless in

A Niche in the Incubator

the mid-1770s, when he was one of the most active contributors to the Gassner scandal.[50] Although he had at first expressed no reservations about Gassner's cures, by 1776 he conceded that many questions still needed close examination. It troubled him, for example, that some of those who claimed to have been helped by Gassner had not really been crippled before. Others had not shown any permanent improvement. Well-attested facts were needed, as the "reasonable Lavater" had demanded. Sartori was also irritated that Gassner dismissed thousands of helpless people, telling them that their condition was merely natural. Was God's Word useless against natural conditions? What happened when "despondent, ignorant people are driven mad and believe that spiritual aids can bring them no further help with their natural illnesses just because exorcism has failed"? Sartori had seen enough to persuade himself that Gassner had real powers, but many questions remained. His "political" doubts were further stimulated by the reports from Sulzbach, where Gassner had stayed in the fall of 1775. There a six-year-old peasant boy was said to have been cured of his mutism, but afterward could speak no better than before. Or what of the Count Vaubert from Burgundy, who had walked without a crutch before he was treated by Gassner, yet afterward was celebrated because he could walk without a crutch?[51] In a sharp departure from his earlier writings, Sartori now voiced the suspicion that certain provinces of the empire were ruled by prejudices in favor of "witchcraft, spirits, and demonic possessions" simply because they were permitted or encouraged by their secular or spiritual princes. Would Gassner have achieved fame if every crippled patient had had to obtain the opinion of an experienced physician before submitting to exorcism? If the prince had threatened to punish those who streamed to Gassner, how famous would Gassner have become? "It was all devilish, and why? Because certain territorial princes permitted it." He now agreed with the sarcastic aphorism of Muratori, that "only those lands are filled with devilries that have a famous exorcist staying there, and only so long as he's there."[52] The great model of prudence in such matters was Empress Maria Theresa's Austria. She was certainly not "Enlightened," but she forbade simple people to go traipsing off to exorcists unless they had been properly examined and certified. Without her caution, princes now ran the risk of reviving witchcraft accusations. Maria Theresa knew how to distinguish the deceitful from the mad and melancholy, and those who hoped to achieve something through a pact with the devil from those who actually did work demonic magic. Following her example, the princes of Swabia and Franconia needed to test in order to exclude patients who were "simple, retarded, crazy, afflicted with illnesses of body or spirit, or with other vehement passions of the imagination, with disordered love or anger," or those who had "inherited deficits from the disordered nature of their parents." One should not simply agree with those who claimed to be possessed, for convulsions could have natural origins and the hysterical and hypochondriacal were often haunted by "horrifying images" which gained control because of their "disordered, thick, melancholy blood." And yet Gassner always determined that such patients were possessed. Why, even Protestant theologians had written better about the proper signs of demonic possession! But Sartori feared that his appeal for serious testing by experts was doomed by the "current state system of ecclesiastical and secular states."[53] Here then were "political doubts" that hinged upon the failure of certain states to follow the healthy example of Austria in curbing superstition.

Oddly enough, another kind of political reaction to the Gassner affair came from certain Protestants who had been attracted to the exorcist and were reluctant to see his system condemned. In contrast to Catholics, who might have to follow their authorities and yield to the archbishops of Prague and Salzburg, one Protestant gloried in his Protestant right to defy the Catholic authorities. Although Archbishop Colloredo was perhaps the "primate of Germany," he was not infallible, he wrote, nor did his theologians include anyone of real wisdom. Instead of thoroughly investigating Gassner, the archbishop of Salzburg had reacted out of a foolish fear of disorder. Halfway through this pseudonymous treatise the unknown author began to blast away insultingly at the secular prejudices visible in the pastoral letters from Prague and Salzburg. Were they not perhaps envious of Gassner? Lacking his faith, had they not turned in wrath, contempt, and madness against him? Was it not both traditional and obvious that the devil could cause physical ills? Was the current age really so enlightened that the pains of hell were only a myth? Had Lucretius and Julian the Apostate had the last word? Of course not. But the theologians of Salzburg were a race of adders, filled with pride and malice.[54] To this author's amazement, the learned of Salzburg did not even sense that reason of state should support Gassner and his doctrines, for theirs was a church that depended upon miracles as a source of money. Instead they represented a secret and treacherous enemy of Rome, a hypocritical wolf in sheep's clothing.[55] We may be surprised to find such symptoms of disappointment and outrage on the part of Protestants, but it is noteworthy that some of this bitterly disillusioned author's arguments were essentially secular and political in nature.

Let us consider one final political note in this discussion. Abbot Oswald Loschert, the Premonstratensian abbot of Oberzell near Würzburg (1704–1785), was one of Gassner's most adamant supporters. His arguments ranged widely over theology, church history, the nature of the empirical evidence for the reality of the devil, and the effectiveness of the exorcisms. In 1749 Loschert had taken an active part in the trial of Maria Renata Singer, subprior of the Cloister of Unterzell, who stood accused of witchcraft and was executed in one of the most spectacular late cases in all of Germany. Loschert had also composed a detailed report sent to Maria Theresa, who had expressed her disgust at the affair.[56] By 1778 it was public knowledge that the emperor had ordered Gassner exiled from Regensburg and that the pope had condemned several elements of his system. For Loschert, however, much remained to be salvaged. He insisted, for example, that the exorcist had not obtained his knowledge of probative exorcisms from forbidden books (such as the *Armamentarium* of Stoiber, the *Flagellum Daemonum* of Menghi, or the *Malleus Daemonum* of Alessandro Albertini a Rocha) but from respected books (listing those of Candidus Brognolo, Gelasius di Cilia, Anton Reichle, and Baruffaldus).[57]

In considering the pastoral letters of the archbishops of Prague and

Salzburg, Abbot Loschert produced a remarkable argument. How could it be, he asked, that men who follow "the views of Espen or Febronius and aim at diminishing papal power and at expanding the power of bishops" could have the effrontery to accuse two bishops (he probably meant those of Regensburg and Chur) of tolerating a form of exorcism that rested on "superstitious formulas"?[58] Here Loschert placed his finger on a sore spot in the German episcopal movement, for it became clear in the 1780s that while Febronius seemed to be arguing for the autonomy of the German bishops, his arguments appealed mainly to the archbishops; as we've seen, the German bishops were divided over Gassner while the great metropolitan princes took a fairly unified stand against him.

Loschert was also determined to see the papal condemnation as one of only practical administrative significance. Pius VI had not condemned exorcisms, of course, and had merely insisted that they should occur "rarely, secretly, and in accord with the *Roman Ritual*." But logically one exorcized more often if demon possession became more common, and Loschert was sure that Gassner's probative exorcisms had proved that demonic assaults were epidemic. It seemed crucial to emphasize that Gassner had not mainly dealt with full-fledged demonic possession but with "devils who torment, sicken, and assault a person inwardly or outwardly." No wonder the exorcisms of the *Roman Ritual* were not appropriate here, for they dealt "only with those obsessed or possessed by the demons and not with bodies vexed with illnesses." And yet even the *Rituale Romanum* provided formulas for "praecepta in nomine Jesu" (i.e., admonitions in the name of Jesus). The German bishops, moreover, had never given up the right to establish their own "special regulations" so long as they did not contradict the *Roman Ritual*. Indeed, Loschert was right on this matter. As recently as 1773 the diocese of Bamberg issued its own Ritual with a broadened understanding of exorcism.[59]

None of these objections could salvage Gassner's system. The tumults he had provoked, the religious excitement, and the revived fears of the devil were too offensive to the peace of the empire; and his probative exorcisms, his lack of appropriate consultation with physicians, and the sensational publicity surrounding his healings had brought the church under a cloud of Enlightened ridicule. For a time the Holy Roman Empire had provided a niche in which his religious revival could take root and flourish, but politically the authorities both secular and ecclesiastical also had effective means at their disposal with which to snuff out such enthusiasms. The lightning bolt of Gassner's healing campaign illuminates both the imperial niches he might exploit and the imperial mechanisms that still functioned effectively to silence this sort of revival.

three
HEALING

> "If all the illnesses that this priest describes have their origin in the devil, and if they can only be treated by exorcisms, then bid our physicians good-bye."
> — *Churbaierische Intelligenzblätter für das Jahr 1774*,
> 12 November 1774

To judge from the countless little portraits that circulated in the 1770s, Father Johann Joseph Gassner was a short, plump, clean-shaven man of modest demeanor. When he dealt with the devil, however, he became vehement and, some said, physically forceful as he touched, stroked, grasped, and finally even wrenched the affected limbs of those who sought his help. From 1774 to 1776 he and his "wonder cures" became a major topic of Enlightened debate in Germany and provoked reflection on a wide range of topics, especially on whether the devil really intervened in the world as a physical force or had physical effects. In the 1760s Gassner had developed a kind of exorcism that was not exactly orthodox, or at least did not follow slavishly the rules laid down in the *Rituale Romanum* of 1614.[1] This was clearly one of the reasons why he got into trouble with critics and with his ecclesiastical superiors, who forced him to stop his mass exorcisms in 1776.[2] One year after Gassner began his healing tour in southern Germany, treating a variety of ordinary ills by working on the assumption that many of them were of demonic origin, Franz Anton Mesmer, as we have noted, went on a healing campaign through some of the same territory. Although Mesmer healed many of the same sorts of miseries, he claimed that his therapy was based on the natural force of "animal magnetism" and not on any supposed casting out of demons. The similarities were striking enough to engage the satirical talents of skeptics and to enrage the perfervid supporters of Gassner. This set

Johann Joseph Gassner, 1775. Contemporaries remarked on the large number of pious images, like this one, depicting Gassner healing various sorts of ailments: the sick, the dumb, and (as here) the crippled. Such images were commonly sold at pilgrimage shrines and displayed on the walls of even humble homes. *Source:* J. M. Söckler, copperplate engraving 1775; reproduced by the kind permission of the Germanisches Nationalmuseum, Nuremberg.

the stage for a noisy debate over the nature of healing, with the forces of Enlightenment ranged against the forces of exorcism.

Gassner and Healing: The Early Years

In this chapter we will look closely at the actual healings conducted by Gassner. The sources for such an examination lie partly in the printed literature of the Gassner controversy, in which we find various reports of eyewitnesses reproduced and criticized at length.[3] But the main sources for this chapter are the manuscript diaries, "protocols," and memoranda taken down by various observers and surviving today in the archives of Feldkirch (Vorarlberg), Munich, Neuenstein (Hohenlohe), and Bamberg.

When Gassner began his healings in Klösterle, he first dealt only with his own parishioners, but already in the early 1760s he began blessing and healing those from nearby regions: from all parts of the Klostertal, from Montafon, Bludenz, Feldkirch, Appenzell, and St. Gall in Switzerland, and even from the south-running valleys of Tyrol such as the Alto-Adige. We are not well informed about his methods in those early days even though he kept several "diaries" starting in the late 1760s. It is clear that the reason he started recording his successes (and only his successes) was his fear that he might one day have to account for what he was doing.[4] But it did not occur to him to record exactly what he did in any detail. Instead, he contented himself with remarks like these:

> Recently a married woman came here from Nassereith in Tyrol suffering with the falling sickness (epilepsy) for many years, and she underwent the test (the "Prob") in the presence of two court officials from here. The result was that she was helped with the above-mentioned illness.[5]

> Christian Big im Wald was crippled (*krum*) with horrible pains; was helped in the presence of the Herr Paumeister [=Baumeister] from here with blessings and restored to complete health although previously all doctoring had done no good.[6]

HEALING

> Franz Riedinger from Bludenz was blind in one eye and was restored to full sight through use of *spiritualibus* [i.e., spiritual aids or sacramentals] here.[7]

These are clearly not the sources from which we can glean much information about what was actually happening, or even what they meant to the participants, and one may doubt whether such memoranda would have done Father Gassner much good if he had been called to account.

Tabulating the Cures

We can, however, tabulate the cures he claimed in order to see what sorts of complaints his supplicants presented. In the "Diarium" that he maintained for 1769 he recorded most of his cures and healing miracles over the previous two years, 1767–1769. If we divide them by gender, we discover that Gassner did not always even make that distinction clear, and sometimes merely remarked that "many" people were helped with a particular problem. Even so, he claimed to have helped over two hundred. (See table 3.1.) From this list it might appear that Gassner was treating an unusually high number of those who suffered from epilepsy (thirteen in all, or about 9 percent of the 140 patients whose ailments can be identified). This was, after all, a disease that had seemed especially mysterious (or even "sacred") ever since antiquity. Several of the other ailments he listed seem to fit into the category some people regard as psychosomatic complaints. But the profile of his patients changed as he became more well known.

In the "diary" Gassner kept for the spring of 1773, he claimed to have healed 130 persons with the ailments listed in table 3.2. From this list we can see that by 1773 epilepsy had fallen from roughly 9 percent to just over 3 percent of all the human complaints. Let us also note, however, that Gassner was obviously also blessing cattle and claiming satisfactory results here too. If there's a placebo response, does it work on cattle? Or only on the owners of cattle? But these early lists also illustrate perfectly Gassner's major innovation. He was

HEALING

Table 3.1 Gassner's Cures in Klösterle: 1767–1769

	Male	Female	Gender Unknown
Epilepsy	2	8	3
"Sick"	4	7	1
Chest *and* heart trouble	3	2	0
Fevers	7	7	2 + "viele"
Blind	5	4	"viele"
Deaf	0	1	
Throat	0	1	
Head *and* face	2	5	
Womb	0	1	
Crippled, lame	13	16	
Cramps and paralysis	1	2	
Pains	4	1	2
Dead [!]	0	1	
Cancer	0	1	
Mad	10	11	
Stomach, vomiting	1	2	
"Dörrsucht" (consumption)	0	1	
Marital impediment	1	1	
"Maul" (lockjaw)	0	1	
Leprosy	0	2	
Could not eat	2	1	
Unknown	1	0	62
Totals	56	76	70, plus two entries listing "viele" many)

Source: Gassner's entries in Diözesanarchiv Feldkirch, Pfarrei Klösterle, 1.2.2.1 ("Diarium I, 1769 mit Nachträgen seit 1759").

obviously treating most illnesses and misfortunes as if they *could* be caused or exacerbated by the devil. He did not discourage the use of medicines but often triumphantly noted that by the time patients came to him, medicine, barber surgeons, and doctors had proved themselves of no use. We find among these hundreds of unfortunate persons none of the classic signs of demoniac possession: no

HEALING

Table 3.2 Gassner's Cures in Klösterle: Spring of 1773

	Male	Female	Gender Unknown
Epilepsy	2	2	
Fatigue	1	0	
"Sick"	0	2	
Chest and heart ailments	1	7	
Shivers and fevers	3	4	
Infections	1	0	
Blind	6	6	
Deaf	3	2	
Cough	1	1	
Throat	0	3	
Headache	2	5	
Womb	0	1	
Testicle	1	0	
Crippled	3	4	2
Pains	20	25	14
Mad	4	4	
Totals	48	66	16
130 in all			
Subgroups of the above:			
Suffering "Maleficium"	2	4	
Children	4	3	2
Marital impediment	0	2	
Cures of cattle diseases			11 owners

Source: Gassner's entries in Diözesanarchiv Feldkirch, Pfarrei Klösterle, 1.2.2.2 ("Diarium II, Frühling 1773").

supernatural strength, no frothing at the mouth,[8] no unaccountable knowledge of distant events. So far as we can tell from these lists, they showed no mysterious ability to *speak* foreign languages they had never learned. Basically, Gassner employed blessings and exorcisms to treat illnesses that looked natural. As I suggested in the first chapter, this is perhaps one of the ways in which the Enlightenment affected his practice: the devil no longer looked as if he were separate from the world of normal appearance. But if we want to understand what he was doing, these records are pretty unyielding.

Fraud? Hysteria?

One of our first responses to such lists of diseases and disorders cured by Gassner is likely to be a search for modern scientific or medical explanations. We may no longer suspect that Gassner was fraudulently falsifying the records or secretly using metal magnets or "sympathetic" materials to obtain marvelous results. I mentioned in the previous chapter, however, that Franz Anton Mesmer felt certain that Gassner was using animal magnetism without knowing it, and a strong tradition within the history of psychoanalysis has tended to agree.[9] And it continues to be common to look over such lists of ailments and to perceive in them (or to choose from them) the psychosomatic complaints and the neurotic or "abnormal" conditions that we regard as characteristic of "hysteria," even though most of the classic conversion hysterias have also evaporated in recent decades. It has long been common to denigrate those religious phenomena one disapproves as sick, "enthusiastic," fanatic, hysterical, or pathological, as Ann Taves points out in her excellent book, *Fits, Trances, and Visions: Experiencing Religion and Explaining Experience from Wesley to James*.[10] The naturalizing language of psychiatry carries with it a flattening effect that eviscerates or devours the neighboring notions of religion and religious experience. Ever since the days of William James, therefore, students of religion have been wise to look for mediating positions rather than opting for the stark dichotomies of natural vs. religious.[11] We need to consider the claims of those who urge a reenchanted nature, a more meaningful science, without necessarily adopting a fully supernatural dimension. This means that we are well advised to ask, at least as a first step, what Gassner was doing. We need to look closely.

HEALING

Better Notes: What Was Gassner Doing?

As Gassner's healing campaign became notorious and controversial, his enthusiastic followers began to take better notes, and Gassner may have learned to be more careful as well (by eliminating his cattle cures, for example) and to speak less and less of witchcraft. Because the sources are not as rich, I will pass over his tour of the region just north of the Lake of Constance, where he impressed many but failed to persuade the cardinal bishop of Constance, Franz Konrad von Rodt, who gave Gassner an hour-long interview and allowed him to try his blessings and exorcisms in his seminary.[12] The picture of Gassner's healing methods clears up considerably from the period in Ellwangen onward. Now we get detailed reports and learn, moreover, that little copper-plate engravings were so commonly sold that, according to the Protestant Augsburg notary Georg Wilhelm Zapf, a copy could be found "in almost every room of the pious while his printed blessing is posted on all the doors of simple and superstitious people."[13] From such images we can obtain an idealized example of the propaganda that at least shows us what Gassner and his followers wanted others to see and experience. Seated at a table, Gassner usually began with instructions and commands to the patient as well as to the demons he presumed were present. In most cases when a supplicant came to Gassner and knelt before him, Gassner might touch him with a small cross or hold his head in his hands. If critical voices among the observers challenged this physical contact, however, he might refrain from stroking or touching of any sort. After a short conversation with the patient, in which Gassner learned the name, origin, and complaint of the person, he undertook to determine whether the devil was present either inwardly or outwardly or perhaps that the disorder was only natural.[14] In most of his early cases he persuaded himself that a demon was at work, and he tried to persuade his suffering patient of the same fact. Much depended upon awakening a sense of trust and on proving that the devil still assaulted mankind in body and soul, and here he drew extensively on his own personal experiences with the devil. Next he urged the patient to obey him to the letter and to believe that the devil was in fact at the root of his or her particular troubles. This was often the most difficult point, and Gassner would proceed by commanding, "If this illness is unnatural, then I command in the name of Jesus that it should show itself at once." Gassner used this *Exorcismus probativus* to move the demon around in the body and to evoke a wide range of horrible symptoms: swellings first here, and then there, fevers, headache, cramps, convulsions, tremors, and pains in one foot, then in the other.

As Gassner moved the demon about, he was also showing the patient that the devil was really there. For this reason he often called his procedures *Praecepta*, precepts, or lessons, in which the devil learned who was boss and the patient learned to trust Gassner and the powerful name of Jesus, but also how to cause his own symptoms to come and go. Sometimes Gassner seemed to torture a patient for up to fifteen minutes with the worst pains and cramps he had ever felt and then dispel them with an *exorcismus lenitivus*. In the most stubborn cases Gassner might take two hours before he was ready to finish off the devil with a final, explosive *exorcismus expulsivus*.[15]

Astonishingly the wished-for symptoms usually appeared whether Gassner spoke in German or in Latin, and often enough a patient would exhibit not just his or her original complaint but horrid, painful convulsions or swellings that he or she had never experienced before. Gassner also proved a master at commanding changes of mood, evoking in quick succession laughter and then sadness, hatred and then timidity or high passion. It also appeared that Gassner was fond of using special hand gestures or strokes. Of course he used the sign of the cross, but he might also grip the hands or head of the patient and place his stole on affected body parts: stomach, chest, lower back, abdomen, hands, or feet.

The View of Gassner's Critics: Physical Explanations

Critics such as Ferdinand Sterzinger were convinced that when Gassner touched his patients, his rubbings, grippings, and manual pressure communicated some secret but natural force. He concluded "that a secret force from the kingdom of nature lies hidden in the operations of Gassner. This rubbing of the exorcist on his belt, the strong pressure on the head of the patient while he pushes with the right hand on the forehead while the left pushes the sensitive parts of the neck, the feeling of the pulses, the shaking, the various posturings, and all of these physical treatments, which I have seen with my own eyes, all give me cause to believe that either a magnetic, an electrical, or a sympathetic force produces these effects, and all the more easily because the power of imagination of the patient is also excited to the maximum, partly by his preaching, partly by his fixed gaze, partly by an immoderate trust in this holy man, partly by the constructed hope for a healing, and other charming fantasies, which are easily capable of confusing the imagination and of moving the vital spirits."[16]

In stubborn cases, Gassner seems to have moved on to ever more energetic measures. According to one sharp critic, he treated a girl whom he regarded as fully possessed by a demon, by grabbing her hair and shaking her head so sharply that the observer thought she would surely lose both hearing and sight.[17]

The worst pains may have been felt by the arthritic and crippled, for Gassner argued that their pains were usually caused or exacerbated by the devil and that a firm faith and some enforced movement might drive away the pain and restore flexibility to limbs that had grown stiff from lack of use. Despite the immediate pains of the procedure, some participants later signed affidavits that the treatment produced real improvements.[18] For critical observers, however, Gassner often went well beyond the limits of good taste and decency, causing one woman to experience repeated assaults of prolapsed uterus, and openly stroking or palpating the possessed breasts of another.[19]

Despite these indiscretions, which critics tried to blow up into scandals (without much success) the most astonishing cures were those worked by Gassner through the use of merely mental commands, or exorcisms in Latin accompanied by secret, inaudible mental instructions.[20] It is no wonder that his fame as a miracle worker spread far and wide and that even crippled and hopeless Protestants betook themselves to Gassner wherever he went. He used his exorcisms to try to

Don Ferdinand Sterzinger, Ord. Theat. (1721–1786). Sterzinger was a prominent member of the Bavarian Academy of Sciences and a spokesman for the Catholic Enlightenment. In the 1760s Sterzinger gained a reputation as an outspoken opponent of "superstition" and of traditional doctrines of witchcraft; in 1775 he emerged as one of Gassner's fiercest opponents. *Die Aufgedeckten Gassnerischen Wunderkuren*, title engraving by J. M. Söckler, 1775; reproduced by kind permission of the Staats- und Stadtbibliothek, Augsburg.

persuade them that conversion to the Catholic faith was the only secure way to keep the devil away, but of course we cannot tell at a distance of over two hundred years whether their conversions were profound or permanent. At the conclusion of a healing episode, he would pray, bless the patient, and prescribe the continued use of relics and holy oil, water, powders, incense, and herbs, all combined with a strengthened faith in the Holy Name of Jesus. Local merchants rejoiced in a strong demand for crucifixes, rosaries, images of Gassner or the Agnus Dei, rings, blessed salves, and devotional booklets.

Participant Observations: Bernhard Joseph Schleis and Abbot Bourgeois

In the enthusiastic but detailed account given (anonymously) by Dr. Bernhard Joseph Schleis von Löwenfeld (1731–1800), we can sense some of the excitement that accompanied a visit to Gassner. This personal physician to the widowed Countess Palatine Dorothea Francisca of the Upper Palatinate-Sulzbach, traveled over one hundred miles to Ellwangen in early March 1775, to see for himself because he had read such contradictory things about Gassner's cures. By the time he got there, the little town of only about two hundred solid houses was teeming with over fifteen hundred foreign visitors. Schleis reported that throngs of sick and miserable ("in soul and body") lingered outside Gassner's house just hoping to glimpse the wonder-worker. Only noblemen and ladies enjoyed unrestricted access to him, however, and others had to try to obtain an appointment. Schleis found out, though, that by paying a few groschen, he could slip past the corporal guarding the door and join a group of observers. Inside he found that an interior wall had been taken down so that visitors could easily see what was transpiring in the next room. There, starting at 5:00 A.M. every morning, Gassner sat at a table with a crucifix to his right. At one end of the table sat a notary ready to take down information concerning each supplicant. Gassner himself was plainly dressed except for a blue stole decorated with red flowers and a silver chain around his neck, from which dangled a piece of the true cross. With each patient, Schleis confirmed that Gassner's first task was to order the illness or complaint to manifest itself. If skeptical doctors were present, he seemed all the more peremptory in calling forth illnesses, sometimes seizing the feet or legs of the crippled, or the head and neck of those with headaches. He often laid his stole on the affected limb or around the head of the afflicted while ordering the complaint to appear. Sometimes this happened at once, but with others it might take ten repetitions. Gassner explained that those who manifested their complaints at once were the "Gut- und Starkglaubige" (those of good and strong faith) while the more hesitant were "Zaghafte und Kleinglaubige" (persons of small and hesitant faith). If a disease or condition did not show itself at all, Gassner held that the person was either naturally afflicted or was perhaps a total unbeliever. In either of those cases, the person was sent away, sometimes with a prayer but with no noticeable improvement. Dr. Schleis was emphatic that Gassner excluded no one, not even those with epidemic diseases or women with monthly complaints, for in his view unnatural diseases could easily hide under the mask of the natural. There were of course truly natural and incurable ailments such as hernia, or a flap of skin that might have grown over an eye, or a badly mended broken leg, but often Gassner claimed, even in such cases, that he could at least alleviate the continuing pain. If a man's lame leg resulted from a damaged Achilles tendon or from a severed nerve, that was natural and beyond Gassner's help. But if it came from *Gicht*, *Gliedersucht*, or *Schlagfluss* (gout, arthritis, or stroke) he might cry out "Oh! This is an unnatural crippling" (O! dieses ist eine unnatürliche Lähmung).[21] Schleis seems to have been fascinated with the element of showmanship here but also convinced that real healing was going on.

Another close observer noticed something else at Ellwangen. A certain Abbot Bourgeois, tutor to the young count of Donsdorf, wrote a description to his brother in Luxembourg emphasizing that Gassner caused symptoms to come and go repeatedly. After cramps that were brought on and then dispelled, patients also suffered waves of contradictory emotions: uncontrollable laughter followed by weeping; frantic singing followed by despair and the melancholy desire to confess.

We would find some symptoms hard to duplicate under clinical circumstances. "He commanded that the pulse in the right arm become weak and barely detectable, but in the left arm it should become strong and fast. Private physicians in attendance felt the right and left pulses and agreed that it was so. The military doctor from Würzburg confirmed all this."[22]

Most strikingly, it now appeared that Gassner practiced until the patient "was convinced of the origin of his trouble and the strength of his [exorcistic] methods, and then he taught him how to help himself in the future and had him test this out [lässt ihn in seiner Gegenwart die Probe machen] in his presence. To this end he commands the sickness [*Krankheit*] to come again, and now the patient has to prevent the outburst, or drive it away if it's already present, with an opposing command, which he issues inwardly in the Name of Jesus. I saw this, and the patients agree."[23] Here Bourgeois described an aspect of these therapies that no one else had remarked upon before. We will notice that as the eyewitness reports became denser in 1775 this aspect became more and more evident.

The Problem of Eyewitness Reports: Who Saw What?

Let us observe that obviously none of the testimony I have cited was impartial. Despite constant claims of objectivity and honesty, those in attendance found themselves either persuaded or skeptical, either willing or unwilling to believe what seemed to be presented. And so all of the scandalous scenes I have read come, naturally enough, from skeptics, while believers are the source for my notions of who was really helped by Gassner's faith healings and exorcisms. There is a hermeneutic circle here that sometimes makes the determination of what "really happened" seem like a sort of historical will-o'-the-wisp. But all historical sources come with their own biases, and historians regularly make a kind of rough and imperfect sense from materials that can never yield up unmediated truths. The best we can do with these reports is notice anomalous details in the accounts of those who basically favored or distrusted the wonder worker.

One of the first deeply skeptical reports came, as we have noted, from the Enlightened pen of Don Ferdinand Sterzinger, the Theatine nobleman from Munich. Already on 12 November 1774 the *Churbaierische Intelligenzblätter* reported the recent publication of Gassner's little guide entitled *Useful Instruction in Fighting the Devil* (*Nützlicher Unterricht wider den Teufel zu streiten*).[24] What caught the eye of the editors in Munich was surely Gassner's explicit attempt to make witchcraft and magic ("Hexerey" and "Zauberkunst") an essential part of the Christian religion and his angry attack on such moderate Enlighteners as Ferdinand Sterzinger, and other heroes of the Bavarian "witchcraft war" of the 1760s, such as "Arduino Ubbidente Dell'Osa" (i.e., Jordan Simon O.S.A., professor of church history and canon law in Erfurt), "Blocksberger" (i.e., Andreas Ulrich Mayer, the chaplain of an Upper Palatine nobleman), C. F. Kautz (an imperial councillor from Vienna) and the "doubting Bavarian" (i.e., Jacob Anton Kollmann). So it will not surprise us that the energetic Sterzinger arranged to visit Ellwangen in December 1774, soon after Gassner had arrived there.[25] On the December 21 Sterzinger watched with amazement as Gassner called forth and expelled "demons" from a series of personages, including the daughter of Bavarian Privy Councillor Protomedicus Johann Anton von Wolter, Baroness von Erdt, who was suffering from convulsions. The "Protokoll" or eyewitness report that Sterzinger published quickly became notorious.[26] Soon the prince elector of Bavaria was sufficiently aroused that he forbade any further discussion of Gassner in Bavaria even as he refused to allow the exorcist into his duchy. As we have already seen, Sterzinger was prepared to grant that Gassner's patients did enjoy some relief of their ailments, even if only for an interval. But he was sure that there was no proof here that the devil was present or that Gassner could move him around or finally expel him.

Starting with Sterzinger's so-called *Exposure of Gassner's Miracle Cures* (Die aufgedeckten Gassnerischen Wunderkuren), debate over Gassner really got under way, and as it developed, one of the basic issues revolved around the nature of the testimony, the number and kind of witnesses, and the detail of the reports that attested to the exorcist's methods. In this game, eyewitnesses were trumps, as we can see from the report of Dr. Bernhard Schleis of Sulzbach. Dr. Schleis told his readers that as a doctor he too had had his doubts about Gassner's marvelous cures. Could there possibly be a magnetic, electrical, sympathetic, or magical force at work here? That was Sterzinger's suspicion, as we have seen, and just the sort of question for which Schleis's medical training had prepared him, but when he visited, he reported that he was unable to detect any hint of fraud or physical means of cure. On one day Schleis was there with two other doctors, a Catholic and a Protestant, and they carefully witnessed cures of many ills, including "epileptic, hypochondriacal, melancholic, furious [i.e., mad], and even [fully] possessed persons," and all who absorbed the influence of Jesus' name were cured. Schleis noted that he himself underwent a treatment for his podagra, a subject on which he had written a book (published in 1767), and he too experienced the relief of Gassner's blessings.

With a great show of medical learning, Schleis noted that recent advances in the understanding of magnets had clarified the marvelous effects of special armatures and devices, and that electrical sparks too could be generated with the right kind of rubbing. "But no!" Gassner used no magnets, and who had ever seen him emit a spark? He admitted as well that the human imagination (*Einbildungskraft*) was always the biggest factor in any successful cure. "Yes, yes, the imagination is according to these philosophers the queen of this world: all luck and misfortune, riches and poverty, victory and defeat consist only in the imagination. So why shouldn't health and sickness also consist of that?" And yet, what pharmacist or surgeon can conquer cataracts and with a word persuade the blind to see? In Ellwangen a Prussian officer who observed Gassner for a time claimed that out of thirty patients no more than two failed to respond to his cures.[27]

So far, I have found no full manuscript record of his Ellwangen campaign (late 1774 to early 1775), but Alois Merz, the zealous ex-Jesuit, wrote in his biography of Gassner that in Ellwangen hundreds of persons of the highest rank now came to him, and that Bishop Fugger ordered the procedures to be carefully reported in order to fend off criticism.[28] Merz claimed that this was done, but that because of the great similarity of all the cases, he simply omitted most. Evidently, Merz was not yet sensitive to the importance of such eyewitness minutes.

The Regensburg Reports

Let us leave aside the details of the reports for a moment and take note of what happened to *Protokolle* in general. The literary battle over Gassner became thoroughly consumed by the question "Who had the better reports?" and this question in turn influenced the actual reports taken down during Gassner's healings. From his stay in Regensburg, for example, the Bayerische Staatsarchiv preserves the actual minutes of Gassner's operations, running from June to September 1775 (see table 3.3). They present a staggeringly full, even if fundamentally biased, record of healing. We are given the name, address, and complaint of over four hundred persons, whom Gassner seemed to help. But now for the first time the minutes record in detail the numbers of persons who could not be helped. And those numbers went up dramatically. On 16 June 1775, no one was listed as sent away without help, but already by June 20, the records include seven persons whose maladies were either natural (such as four cases of profound blindness) or whose mental condition made it impossible for them to take in Gassner's message. Several of these latter were described as melancholy or "schwermütig" or half-wits and fools ("eine halbe Nahrheit bemerkt," "verwiesen . . . weil sie nur mit halber vernunft befunden," "wegen Abgang des Verstands oder munteren Vertrauens"). This was a new level of self-denying reportage, but after July 4, the numbers of those dismissed with no cure skyrocketed. As the minutes became more and more scrupulous, it became clear now that those who had to depart with no help actually outnumbered those Gassner could help.

It is of course possible that Regensburg was simply a less enthusiastic place for faith healing, that the conditions in Ellwangen could not be so easily reproduced. After all, even Jesus had had trouble with the

Table 3.3 Gassner's Cures in Regensburg: June–September 1775

	Male (m)	Female (f)	Dismissed without Help (d)	Totals (m, f, d)
16 June	8	8		
20 June	12	9	8	
21 June	9	8	3	
23 June	10	14	25	
27 June	13	12	21	
28 June	3	9	26	
30 June	4	6	10	59m, 66f, 93d
4 July	3	13	8	
5 July	6	4	43	
7 July	5	6	25	
11 July	1	9	24	
12 July	4	8	21	
14 July	6	2	35	25m, 42f, 156d
18 July	14	5	50	
19 July	1	3	19	
21 July	10	18	29	
26 July	1	5	8	
28 July	2	3	38	28m, 34f, 144d
1 August	6	7	40	
2 August	1	3	25	
4 August	2	9	24	
8 August	0	7	28	
9 August	5	2	39–42	
11 August	2	8	38	16m, 36f, 194–197d
16 August	2	3	35 + "viele"	
18 August	4	5	16 + "viele"	
22 August	8	6	21	
23 August	5	7	49	
25 August	4	8	16	
29 August	5	8	15	
30 August	8	6	17	36m, 43f, 169++d[a]

HEALING

Table 3.3 (*continued*)

	Male (m)	Female (f)	Dismissed without Help (d)	Totals (m, f, d)
1 September	0	8	9	
5 September	4	5	19	
6 September	1	1	11	
12 September	9	11	26	
13 September	0	1	11	
15 September	5	2	4	19m, 28f, 80d

ᵃSome entries implied that several extra persons were dismissed. This is indicated by the plus sign; for larger numbers implied, the double plus sign is used. Source: Bayerisches Hauptstaatsarchiv, Munich, GR 1210/20.

people of his own home district and could work no miracles there (Mark 5:5–6). But it is easily possible that what had really changed was the nature of the eyewitness minutes. Increasingly we see what one report from Ellwangen had mentioned, that Gassner was not fully successful with a patient until she or he *learned* to control his or her symptoms.[29] By the summer of 1775 it appeared to some of Gassner's proponents that what he was really doing was teaching tormented people to intensify and then to dismiss their pains themselves, with the help of Jesus.[30] But if this is what he now seemed to be doing, it was becoming clear that some cases were beyond his instruction. The numbers of those dismissed with no help now ballooned to numbers that exceeded those cured. As we can see from table 3.4, those dismissed in this way rose from 42 percent of supplicants to almost 80 percent by August. I suspect that Gassner's healing methods were actually shifting under the scrutiny of skeptics and medical observers, and that he was increasingly using exorcism as a way to teach people how to manage their pain and control their symptoms. He was still "thinking with demons," but he was doing something new.

The ailments Gassner was treating remained as diverse as ever. The minutes from Regensburg allow us to list the cases from the first

Table 3.4 Summary of Gassner's Regensburg Healings:
June–September 1775

Dates	Male	Female	Total m + f	Dismissed	Dismissed as Percent of Total
2nd half June	59	66	125	93	42 percent
1st half July	25	42	67	156	70 percent
2nd half July	28	34	62	144	70 percent
1st half Aug.	16	36	52	194–197	79 percent
2nd half Aug.	36	43	79	169++	68 percent++
1st half Sept.	19	28	47	80	63 percent
Total persons seen:		1,268 ++			
Total healed:		432			
Total dismissed:		at least 836			

Source: Bayerisches Hauptstaatsarchiv, Munich, GR 1210/20.

twenty days of his campaign there (see table 3.5). We notice that epilepsy was now fairly rare but that "pains" and lameness of various sorts, arthritis, crooked hands and feet, along with shakes, tremors, and convulsions were the most common complaints. A large number of patients also came with eye and ear troubles or with neurological disorders. Explicitly psychological problems were by no means the most common complaints of these troubled souls.

The Sulzbach Reports

In September 1775, Gassner traveled to Sulzbach, where the widowed Countess Palatine Francisca had invited him, doubtless at the instigation of Dr. Bernhard Joseph Schleis, who had become one of his most articulate proponents. Here we are not told how many Gassner could *not* help, but according to Schleis, who signed a large number of these minutes, the key came when Gassner got these patients to take charge of their symptoms, to piously get rid of troubles when they returned (see table 3.6). As he told eleven-year-old Isabella Enhuber (25 September 1775):

Table 3.5 Symptoms of Those Healed by Gassner in Regensburg: 16 June–4 July 1775

	Male	Female	Dismissed without Help
Epilepsy	3	2	1
Swellings	2	4	
Pains	11	9	
Lame feet ("crooked feet")	7	2	
Short foot	1	2	2
Lame hands ("crooked hands")	1	2	1
Headache	3	2	
Faint/weak	2	1	
Tremors, shakes, convulsions	9	14	1
"Serious illness"	0	4	
"Womb"	0	2	
Nausea/can't eat	2	1	
Paralysis	4	2	
Can't walk	2	1	
Asthma/lungs	2	6	
Eyes (blind, dim, painful)	12	4	5
Hearing	4	12	
Anxious	1	1	
Unconscious spells, trance	0	2	
Dizzy	0	1	
"Fury"	1	0	
Melancholia	0	1	
Secret concern	1	0	
Obsessed (seemed possessed)	1	4	1
Dismissed with no description or diagnosis[a]			90
Total[b]	69 (47 percent)	79 (53 percent)	101

[a] After 4 July 1775 the numbers of those dismissed ("verwiesen") rose dramatically.

[b] A total of 148 patients were helped with at least one symptom; 101 were sent away either because Gassner determined that their conditions were natural or because they were so sad, despondent, or depressed that they could not be taught to trust.

Source: Bayerisches Hauptstaatsarchiv, Munich, GR 1210/20.

He reminded her again that perhaps in later years she would be overcome with such pains, and she should then remember at once that they came from the devil. So she should quickly expel them for these pains are imposed on the good and the wicked alike, but the Enemy especially attacks those of her temperament [of the same temperament]; so she should strive daily or more often, even hourly, in this battle, and command the devil in the Name of Jesus, that he should depart from her immediately with all his assaults on her body and soul.

Table 3.6 Gassner's Cures in Sulzbach: 21 September–11 November 1775[a]

	Males	Females	Indeterminate	Total
21 September	12	10		22
21–23 September	1 Graf			1
22 September	1 Baron			1
23 September	9	18	1 Kind	28
23 September	1	3 noble ladies		4
24 September	3	11	1 Kind	15
25 September	11	10	1 Kind	22
26 September	2	3		5
27 September	3	4	"viele"	7+
27 September	12	21		33
28 September	7	11	"viele"	18+
28 September	2	4		6
29 September	8	21		29
30 September	6	24	"einige"	30+
30 September	7	1		8
1 October	8	18		26
1 October	1	3		4
2 October	1	9		10
2 October	21	19	"einige"	40+
3 October	21	8		29
4 October	5	8		13
Totals:	142	206	3 +	351 +
	40 percent	59 percent	1 percent +	100 percent

[a]Signed and sealed by Bernhard Joseph Schleis von Löwenfeld. *Source:* Bayerisches Hauptstaatsarchiv, Munich, GR 1210/20.

Over and over now, the eyewitness reports record Gassner's success in teaching people to cause their pains to come and go. To take only one example, the noble lady Maria Anna von Schezzer came complaining of anxiety, weakness, headache, and toothaches.[31] Gassner immediately commanded a demonic "wind" to swell up into her chest, and her whole body began to shake with "hysterical movements" until she could hardly breathe. With the command "Cesset ista Agitatio," she became calm at once. Then he evoked headache alone, and she fell unconscious, but with the command "Iterum bene se habeat" she came to herself again. Next came her toothaches, and the headaches again; then "Sie solle alles zugleich fortschaffen"—*she* was to get rid of them all at once. Finally Father Gassner prompted all of her painful affects, cramps, and pains to come at once, and "she drove off every attack with courage and perseverance" and departed full of consolation. What had happened? What had she learned?

Gassner's Return to Ellwangen: The Politics of Healing, 1777

When Gassner was summoned back to Ellwangen by the bishop of Regensburg in October of 1777, a year and a half after Pius VI had directed that he not perform so publicly or so promiscuously ever again, it was evidently part of a campaign to change the minds of the Curia in Rome. High nobles from Hohenlohe and Württemberg, among others, were there assembled, and Alois Merz, the ex-Jesuit of Augsburg, was also present to witness and record the wonders from October of 1777 (see table 3.7).[32]

What can we say about such a list? For a start, we may be impressed by the numbers of noblemen and noble ladies who claimed to have found relief from their ailments. Of course, it was also true that when such personages were involved, they were almost sure to be recorded, and so their appearance in the list makes a larger impression than it would have if we had complete records. It is also true that by 1777 Gassner had been condemned by both the pope and the emperor, so that these cures were also politically delicate, aiming at changing the minds of those in Rome who had engineered Gassner's condemnation.[33]

Table 3.7 Gassner's Healings in Ellwangen in 1777[a]

Princes and Freiherren (6):
   Carl Albert Count of Hohenlohe Waldenburg and Schillingsfürst
   Count de Faubert, Grand Bailif d'Épée de la Province de Bourgogne
   M le Baron de Silwestolpe
   Baron von Preysing
   Freyherr von Lochner
   Freyherr von Gravenreuth
Ladies and Gentlemen (28):

Ladies	22
Gentlemen	6
Lower and Middle Class (183):	
Women	103
Men	80
Children under Age 12 (15):	
Girls	7
Boys	6
Unknown	2
Totals:	
Female	132 (57.4 percent)
Male	98 (42.6 percent)
Unknown	2
Total	232[b]

[a] The Protocol of these healings was witnessed by Carl Albrecht Prince of Hohenlohe und Waldenburg, Ludwig Eugen Duke of Württemberg, Gandolph Ernst Count of Kürnberg and Cathedral Canon of Salzburg and Canon of the Provostry of Ellwangen. The first seventeen were attested to by "Francisca, widowed Countess Palatine of Zweibrücken" herself, the mistress and employer of Dr. Bernhard Joseph Schleis.

[b] These numbers include ten Lutherans and one Catholic convert from Württemberg.

Source: Data extracted from [Oswald Loschert], *Altes und neues System* ([Frankfurt, Hanau, and Leipzig], 1778).

HEALING

Trying to Explain

There are dangers in reducing the experience of demonic possession to some supposedly more fundamental psychopathological condition, to neurosis, hysteria, psychosomatic disorder, and so forth. To avoid flattening out the experiences of other cultures and assimilating the variety of humankind to our own parochial experience, we need to preserve the integrity of the language-world within which such disorders have their reality and in which we experience them. The language we use is not just an interchangeable set of arbitrary labels but a framing and shaping environment that actually alters what we experience. In short, a rose by any other name would not smell as sweet, for the fragrance of roses is part of a whole culture in which roses have a complex historical and symbolic function. Just as food "tastes" better if it is beautifully presented, other foods may revolt us once we learn their names or what their names connote. Doctors often show that they know this as they disguise diseases under the cloak of mysterious-sounding Latinate names.

In a thoughtful book about the miracles at Lourdes in the years after 1858, Ruth Harris noted that the efforts to medicalize and explain the healings there were part of a doctrinaire positivist campaign to take the Catholic Church out of French politics and the spirit out of the world in general. Interestingly, that effort withered in the years after 1890 as the Catholic Church responded with ever better documented case histories of undoubted and frankly unexplainable cures.[34] We are entering the contested realm between the claims of experience and the claims of orthodox naturalism. Harris insists, I think rightly, that we should not blindly reduce miracles to autosuggestion, placebos, or unprecedentedly successful psychotherapy, as if we can explain satisfactorily everything we find in our records.[35] She interprets the miracles of Lourdes and elsewhere as examples of self-transformation, in which afflicted persons learn to take a different attitude toward life and toward their place in it. She also openly admits that some of the cures achieved at Lourdes truly have no physical or psychological explanation.[36] I am tempted to say something similar about Gassner. Clearly he achieved results that could not be easily explained either then or now, and he was doing so, in part, by transforming the frame within which people understood their own sufferings, making them somehow more intelligible and tolerable. In claiming that we should retain the categories within which people thought and experienced their religion, I do not wish to disclaim all interest in explaining (in our own terms) what we find in the past. But the number of cures Gassner achieved and the speed with which he achieved them (in minutes or hours at the most) hardly fit with what we understand about placebos today.[37] Moreover, the concept of the placebo has the strange effect of colonizing territory for medicine even as it admits an efficacy beyond our current abilities to explain. When we say that a particular medicine works by way of the placebo response, we mean that it seems to have an effect that we cannot otherwise explain, but we do not mean that it works instantaneously or miraculously. As Ed Cohen has shrewdly remarked,

> Instead of having to recognize, let alone appreciate, that other kinds of ameliorative agency may be grounded in different ways of making sense in and of the world, perhaps having their own specific forms of efficacy, the placebo concept allows bio-medicine both to diminish and to annex these alternative forms of healing agency for its own purposes. To designate an experience of healing as a "placebo effect" is not only to set it apart from the "real" domain of bio-chemical causality (while retaining the hope that some day a bio-chemical explanation may appear to account for this seeming deviation) but also to restrict the extent to which its existence can appear as a credible alternative to the deterministic claims of bio-medicine.[38]

In trying to learn from the indigenous categories of the people under study, I am similarly encouraged by the studies of Thomas Csordas, an anthropologist. In a study of a young man who impressed charismatic healers as demon possessed but appeared to psychotherapists to be suffering from psychosis, Csordas emphasizes the priority of embodiment, and the existential basis of suffering, which comes before all efforts to name or categorize the problem.[39] Moreover, the metaphors of disease and disorder on the one hand and of demons and possession on the other are simply not mutually reducible to each other: "Where these two entities diverge the most is precisely in their rhetorical properties or possibilities. The fact that an evil spirit is a first-person process with an intentional history [that is, it has a will and an evil purpose] rather than a third-person process with a natural history [that is, diseases are merely natural evils] means that it [the demon] can be questioned and commanded. Hence, it can be manipulated in its intimate relations with the afflicted person.... Moreover, because each disease implies a different natural history, it also implies a different treatment."[40]

In contrast, charismatic healers and exorcists usually have the same remedy for all demonic afflictions. Csordas defends the view that one's specific culture or subculture makes a difference in the experience of suffering and affliction. Arthur Kleinman, a medical anthropologist, has also urged the cultural untranslatability of many disease entities and diagnoses and their essentially irreducible experience.[41] This can sound all very sensitive, politically correct, and well-intentioned, of course, until we reach the apparently logical conclusion that if a person thinks she or he is possessed, then biomedical psychotherapy should simply give way to the exorcist.[42] This conclusion is not always happy. Several scandals have erupted in recent years when psychiatrists have tried to cast out demons. One trouble is that merely *thinking* oneself possessed was, traditionally, never a sufficient proof (either for charismatic healers or for the Roman Catholic Church) that one really was possessed. Traditionally the *Roman Ritual* required the assurance that no natural explanation could be found before one regarded some preternatural condition as demonic.

So when we are tempted to explain religious phenomena by invoking "suggestion" or the placebo response, please notice that we may be merely replacing one mystery with another. Recent studies of the placebo response have suggested just how inscrutable it seems and how far we are from understanding it.[43] We do not advance very far if we declare wondrous cures to be nothing more than the effect of a principle we do not understand. One point of connection does seem promising, however. It's been suggested that when placebos seem to work, they do so by mobilizing habits, expectations, and symbolic representations.[44] Surely Gassner was doing that by trying to deepen the trust of his patients in the healing power of Jesus, and by placing their sufferings in a broader, more meaningful religious framework.

When we confront the mysteries of healing, therefore, the deeper question might be: What sort of explanation or understanding gives us as observers comfort? Of course, comfort is not a criterion for truth, and some of us would insist on the importance of "uncomfortable truths." But uncomfortable truths can cut both ways, disillusioning the illusioned, and reenchanting the disenchanted.[45] What sort of answer do we find satisfying? For some, the availability of miracles is *the* greatest comfort available in this life, while for others the reassuring sense of the world as a regular, orderly place of purely natural processes (rather than of demons or miracles) marks the major advance of the modern mind. Historians do not have to decide between these views, but I find that leaping to a ready-made, modern, medical, psychiatric explanation usually keeps me from hearing what all of my historical subjects are talking about. As historians, as human beings, one of our first jobs is to attend with compassion to what was going on for all those who inhabited distant times.[46] And what Gassner seems to have been doing by the end of his career was providing religious instruction by which afflicted persons could take charge of their ills by placing them in a larger framework of Christian meaning. Psychiatrists will not agree on what to call that, but it must have been a considerable relief for many of those who so eagerly sought him out.

four
INTERPRETATION

> Far be it from us to accept as dogma that the devil can physically enter into people, either individually or as legions; that the devil makes them sick; that the devil joins with them in a pact; that magicians and witches can deploy the help of the devil—We must refute all these things, rooting them out like weeds that smother religion.
> —Johann Salomo Semler, *Samlungen von Briefen und Aufsätzen über die Gassnerischen . . . Geisterbeschwörungen*

> So what if there were persons who contrived to see the effects of Satan everywhere, physical possessions and apparitions of spirits? These were mere errors of the times and not a necessary result of the doctrine that sometimes evil spirits cause certain effects in particular people.
> —Georg Friedrich Seiler, "Gedanken über die Frage: Sind böse Geister, und haben sie einen schädlichen Einfluss auf den sittlichen Zustand der Menschen?"

In March of 1775 the physiognomist and Zurich pastor Johann Kaspar Lavater wrote to Johann Salomo Semler, the great theologian of Halle, imploring him to investigate the miraculous healings of Gassner, about whom Lavater had been reading for several months. Lavater did not choose Semler at random or only because he was already well known as one of Germany's leading theologians, a founder of "neologist" interpretation, an approach to Scripture that started with the assumption that the Bible was a human document, to be understood within a historical context. Many Lutheran readers would have also recognized Semler simply as *the* expert on modern demonology. If Gassner was to make sense in a Protestant context, he would have to make sense to Semler. But just as Catholic controversialists received or understood Gassner in a context infused with fears of reviving the witchcraft trials of just a decade or so earlier, so in the Protestant North, too, news of Gassner fitted into a framework that had developed over the previous fifteen years. We should recognize that it wasn't only German Catholics who found themselves facing the devil in the mid-eighteenth century. And such issues were not merely theoretical.[1]

"The Lohmann Woman": Demons or Angels?

In 1759 a twenty-one-year-old woman named Anna Elisabeth Lohmann, the daughter of a hops dealer from Horsdorf in the Saxon duchy of Anhalt-Dessau, fell into seizures and visions, first coming from the devil and then from angels. After several amateur efforts failed, she followed the advice of one of her angels and went to the Lutheran pastor, Gottlieb Müller of Kemberg for help. Müller took her visions seriously and decided that she was actually possessed by demons. Using his own formulas, he tried to exorcise her twice in mid-1759 and then published an account of these affairs. Publicity brought disapproval, however, from the general superintendent in Wittenberg named Hoffmann, who remembered all too well a recent series of scandalous "spirit possessed" Protestant girls.[2] The Ecclesiastical Ministry in Dresden ordered Müller's little publication confiscated and decreed that he should cease publishing on the matter. Anna Elisabeth Lohmann was also ordered arrested, but in the meanwhile she had returned to her home in Anhalt, where the Wittenberg and Dresden authorities could not touch her. But she was sent to a poorhouse in Dessau, where she was confined, separated from others, threatened, and beaten in an ultimately successful effort to get her to eat and to control her visions or at least stop talking about them.[3]

Pastor Müller was not so easily silenced. He could not be treated as crazy or possessed, and as an educated man, he appealed to educated opinion in the newspapers of Berlin, Altona, and Hamburg, and to the universities of Wittenberg, Leipzig, and Halle. These appeals ignited a minor theological storm as various luminaries sprang (mainly) to attack Müller and his notions of demonic influence.[4] The most important of these came from the pen of the increasingly famous "neologian" Johann Salomo Semler, who mounted an unnecessarily massive assault on poor Pastor Müller.[5] At that point, in late 1759, Semler could object that Anna Elisabeth did not display the three classic signs of demonic possession (knowledge of hidden things, knowledge of foreign languages she had never heard, or supernatural strength), and he went on to point out that the other "lesser signa" don't prove anything since they could appear as purely natural phenomena: such signs as blasphemy, screaming, inhuman eating habits, or pains in the extremities. It is of interest that Semler here adopted the cardinal signs of possession listed in the Catholic *Rituale Romanum* of 1614, but there was nothing too unusual in a Lutheran doing that. Johann Heinrich Zedler's Lutheran-orthodox *Universal Lexicon* had done the same in its entry on demonic possession from the year 1733.[6]

Interestingly, however, Semler went on to doubt the value of all empirical data with respect to possible demoniac possessions, claiming that even the Evangelists might well have been mistaken in thinking that someone was possessed. Even millions of eyewitness reports would only show us that in a given case demonic possession was possible. And the truth was, as far as Semler was concerned, that possession seemed flatly impossible on metaphysical grounds. This left Semler with a major problem, of course, for Holy Scripture spoke often of demonic possession, at least in the gospels, and despite a great deal of sifting and citing, Semler admitted that he was confused, concluding, "truly certain persons were possessed back then [in the time of Christ], although I do not have the same concept of this possession as one commonly assumes." Most ominously, perhaps, Semler claimed that even if the Evangelists did speak of demoniac possession, they were only using the language of their day, which did not bind modern Christians to accept their idea as a reality.[7]

Semler and Demoniac Possession

In his barely concealed confusion and in his efforts to find a satisfactory formula, Semler obviously sensed that this little Saxon incident had raised much larger issues, and so later in 1760 he wrote a thesis on demon possession in the gospels (*De daemoniacis, quorum in Evangeliis fit mentio*), dealing now with a subject, as he said, that touches "the very foundations of the Christian religion" (ipsa christianae religionis fundamenta).[8] Here he started off with the work of the seventeenth-century English polymath Joseph Mede (and with a work he merely cited as *Enquiry into the Meaning of Demoniacks in the new testament)* and developed the idea that even the biblical examples of demoniac possession were actually cases of natural illness, and especially madness.[9] Heaping scorn on Catholic miracles and pilgrimages that had as their purpose the expulsion of demons, he burst out, "O barbaricum stoliditatem, si ad religionem, quidem ceteris meliorem, haec sacra insania, maxime pertinere dicatur." But then, what of Christ's miracles? This should be of no real worry, he claimed, for the fact was that Jesus' miracles were still intact, because he was still curing terrible madnesses and other ailments "extra omne naturalium subsidiorum remedium."[10]

Here we notice Semler's well-known eagerness to demythologize Scripture, to find less "superstitious" explanations for the mysterious foundations of faith.[11] In so doing he plowed through a heap of ancient Greek and Jewish citations to discover that *daimonas* for most Greeks were nothing more than the nonmortal part of man, so that good men produced good *daimonas*, and bad men were survived by bad *daimonas*. The "superstitious Jews" foolishly thought they could expel demons through the use of special roots and herbs in a way totally different from the methods of Jesus. The basic point was that the ancient world was buzzing with false and foolish ideas; for the ancient Greeks and the Jews "all things are full of demons, and they are able to invade men and drive them mad." So naturally they used turns of phrase like "habet daemonem" or "est *daimonizomenos*" when all they meant to say was that the person was sick or mad. For Semler this was no reason to conclude that a demon as a kind of substance had taken a seat in human beings ("daemonem, substantiam ipsam quandam, in hominibus sedisse"). This was only a manner of speaking ("phrasis historica"), and the Evangelists were Jews who simply adopted this turn of phrase ("hanc loquendi consuetudinem servaverint") in order that the magnitude of Jesus' miracles should be the more easily understood. Indeed, even if Jesus' disciples *thought* that the possessed really were possessed, that was not in itself a good enough reason for modern Christians to agree. For Semler, the apostles were actually full of the false opinions of the Jews of their day. After all, they had foolishly expected Jesus to return as an earthly ruler. And Jesus may well have thought that this was not the time to correct all of these popular errors. He had more important work to do. If these arguments did not clinch the matter, Semler raised the stakes unfairly, it seems to me, and denied that Jesus anywhere insisted on corporal demoniac possession as a doctrine upon which salvation itself depended.[12]

A Prior Crisis of Enlightened Demonology: England

In staking out this position, Semler was dealing more extensively and more flexibly with the problems of demon possession than other Germans of his day. But from the very beginning of his treatise he indicates that the English had already ventilated many of these matters. In truth, we could call the Lohmann affair the second literary-diabolical crisis of the eighteenth century, but only if we recognize that the English had suffered through a first polemical crisis, starting in 1737. In that year the zealous controversialist Arthur Ashley Sykes (1683 or 1684 to 1756) published anonymously a treatise entitled *An Enquiry into the Meaning of Demoniacks in the New Testament*.[13] Here we find already many of Semler's themes: that the demons of the ancient Greeks were *not* devils but the souls of dead men, that such demons do not in fact have any power over men, that many superstitious Greeks and Jews attributed all manner of natural illnesses to demons even after Hippocrates had destroyed the idea, and that therefore in every instance of New Testament demon possession we can correctly find nothing more than madness or epilepsy.[14] In an act of courageous fancy Sykes opined that when Jesus cast out the demons from the Gadarene demoniac, the 2,000 swine were driven mad by a sort of infection that passed from the "possessed" madman into the pigs.[15]

This inflammatory treatise kicked off what I'm calling the first literary crisis of the devil in the eighteenth century, for it exploded in the next couple of years into over a dozen tracts by opponents and defenders.[16] Some of this controversy was well known in Germany, and Semler had certainly seen some of its constituent parts.[17] At issue was the now vexed question of how one might best use non-Scriptural sources to understand the terminology and thoughts of the writers of Holy Scripture. The 1720s and 1730s were also the decades of high dispute over the nature of miracles, and several of the demonologists took part in that debate as well, criticizing either the evidence for or the very possibility of New Testament miracles.[18]

Semler's New Approach to Scripture

Semler knew this debate and found it useful in clarifying his own ideas about the extent to which Christians should be bound to the words and ideas of Holy Scripture. And the topic gave him no rest. In 1762 he went over the recently plowed field in German, citing again all the ancient and modern literature and responding to the recent criticism he had received from the University of Jena. He summed up his conclusions under six heads:

1. That Jesus did indeed work miracles.
2. That the Jews of old, however, had attributed many ills to evil "*Ruach*" even as the ancient Greeks thought that *daimones* were the souls of evil men.
3. That the Old Testament does not speak anywhere of physical possession by demons.
4. That, crucially, people do not have the same ideas at all times, nor does God command us to agree on this particular subject.
5. Indeed, even some of the church fathers disagreed concerning demonic possession.
6. And some of the best Christian exegetes did not understand demons as the Jews had done.

As we can see, Semler's thinking about demons had jolted him to consider very wide-ranging conclusions indeed. He repeated and clarified his conclusion that since the miraculous healings of Jesus were not in question, it was of little moment whether demons actually infested sick persons. Indeed, even certain medieval theologians had agreed that "demonic possession" was only a term for sickness. One of his most general conclusions was that Holy Scripture should never be used as a teacher of physical knowledge, for such ideas vary and develop. Perhaps consciously echoing Galileo's claim about Scripture and science, Semler argued that "the dogmatic truths of Scripture never refer to physical things."[19] Our ideas concerning the sphericity of the earth and our understanding of dew and lightning are just a few examples of areas in which we are more advanced than the ancients. And it seemed undeniable to Semler that the ancients, even the Evangelists, believed far too much in spirits.[20] In the hands of neologists such as Semler, Scripture was not to be equated with the Word of God even if it might "contain" God's Word. The problem of demons pushed Semler to regard the Bible as a historical document with human origins.

Thus Semler had moved far toward what Hans Frei called the "eclipse of biblical narrative," for, despite the Bible's historical origins, Semler was seeking to capture an essential message of Christ that could be phrased in other words, to recharacterize the essence of his spiritually healing message.[21] He was not just retelling the story but trying to extract the meaning from the encrusted sarcophagus of nonsensical ideas. So his move was not just a gesture of nascent rationalism or of accommodation to the world, and not just a rejection of Orthodox hermeneutics on general principles, but an effort to find out where and how Scripture might be effectively *applied* to the problems of life. The trouble for Semler was that Catholics weren't the only ones to find Gassner fascinating or even inspiring. If it had been only Catholics, they might have been safely ignored or contemned, which describes the normal approach of most Protestants throughout the eighteenth century to Catholic "superstition," revealing an ignorant but sovereign contempt that proceeded from two centuries of theological impasse. No, frankly, his more serious problem lay with those *Protestants* who took Gassner all too seriously.

We should be careful, however, not to replicate in our studies the haughty disdain for Catholic thinking that we find in most Protestant sources. Indeed, this is a sore point in Enlightenment studies generally. Most scholars have been so intent upon following the trail of nascent modern thinking that they have resolutely ignored Catholic biblical criticism and Protestant orthodoxy as well.[22] Here we cannot take on this large task, but we can notice that some Catholics, too, had their difficulties with demons.

Gassner and Catholic Biblical Understanding

English and German Protestants were by no means the only critics of traditional theology and the demonology that came with it. In the midst of Catholic opposition to the Jesuits and the dogmatic and polemical theology they represented, a more historically oriented Catholic pedagogy took root in some universities, in Würzburg and Bamberg, for example.[23] It is one of the ironies of the history of exegesis that by the mid to late eighteenth century, as "advanced" German Lutheran exegetes were leaving a literal interpretation of the Bible behind, that niche could now be filled by avant garde Catholic scholars, who opposed scholastic and Jesuit biblical exegesis in favor of a more literal approach. Until the Lutherans abandoned this approach to Scripture, any Catholic taking up such a stance might easily be accused of sympathy with Lutheran "heretics," but from 1750 or 1770 onward, such a hermeneutic was no longer so exclusively identified as Lutheran.

On the basis of a literal and increasingly historical hermeneutic, Enlightened Catholic thinkers increasingly found the notion of physically dangerous demons silly and unbiblical. The Theatine Ferdinand Sterzinger of Munich had ignited a noisy discussion of these matters in October of 1766 with an "Academic Address" delivered to the Bavarian Academy of Sciences. Although the academy forbade the discussion of religious questions, Sterzinger declared that witchcraft was no more than a laughable fairytale accepted only by ignorant common people but regarded by the learned as a "vulgar chimera, a trumped-up fiction." He was joined by other reform Catholics, who eagerly exploited the discrepancies between traditional views of demons and spirits and what a more learned biblical exegesis was turning up.[24] According to Wolfgang Behringer, objections to the traditional interpretation of key biblical passages had serious limits because in many verses the devil seems to have real and powerful physical effects. Getting beyond them required a wholly new understanding of reality. For Behringer, therefore, the crucial basis for denying witchcraft and the physical influence of demons was the abstract system of reason constructed by Christian Wolff, according to which demons were simply ridiculous, and indeed Sterzinger did mention Wolff fleetingly. But here Behringer reveals his modern bias toward arguments that often seem more persuasive to us than they did to Catholics (and many Protestants) of the eighteenth century. To me it is crucial that Sterzinger and his backers were willing to engage their opponents on the contested ground of biblical interpretation. When Fortunat Durich, OFM de Paula, attacked Sterzinger for misunderstanding the biblical words *hartummim* and *belahatehem* (i.e., *lehatim*), Aloys Wiener von Sonnenfels, a Viennese professor of Hebrew and convert from Judaism, came to Sterzinger's defense.[25] These were Old Testament words for the Egyptian magicians and enchantments (e.g., Gn 41:8; Ex 7:11; Dn 2:2), crucially the most powerful examples of effective magic in the Old Testament. If it could be shown that even the Egyptian enchanters could accomplish nothing more than illusions, then one might proceed with proofs that the traditional teaching on the devil granted the evil one too much earthly power. We need to recognize, therefore, that the new style of exegesis defended by Semler in Halle had a parallel among reform Catholic theologians in Bavaria and Austria, one that aimed at arriving at a literal interpretation of Scripture that would not conflict with the best Catholic traditions.[26]

Sterzinger also depended for some of his views on "good Catholic authors," such as the Italians Girolamo Tartarotti (1706–1761), the abbot of Rovereto in the Trentino; Ludovico Muratori (1672–1750), the learned librarian of Modena; Scipione Maffei (1675–1755), the skeptical antiquarian of Verona; and the Italian-sounding "Arduino Ubbidiente Dell'Osa" (humorous pseudonym for Jordan Simon of Erfurt, an Augustinian canon, who was, therefore, "dell' O.S.A."). These citations remind us of the warm cultural relations between South German Catholic states and their North Italian counterparts only a hundred miles or so to the south.[27] Together these reforming Italians of the first half of the century had attacked the cumulative late medieval concept of witchcraft, pointing out that the biblical basis for notions of the witches' pact, flight to the sabbath, sex with the devil, etc., was negligible. Muratori was also famous for his advocacy of toleration, simplified religious observances, and neighborly love as the core of Christian belief, a core that did not comport well with scholastic (Jesuit) dogmatics or with the "baroque" beliefs of those who demanded intolerance of new ideas, suspicion of neighbors, and ritual protections against demons.[28] Maffei had gone further and had claimed that magic and all sorts of supernatural interventions in nature were flatly impossible.[29] These Italian Catholics frequently noticed the differences between the world of the New Testament and their own, and used these differences to discredit cultural practices and beliefs that seemed superstitious. In this way a literalistic reading of Scripture could serve as an instrument of "Enlightenment."

We noticed earlier that when Ferdinand Sterzinger first took notice of Gassner's healings in Ellwangen, in December of 1774, he relied for his criticisms upon what he claimed he had seen with his own eyes. But he was also astonished to find a Catholic priest using exorcistic formulas in ways that did not conform to the injunctions of the *Roman Ritual*. Gassner's division of demonic attacks into three sorts, adding "circumsessio" to the traditional "obsessio" and "possessio," seemed unorthodox to Sterzinger, deriving as it did from the works of Girolamo Menghi, Candido Brognolo, Stephan Coletus, and Ubald Stoiber, all of whom had been placed "for that reason" on the Index of Forbidden Books.[30] Invoking the healings of Jesus, Sterzinger asked sharply where had Jesus and his apostles ever tried to evoke illness or seizures before trying to cure them? Where had anyone taught that most disorders might be of diabolic origin? Where can we find that Jesus healed only the unnaturally ill? Why wasn't Gassner content to follow the tests set down by the *Roman Ritual* of 1614?[31] Notice that Sterzinger's critique was repeatedly grounded not in some abstract Wolffian or Leibnizian appeal to reason, but in what we can recognize as Enlightened biblical criticism.

In an appended "Catechism on the Doctrine of Spirits" Sterzinger went further and took up a claim that one could find also among the English and North Germans of the eighteenth century: that Christ had chained all the devils in hell, so that they are not nowadays permitted to swarm at will through the air. For the topic of demons, this was closely akin to the common Protestant claim that the age of miracles had ended with the primitive church. But because the effects of demons were not literally miraculous (they were preternatural rather than totally unnatural), one needed a separate and compelling reason why demons could no longer act as once they had. Thus Sterzinger stressed again the cardinal proofs of demonic possession as specified in the *Rituale Romanum:* speaking strange foreign languages, stating correctly what was happening in some distant land when one could not be expected to guess correctly, finding truly hidden objects of which one had no knowledge, and reading the thoughts of others. Without these proofs, "possession" was nothing more than a malicious fraud; such poseurs should "have the devil beaten out of them."[32] Sterzinger's reliance on the *Roman Ritual* shows how, in skillful hands, it could be deployed as a profoundly skeptical interpretation of demonic possession.

Notice the variety of authorities invoked here: the skeptical witness of one's own eyes, a carefully weeded garden of ecclesiastical history, along with the *Roman Ritual* of 1614, and a strict or Enlightened and literal interpretation of the Bible, a style of exegesis that did not take marching orders from medieval scholastic theologians. Crucial for Sterzinger, as we have seen, was his fear that a revived belief in demonic possession would lead to a revival of witch hunting. It may have been the ferocious attack by Sterzinger, indeed, that prompted

Gassner and his followers to change course and to drop their references to witchcraft and *maleficium*. In the emerging literary and theological battle of the mid-1770s, and in the hundreds or indeed thousands of cases of which we have eyewitness records, we have seen that Gassner dropped all efforts to detect *maleficium*, i.e., illnesses derived from charms, spells, and witchcraft of magicians or witches. Our exorcist learned to suppress these questions and to concentrate just on healing. I think that in so doing he was following the best biblical criticism of his day, a reading of Scripture that set forth the example of Jesus' exorcisms as the model for the modern exorcist. As Sterzinger and others never tired of pointing out, Jesus had never diagnosed the operation of witchcraft among those he regarded as demoniacs. So instead of looking for *maleficium*, Gassner paid increasingly exclusive attention to those "unnatural disorders" caused directly by the devil. But in the last years of his life he also increasingly did away with the distinction between natural and unnatural illnesses, now teaching flatly that "all diseases come from the devil," and "medicines are only for those without faith," as he put it in March 1779, shortly before his death.[33]

Gassner's Catholic Defenders

The staunchest defenders of Gassner's healings were members of South German religious orders and especially the ex-Jesuits, many of whom had retreated to Augsburg, where for a long time the papal decree dissolving their order was not even published.[34] From there the presses poured forth pro-Gassner material: sermons, reports, dialogues, scathing attacks on the Enlightenment, and printed replies to skeptics such as Sterzinger.[35] The most energetic of these ex-Jesuits was the cathedral preacher of Augsburg, Alois Merz, who happily took up the cudgels against Protestantism, Josephinism, and the Enlightenment as often as possible, contributing manfully to the poisonous confessional atmosphere for which Augsburg was well known in the late eighteenth century.[36] His office in the Augsburg cathedral was that of "Kontroversprediger," and his bitter, divisive, scathing sermons were models of their kind.³⁷ Realizing the force of Sterzinger's biblically based objections, Merz published in 1775 a treatise with the title "Solid Proof that the Means by which Gassner Heals Diseases is Consistent with the Principles of the Gospels and the Opinions of the Earliest Church."³⁸ Taking up the claim that Christ had bound the devil and all demons in hell, Merz retorted that such a view undermined all Christian morality, for it was the devil who continually tempted humankind to evil.³⁹ He claimed further that Gassner's methods of using trial exorcisms were exactly what the apostles and the Church had taught for centuries.⁴⁰ It was indeed a mark of Gassner's care that he was willing to test to see if the devil was in fact present. If he was unable to effect a cure, he regularly concluded that the unfortunate condition was natural and hence beyond his means to remedy.⁴¹ Merz exultantly cited the testimony of a Protestant physician, who had attended Gassner's operations in Ellwangen, to the effect that "no earthly medicine" could produce the remarkable results that Gassner's exorcisms achieved. Merz also reveled in the apparent humility of Gassner's claims, for when asked if he regarded his cures as "miracles," Gassner had wisely said "No," that he was merely exorcizing or blessing. But just as such illnesses were not wholly natural, so too their remedies were not entirely natural either.⁴² Merz was apparently resuscitating the moribund concept of the preternatural so that he could carve out for Gassner a kind of space for spiritual healing without making pretensions to full (and therefore saintly) miracle-working.⁴³ Or, perhaps wisely, they refused to speculate about how the sacramentals worked and contented themselves with the explanation that the devil had to respect the name of Jesus and the rituals of the church. The Catholic Church had long denied that the blessed sacraments (and, for some, the sacramentals as well) depended upon the piety or character of the priest.

Merz had a much easier time of it when he moved on to the traditional claim that the devil had at all times possessed men in both body and soul. Christians, he claimed, have also at all times sought help in the holy name of Jesus, citing a long list of church fathers as well as such Jesuit authorities as Petrus Thyraeus and Martin Delrio. Like the skeptical Sterzinger, Merz also cited the authority of his own eyewitness, "although I could only stay as an observer for a few days."[44] Merz made short work of the suspicion that Gassner was deploying secret magnets or the occult forces of sympathy: "I will never persuade myself that a magnet could have such an effect on the minds [*Gemüther*], or the passions and thoughts of men. These patients are driving off their illness, even in the absence of the exorcist, purely by thought." These effects had been attested by princes, imperial counts, generals, lords, physicians, and even Protestants, who had all agreed that their gruesome symptoms had to be "completely unnatural [vollkommen unnatürlich]." Ignatius of Loyola had explained how easily we think a condition natural when in actuality it's the attack of a demon, and exultantly Merz showed that Martin Luther himself agreed on the point.[45] It was a constant nuisance to Lutheran apologists of the 1770s that their Catholic antagonists had learned so well to cite Scripture and the works of Luther, for it reminded them of how far they had in fact drifted from the historical-literal and prophetic sense of the Bible and from their moorings in early Reformation theology.[46] For the belligerent preacher of Augsburg (his official title as *Kontroversprediger* required him to preach regularly on current controversies), these points were all opportunities to reassert the conservative Jesuit message and to revive the "witchcraft war" of less than ten years earlier, and this time on more favorable terrain. While the early modern notion of witchcraft was largely a late medieval composition, demonic possession was an idea with a profoundly biblical basis. It seems clear enough that a literal-historical reading of the gospels favored the view that Jesus himself had cast out real demons. But as Catholic exegesis caught up with that of Martin Luther, we have found Johann Salomo Semler developing a historical-critical exegesis that claimed to move the Bible into the modern world.

Altogether, Merz wrote over ten separate works, large and small, defending Gassner.[47] Although Merz constructed a modern ex-Jesuit defense of Gassner that eliminated or sharply curtailed references to witchcraft and hexing as causes of demonic possession, not all of Gassner's supporters were so careful. Indeed, the abbot of the Premonstratensian Abbey at Oberzell, Oswald Loschert, became one of the most prolific defenders of the notion that the devil was constantly at work in the world, not only possessing those he could, but allying himself with witches and magicians to increase his influence and to magnify his destructions. It was no accident that Abbot Loschert defended Gassner, for he had been one of the active prosecutors in the trial of Maria Renata Singer, the subprioress of Unterzell, who was executed for the crime of witchcraft in 1749 (certainly one of the last witches to be executed on German soil).[48] Of course, the context of the Gassner debate often explains a given participant's point of view, but this is obvious in the case of Oswald Loschert, whose many works for Gassner served also to justify his own lifelong campaign against the devil.[49]

We have examined Loschert's political considerations of Gassner (chapter 2), but here we must notice that the abbot of Unterzell sometimes seemed ready to jettison medieval and early modern accounts of demonic possession and to rely on a close reading of Jesus' miracles. From Scripture one could learn that there were several sorts of demonic attack (obsession, possession, bewitchment, and even circumsession), that demons often spoke from the bodies of the possessed, that an exorcist might force them to tell the truth, that possession did not necessarily depend upon *maleficium* of any sort, and that therefore the search for witches or other *Teufelskünstler* was both dangerous and wrong. Rural people were always too quick to accuse their neighbors, Loschert maintained, but the model of Scripture pointed the right way to healing without bandying about destructive accusations of witchcraft.[50] To reach such conclusions, Loschert depended upon a literal reading of Scripture and was able to dispense with much of the scholastic apparatus that Enlightened critics so harshly ridiculed. In his "Fourth Open Letter," published in 1776, Loschert took learned exception to the tactics of Semler and other Enlightened contemners of a literal reading of Scripture. Applying an allegorical reading, as Semler did, ran the risk of eviscerating the Scriptures and of seeing only what one wanted to see in God's Word. This seriously intended riposte to Semler provides striking evidence that even hard-bitten Gassnerites were acquainted with Enlightened biblical criticism and able to attack its weak points.[51] They were neither so ignorant nor so defenseless as students of the Enlightenment have usually assumed. It is also ironic that Martin Luther had begun his religious revolution with an attack on allegorical and metaphorical readings of Scripture. Now, in the late eighteenth century, the tables were turned, and advanced Lutheran opinion had adopted allegory, while conservative Catholic readings favored a more literal approach.

Protestant Reactions to Gassner

Let us return now to the question of Protestant reactions to Gassner. It is one of the more remarkable aspects of the Gassner scandal that Protestants got so thoroughly enmeshed in it. Whereas it might have remained a purely Catholic or South German controversy, Protestant scholars and polemicists from all over the German-speaking world took part, and the lines of division were not always what we might have predicted.

With most theological issues, to be sure, Lutherans and Reformed Protestants were content to notice, disagree, ridicule, or comment exclusively upon the views of fellow Protestants. They high-mindedly ignored Catholic theology and Catholic events. Similarly, for Catholic theologians the Lutheran and Reformed camps set forth their arguments on such radically different grounds — with so thoroughly alien a set of proofs — that it was usually easier and more natural to ignore them.[52] In the case of Gassner it was different, and not only because so many ordinary Lutherans ignored the admonitions of their pastors and betook themselves to the wonder worker in search of healing. Gassner frankly fascinated certain Protestant theologians, and especially the Pietists.

The Württemberg Pietist and instrument maker Philipp Matthäus Hahn maintained a reserve about the supposed miracles taking place not far away in Ellwangen, but from his correspondence we learn that Friedrich Christoph Oetinger had gone to see Gassner's operations.[53] It's not clear how Oetinger reacted, but we know much more about the fascination expressed by the enthusiastic physiognomist of Zurich, Johann Kaspar Lavater, who first learned of Gassner's healings at the end of 1774. The Pietist pastor of the Orphanage Church in Zurich wrote at once to the Catholic exorcist asking for personal contact, and with a favorable reply in hand, Lavater now undertook a vigorous campaign to obtain for Gassner a full and impartial investigation and verification of the wonders he was performing. That was the reason he turned to Semler, as we've seen — a complication to which we will soon turn. For Lavater the crucial context was not Gassner and the devil, for Lavater actually expended little time or effort on the demons of the New Testament even though he did preach voluminously on sin and even on Satan as tempter.[54] No, for him Gassner represented a chance to see or experience directly the transcendent. From 1768 on Lavater had pursued a whole series of possible proofs that the Christian life brought with it tangible "gifts of the spirit." He was forever asking friends and acquaintances to send him reliable reports of extraordinary "phenomena and experiences" (*Begebenheiten und Erfahrungen*), by which the world of spirit could be examined objectively, even scientifically. Indeed his famous work on physiognomy from 1772 (and expanded thereafter) was meant to contribute to this effort by showing how the character or spirit of a man was visible in his facial features.[55]

For Lavater, Gassner seemed like a dream come true, and he wrote to the Swiss expatriate and Hannoverian royal physician Johann Georg Zimmermann, challenging him to join others in investigating Gassner's methods and results.[56] Zimmermann seemed like a reasonable choice, but the doctor remained unpersuaded that Gassner's cures, even if genuine, depended upon actually expelling demons. As Zimmermann put it later, believing in such demons "was just too much for our time." In short, Zimmermann regarded Lavater as self-deceived, even though he admired the Zurich pastor for possessing charismatic influence over the imaginations of others.[57]

Zimmermann, therefore, did not undertake the investigation that Lavater hoped for, and yet Lavater was all too aware of the crippling bias in the Catholic accounts he had read. They could not provide the proofs he continued to hope for. Lavater was, however, even more incensed at the dismissive ridicule and scorn which Enlightened deists and Protestants heaped upon Gassner despite their total ignorance of what Gassner was achieving. Repeatedly he challenged his complacent evangelical colleagues to recognize that Gassner presented facts (*FACTA*) that cried out for examination. With disappointment he sharply criticized the worldly wise: "It's easier to laugh than to investigate."[58] Although Lavater burned for months to make a pilgrimage to Ellwangen to see Gassner for himself, his friends persuaded him that Gassner was so controversial that a trip might well do Lavater's cause more harm than good. In the meanwhile, too, Lavater obviously read Sterzinger's highly critical account of his encounter with the faith healer, an account that seems to have sobered Lavater, so that he postponed a meeting to the summer of 1778, well after the Gassner storm had passed.[59] For our purposes the crucial point is that for Lavater, with all his reservations about rationality, with all his "lust for wonders" (*Wunderlust*), Gassner presented a potentially key example of how the spirit works in this world.[60]

The last sort of theological or religious response to be considered is that of the Enlightened Protestant North. As we've seen, one of the scholars whom Lavater challenged to investigate the Gassner affair was Dr. Johann Georg Zimmermann, a fellow Swiss who was serving as personal physician to the royal court of Hanover. Although the skeptical Zimmermann refused to get personally involved, in his popular reflections on solitude and loneliness, he thought about Gassner's strange effectiveness. For Zimmermann it was obvious that the Catholic exorcist had cured real illnesses:

> Gassner really did heal through his exorcisms, instantly and enduringly, for these really were sick persons, whose cases I know and whom I and other much more skilled doctors could not heal. But we too would have healed them if only we had the sort of influence over the souls of mankind that all doctors ought to have. And yet I believe as little that the devil causes any sort of illness as I do that one can get rid of any sort of illness by getting rid of the devil. I am, however, well persuaded that Gassner cured the nerve-sick by means of his extraordinary mastery over the imagination and nerves of ordinary people.[61]

INTERPRETATION

For Zimmermann, Gassner's effective cures did not work by casting out demons; instead Gassner had the power of charismatic authority. In just such a manner St. Anthony had cured people by "casting out demons" that people did not really have. He was the "Gassner of his age." And it was in just this manner as well that his friend, the great-spirited Lavater, had overwhelmed the feelings or sentiments of women and other suggestible people, so that by expecting miracles, they saw miracles.[62] For Dr. Zimmermann the imagination was stronger that any human understanding, producing joy (the life of the soul), but also fanaticism and psychic convulsions (the death of the soul). Gassner's deceptions, unfortunately, were calculated to take advantage of just these characteristic human weaknesses. Zimmermann's emphasis upon the imagination and the sentiments reminds us forcefully of the burgeoning interest in the ways that the mind could be found "in the body" and the "body in the mind," to take Jerome McGann's phrase as a pointer to the age of late-eighteenth-century sentiment and sensibility.[63] By the 1770s the belief that the powers of the human imagination could trigger genuinely physical reactions was commonplace. Of course, physicians had long held that pregnant women had to be careful or else their fantasies might affect their unborn babies; and terrors of various sorts were thought to have physical effects upon those of "soft" natures. But the cult of sensibility took this view and generalized it so that all the powers of the imagination were now thought to have previously unsuspected force, and not just upon ladies and others of a delicate disposition. This conclusion provided a means by which intellectuals could comfortably naturalize visions, religious conversions, the sublime, and miracles of all sorts. No wonder so many thought they could explain both Gassner's and Mesmer's successes through the startling powers of the *Einbildungskraft*.

Neology and the Demons

The other major intellectual to whom Lavater appealed was, as we have seen, Johann Salomo Semler of Halle, this time hoping that Semler would journey to Ellwangen to investigate the world of demons that Gassner had put on display. This was, after all, a topic to which Semler had devoted himself ever since December of 1759, when he had first undertaken to debunk the Lohmann affair. But Semler was also making a name for himself as a "neologian," or "neologist," a critical scholar who mediated between orthodoxy and rationalism and who drove home the central point that the New Testament had grown and developed like any other ancient body of texts, subject to all the human pressures and vicissitudes of any human artifact. In Semler's eyes the Word of God should, therefore, never be equated with the mutable and fallible text of the canonical Scriptures.[64] We have already seen what this meant in general terms from Semler's works on demons from the 1760s, but it remained one of his favorite themes.[65] No wonder Lavater turned to him.

In that Semler's methods were historical and philological, the professor refused to accept Lavater's challenge in 1775, much as he had earlier refused to visit Anna Elisabeth Lohmann. Instead he answered Lavater in an open letter in the *Hallische neue gelehrte Zeitungen*, claiming that Gassner's cures were not really exorcisms at all, but psychologically effective faith healings at best (and possibly fraudulent or self-deceived at worst). He had not changed his mind about the gospel demoniacs, whom he still regarded as essentially madmen or epileptics, and whom Jesus healed miraculously but without really ejecting any demons. Of course one might cross-examine Professor Semler and ask why it was then that Jesus and his disciples so regularly referred to demons and so often conveyed the impression that such spirits were the effective agents of chronic disorders. Here Semler relied upon his reading of that now forgotten English literary-theological battle over the gospel demoniacs, which had taken off in 1737 and which we have already considered briefly. That controversy had come to a head early (in the years 1737–1739) but had never entirely died away (for there were continuing contributions to it in 1750, 1760, and then again in the 1770s). In 1775 the key English work was by the independent Hugh Farmer (1714–1787).[66] In these English controversial works, which number well over twenty titles, the crucial theological question was how to interpret the Greek words *daimōn* and *daimonia* in the New Testament.

As we have seen, scholars had realized that while the King James translators had regularly spoken of "devil possession," the Greek New Testament actually spoke in every case of *daimōn* and *daimonion*. So liberal exegetes decided that the sensible thing to do was to translate these words with *demon* and to speak of *demon possession*. If this was a significant difference, it had to make an exegetical difference, and the next step was to uncouple the devil from demons, claiming with some justice that their union was a later doctrinal imposition, a theological interpretation unsupported by the text. It seemed increasingly clear that the first-century Greek and Jewish world had spoken of many sorts of unclean spirits or demons, not all of them ranged in an elaborate military hierarchy or monarchy with Satan at its head. With some fancy stepping Arthur Ashley Sykes and his partisans could try to preserve the doctrine of the devil as a fallen angel and the spiritual origin of sin while at the same time reducing demons to the status of ghosts and other superstitious illusions.[67] The real exegetical trouble came, as we have seen, when one asked *why* Jesus and his apostles had spent any time curing people of illusory ills, but Semler was ready enough to follow Balthasar Bekker, Sykes, and Hugh Farmer, in claiming that Jesus had merely adopted the hopelessly superstitious language of the Jews of that day. This left the reader wondering whether Jesus' accommodation of the common superstitions of his time meant that he himself bought into them to any extent. If not, it could appear that he was actually lying or deceiving rather than merely accommodating the errors of his countrymen. Did he not stand for the truth, after all?

This question shows just how dangerous the fire was with which Semler was playing. He could tell from the debates in England from the 1720s onward that those who took his positions on demons could easily drift into the denial of miracles altogether, into Arianism or Socinianism, or into full-scale naturalism. Suspicions of this sort had cost Johann Jacob Wettstein his pastoral position in Basel in 1730, and Wettstein was the sort of biblical scholar Semler admired. Not only had he produced a new, critical edition of the Greek New Testament (1751–52) using more manuscripts than previous editors, but Semler thought highly enough of Wettstein's earlier *Prolegomena* to the study of the New Testament to publish, in 1764, a new edition of it, with his own editorial comments.[68] Semler was careful not to run the same risk, and repeatedly emphasized throughout his career that the devil certainly existed, even if his chief effects were on the moral life of mankind, rather than upon the body.[69] He essentially argued that "demon possession" was merely the term Jesus used to mean madness, but as we have seen, it was conceivable that Jesus had used the expression because he had more important things on his mind than correcting all the foolish and superstitious errors of his day. Here Semler's neologist friend Ernesti drew the line. It was one thing to claim that the New Testament demons were really only the "ghosts" of the dead, and it was as clear to Ernesti as it was to Semler that Christians need not accept all the beliefs of the Evangelists themselves. But it was too much to claim that the Evangelists (or perhaps even Jesus) used the false and superstitious idea of demons without sharing it themselves. To Ernesti that claim seemed flatly heretical and dangerous. So, Semler fudged and left himself a loophole; if finally cornered, he might respond that God could even have made an exception to His general commitment to reason, and therefore could have even permitted the existence of genuine, physical demonic possession.[70]

Reimarus and the Deists

Some of Semler's contemporaries were ready to go further even though they too knew that they were running an obvious risk. We now know that Hermann Samuel Reimarus (1694–1768), the Hamburg philosopher, orientalist, and deist theologian, worked for some thirty years on a private manuscript which he never dared to publish. Even after his death, his family kept the secret, and when Gotthold Ephraim Lessing undertook to publish the "Fragments" of an "anonymous" (the work we now know as Reimarus's *Apology*), he pretended that he had discovered it in the ducal library in Wolfenbüttel, where he was librarian.[71] The publication in the 1770s of these *Fragments* provoked what was surely the most important theological controversy of the German Enlightenment, one that set off shock waves into the nineteenth century, affecting generations of work on the life of Jesus. In that work, Reimarus moved beyond common platitudes such as God's benign attitude toward mankind, his reasonable rule, and the way in which all religious truths must accord with nature and reason.

In his *Apologie* and in the *Fragments* of it that Lessing published, Reimarus argued that we have no good reason to think that the Old or New Testaments were the inspired Word of God, no reason to accept the miracles they recount, and above all, no reason to deny that Jesus was simply mistaken about his role as the Messiah. In the view of Reimarus, the disciples probably stole the corpse of their crucified leader and then falsified the accounts of his resurrection, proceeding to create a miraculous religion in place of the wise and morally uplifting teachings of Jesus. All talk of biblical revelation was therefore deceptive nonsense. It is now well known that Reimarus had studied the English deists carefully, but no one to my knowledge has paid any attention to his treatment of demonic possession.[72]

Reimarus dealt with the figure of Satan and with Jesus' false miracles in several places,[73] but he dealt with demons most explicitly in a discussion of the apostles' use of "miracles" as a means to spread the newly invented religion. Reimarus emphasized that Jesus only worked his apparent cures where people believed in him, and one important problem was that others actually seemed to work such wonders as well, men whom Jesus characterized as false Christs and false prophets, who used the power of Satan (Mt 24:24; 2 Thes 2:9–11). But all of these wonders and miracles were false. Echoing the fashionable anti-Jewish sentiments of the eighteenth century (including even some of the Enlightened), he held that demonic possession flourished in those days because the Jewish people were so superstitious that they regarded melancholy and madness, or indeed all diseases, as originating in evil spirits.[74] "In this way all of these became supernatural among the Jews and Christians of those days, both the diseases and their healing. And the devil back then and the false prophets too, using his help, could also work signs and wonders, which could not be distinguished from the true, and so even the chosen faithful could have been easily seduced."[75]

For modern Christians, however, the question was not only whether God *could* have worked miracles in order to achieve his purposes. "Instead, [the question was] whether he actually did them and for this specific purpose." To answer that question one needed the witness and narrative of other people who could not have been mistaken in their accounts. Unfortunately, if one assumed that miracle accounts were reliable because the narrators were "viros theopneustos" (men inspired by God), "then we land in a vicious circle, for the miracles prove their Theopneustie [divine inspiration], while their Theopneustie depends upon the miracles, without which no person could be free of human errors and weaknesses."[76]

With respect to the demonically possessed, Reimarus remarked acidly that all of these stories "depend on the false opinion of the Jews of that time that all diseases, and especially epilepsy and madness, came from evil spirits, who took over the body and soul of men, and who had to be expelled by a higher power and by specific words and other means." He added that the recognition of the possessed as epileptics and madmen was beginning to dawn on "reasonable theologians," citing Balthasar Bekker, Arthur Ashley Sykes, and Nathaniel Lardner, and later Conyers Middleton. But "where people have so little understanding of nature and are so superstitious that they immediately think of supernatural causes, speak at once of demonic possessions and the conjuration of spirits, where Satan can perform miracles just as easily as God himself, there is the real market for thaumaturges [wonder workers], who can then make their illusions."

Thus Jesus and his disciples betrayed either their own superstition by blaming the devil for the faults of nature, or they exploited the false opinions of the common people in order to obtain for themselves a respect they did not deserve. Why didn't Jesus explain to his disciples just how the false Christs to come would perform false miracles? How did they perform their tricks? Why not teach how to uncover their frauds? The disciples might have received a sure criterion by which false miracles could be distinguished from the true so that one could not be deceived. But no, Jesus did not do this because his miracles too were "suspect"; even he could not work wonders where people did not believe in him or when the Scribes and Pharisees demanded miracles.[77] Obviously Reimarus had no time for fine talk about Jesus' accommodation or his will to reform the superstitions of the Jews; for Reimarus, Jesus and his apostles were part of the problem. So we can easily see that in his speculations, Semler was coming close to outright deism.[78] No wonder Orthodox Lutherans held tightly to more traditional views. Even if recent cases of Catholic possession and exorcism were nonsense in their eyes, that provided no reason for them to doubt the literal reality of possession and healing in the New Testament.

The Response of the Orthodox

The most zealous "advocate for the devil" was probably Heinrich Martin Gottfried Köster (1734–1802), a well-known historian, pastor, and writer on children's education in Giessen.[79] In a sarcastic pamphlet entitled "Humble Plea for Instruction from the Great Men Who Don't Believe in the Devil," Köster heaped scorn on those who seemed to be claiming to be stronger than Christ and all his apostles. For the Savior only weakened the devil and the associated Jewish superstitions, but the so-called "great men," by which he seems to have meant not only Semler but also the "naturalists," had banned the devil entirely and threatened to turn Christianity into nothing more than empty moralizing ("eine blosse Moral").[80] If doctrine is to be simply chosen freely, why not get rid of the atonement, original sin, Christ's divinity, and hell as well? Once we turn the demon-possessed into sick people, then it's easy to turn the devil into a mere "un-thing" ("Unding"), but where in Scripture was there any hint that Jesus cynically used the prejudices or superstitions of his listeners? And why should we think that God could not have given the devil the power to harm people? Just because God was wise, just, and good? Köster realized that this was a merely a priori argument that would eviscerate Scripture if it were turned loose. Essentially Köster insisted that we have no right to judge what was "unnecessary" in Scripture, for if we arrogate to ourselves the right to decide on doctrine, we could wind up with nothing more than our own prejudices. Christianity would become a mere compilation of our own whims and desires. And yet, Köster affirmed, there were many cases in Scripture where we are asked to believe because we have witnesses or solid accounts of experiences, even though we do not know *why* something is so. Why is the devil in the world? We don't know. Why is God a trinity? We don't know, but God must have His own good reasons.[81] With this keen-eyed attack, Köster did not disarm the neologist Semler or "naturalists" such as Reimarus, but he surely placed his finger on a sore point. Indeed, how could Semler claim that he was treating Holy Scripture as a human document and still retain a sense of divine revelation?

Köster did not let it go at that. Between 1778 and 1797 he published a journal that reported on the "latest religious phenomena," and was keen to record the news on the demonic front. He noticed, for example, that in response to the "Humble Plea" of 1775, many learned men had written to defend their ideas while denying that they were "great men." Now Köster turned to the interpretation of the New Testament and the claim of some that the devil could not even be found there. To be sure, no one denied that *daimōn* and *diabolos* appeared as words, but the real question was what they meant. Should one claim that all the tricky passages of Scripture were simply figurative? Clearly not. But Semler and the English demonologists had also emphasized that superstitious Jewish ideas of demons had proliferated after the Babylonian Captivity. But, even granting that, could it matter crucially where or when the Jews had obtained their ideas? The real test of doctrine, in Köster's view, was whether the Jews were mistaken in believing their world full of demons and whether such an idea was totally foolish and contrary to reason; actually, as far as Köster was concerned, the devil and demons made a lot of sense.[82]

By 1778 Köster was able to review a host of responses that his little pamphlet had generated. Obviously the dispute had touched a sensitive nerve. Johann Carl Bonnet, pastor in Niederkirchen in the Palatinate, for example, composed a "Most Humble Answer by a Minor Rural Pastor to the Humble Plea" (*Demüthigste Antwort eines geringen Landgeistlichen auf die demüthige Bitte um Belehrung and die grossen Männer, welche keinen Teufel glauben*), in which he claimed to believe in the existence of a devil but denied that Christians can obtain any clear view of his actions or powers from Scripture. Surely no one should deny that Jesus and his disciples often used picturesque and figurative language, and they were not deceiving anyone in so doing. Similarly, the ancient Jews were full of foolish prejudices and superstitions that Christians could not be expected to believe. So in the end, Bonnet insisted on a devil, but not necessarily a personal devil.[83]

Another contribution of this sort came from an unknown author who sarcastically asked, "So Is the Devil Really Now a Nothing?" (*Sollte der Teufel wirklich ein Unding seyn? eine Frage und Bitte an die Theologen unserer Zeit*). Explicitly attacking Semler and Teller, and implicitly Friedrich Nicolai's *Allgemeine Deutsche Bibliothek* as well, the author claimed that the devil was much more than merely a "Chaldean fantasy." It was true that modern philosophers thirty years earlier asserted that whatever they could not understand could not exist, "but now that in our day we place more weight on experience and witnesses, and now that philosophers no longer say that this or that cannot be just because it does not seem possible to them," it seemed better to say that many things exist of which we have no understanding. Even the recent discoveries of science seemed to strengthen this conviction, for the most recent years had brought news of "an animal in the northern waters that is as large as an island"; of a polyp which could be cut into pieces, but whose pieces could grow into a whole worm again; and of an insect ("das Radthier") which could be dried out for more than two years and then come to life again. Scholars did not doubt the existence of such creatures, and similarly should not doubt the well-attested existence of demons. Since he was writing to theologians, the author assumed that he did not have to defend the credibility of Scripture and could confine himself to the question of whether the Bible gave witness to the existence of Satan. He regarded that question as open and shut. If one doubted so well-attested ideas, "then there will be no certainty in any biblical exegesis at all."[84]

In answer to this little pamphlet Pastor Conrad H. Runge (1731–1792) of St. Ansgar's in Bremen wrote a stout volume of 426 pages. He first ridiculed the ignorance of the anonymous author, who evidently knew neither the requisite ancient languages nor the rules of scriptural interpretation and so ran the risk of vastly exaggerating the role of the devil and of demons in the world. Both the heathens and Roman Catholic priests exercised their dominion, Runge claimed, by inculcating an unreasoning fear of demons in the minds of simple people. With such fears one could destroy all morality and all knowledge of God, Providence, and religion. With a great show of learning, Runge claimed that his pamphlet opponent had ignored important distinctions and thrown out wild allegations of Socinianism and Sadduceeism. He did admit, however, that certain modern theologians such as Bekker, Wagstaff, and Lardner "and our recent Germans" had indeed gone far toward allegorizing all of Scripture in an effort to get rid of the devil, but one could not easily escape the fact that Jesus and His apostles did use figurative language, allegories, and parables, thus posing serious problems for the modern interpreter. It seemed undeniable that a full doctrine of the devil had developed late in the Old Testament and that Chaldean influence was likely, but this showed the wisdom of God in not overburdening the Jews with all of the truth too early in their spiritual life. In theology Runge seems to have favored some of the views of Bishop Warburton (for whom demonic influence was mental and moral rather than physical), Hugh Farmer, and other English authors.[85] His efforts to mediate between Semler and the credulous had produced a dust storm of erudition and little clarity.

These publications brought Köster back into the fray, and he concentrated on the now extremely contentious issue of whether Jewish ideas of demons were nothing more than superstitious imports from

Chaldean culture. With an enviable grasp of the requisite languages, he tried to show that the origins of Jewish beliefs and ideas were not so easily categorized and dismissed.[86] In his *Recent Religious Phenomena* for 1778, Köster continued to blister those who published tiresome little pamphlets that only confused the major issues and provoked anger and strife. It was becoming hard to know what the really important points were. But by 1778 the visionary ideas and experiences of Emmanuel Swedenborg (or at least someone writing in the name of Swedenborg) had been stirred into the mix, and Lutherans were also troubled by a massive but anonymous "Attempt at a Biblical Demonology" (actually by Otto Justus Basilius Hesse) which Semler had published with an introduction.[87] Köster protested that even if the "possessions" recounted in the New Testament were only diseases that doctors now recognize as natural, one might still attribute the diseases to the devil, and this dissolved into the question "whether a spirit can have effects in a body"; but that question was easily answered even by doctors, for everyone knew how much force the soul has through "the stirred up force of imagination in the body." If the soul can do this in its own body, then it seemed true enough that another spirit could do the same, especially in view of the fact that we do not really understand much about the nature of spirits.[88] Köster conceded that Hugh Farmer's essay on biblical demonology was the "most prominent" of the writings against a literal interpretation of demoniac possession, but then mounted a refutation aimed at most of its assertions.[89]

Köster also noticed that while the Protestant debate concerned the powers of demons and the devil, the Catholic debate about Gassner concentrated rather upon the reality of Gassner's cures, and therefore had a different center of gravity. That was not the whole truth, however, and even he took note of an anonymous Catholic work on the theory of diabolical effects in this world.[90] With a refreshing openness to Evangelical authors as well as to the whole of church history, this work defended the notion of demonic possession and the continuing need for exorcism. The mere fact that superstitions had crept

INTERPRETATION

into such practices did not disprove the central core. Here again, Köster revealed that in opposing the "naturalists," he was as willing as Lavater to seek help among the Catholics.[91]

These polemical publications produced at least one conversion, a testimony to the fact that vehement debate sometimes (but rarely) did more than amply offend one's opponents. Christian Wilhelm Kindleben (1748–1785), the pastor and poet (and author of the well-known student drinking song "Gaudeamus Igitur," 1781) admitted in 1779 that he had written the little book proving the "nonexistence" of the devil, but after reading Köster and the other contributions to this noisy debate, he was ready to concede that the devil does exist, that he could indeed possess human beings, and that medical explanations could not account for all of the sufferings that were called demonic.[92] In his view, the struggle over the devil was "epoch-making in the learned annals of the eighteenth century," one in which scholars had written "almost a whole library in miniature concerning the doctrine of the devil." He now ruefully admitted that he had by no means disproved the existence of the devil and went further to confess that in his view the exegetical theory of accommodation had been misused or extended so far that Holy Scripture was in danger of being transformed into a mass of figural imaginings. He trusted Semler's theory no more and vowed to write no more about the devil.[93] Reviewing this retractatio, Köster laughed at Kindleben's foolish hope that he might single-handedly end the controversy over demons by finally admitting that the devil did indeed have earthly powers, and indeed the theological struggle continued on into the 1780s, although with less intensity.[94]

Conclusion

Gassner's healings thus produced a deep and wide theological debate, both among Roman Catholics and among German Protestants. We have here taken the time to notice only the most often discussed or the deepest issues, but it is truly surprising how many persons contributed to these disputes and how widely they were reported in the journals and newspapers of the day. In this chapter we have also taken notice only of the religious issues, but there were contributions from the medical establishment and from politically motivated writers as well. Some of these will form a basis for the fifth chapter, where I will outline the implicit rules of these debates, the kind of decorum that developed or broke down. But here we may conclude that for Catholics the chief questions were two: (1) whether the devil could now cause the sorts of physical ills Gassner's patients presented and (2) whether Gassner's blessings and exorcisms were appropriate. The Catholic world was badly divided on these issues in the 1770s, and Gassner provided a focal point for many of these divisions. For German and Swiss Protestants, however, the main issue raised by Gassner was not whether the devil could possess people nowadays and certainly not whether exorcism worked. Most Protestants agreed that this was an ill-founded notion and a superstitious practice. But the debate had triggered a much more important debate among Evangelicals about the interpretation of Scripture. Johann Salomo Semler found in the current disputes over demonic possession such a fascinating and vexing problem that he became obsessed with demonology, using it as a pivot on which to turn his biblical exegesis in a new direction. Semler's neological theology and the English writers upon whom he depended went far toward transforming the Bible into a simple mirror of their own moral thoughts. Difficult passages and "obsolete" ideas could be treated as so much heathen mythology or Jewish superstition and then swept away with sovereign contempt; but as critics noted, there was little assurance that this was really what God had meant when he set down his Word in flesh and ink. So the "third crisis" of the devil in the eighteenth century raised large and troubling problems for both Catholics and Protestants, problems that have not disappeared over the past two centuries even though they now appear in different dress.

five
CONVERSATION AND RIDICULE

> Ridicule often decides things better than bitter argument.
> — Horace, *Satires*, 1.10, 14–15

> It is easier to laugh than to investigate.
> — Johann Caspar Lavater (Frankfurt, 1775)

When we consider the form of the Gassner controversy, one remarkable feature stands out: the unbridled joy several of the combatants felt in laughing at their opponents. The lust for laughter was not quite legitimate in the eighteenth century, however. Critics adopted medical analogies to condemn the barbarous ferocity, the "furor" of the satirist, his blood lust for revenge or for conquest. Moralists in Germany condemned satire and allied forms of criticism as failures of neighborly love, and made it hard to claim that one had only the welfare of one's foolish antagonist at heart.[1] And yet the claims of ridicule continued to make their way. One reason was that many of the foundational works of Western literature and religion seemed to model or even authorize sarcasm and the satirical correction of others' errors. Even God Himself could be found ridiculing His own creatures; when He discovered Adam's disobedience in the Garden, He remarked with sarcastic humor: "Behold, the man [Adam] has become like one of us, knowing good and evil" (Gn 3:22). Of course satire, sarcasm, and ridicule are not identical, but they all depend upon witty deprecation, a derision that bites.

Some were even willing to apply the test of laughter to truth itself. Anthony Ashley Cooper, the Third Earl of Shaftesbury, was famous throughout the eighteenth century, and throughout Enlightened Germany, for claiming that one of the tests of truth was ridicule.[2] "Truth, 'tis supposed, may bear all lights; and one of those principal lights, or natural mediums, by which things are to be viewed . . . is ridicule itself, or that manner of proof by which we discern whatever is liable to just raillery in any subject." It is not clear that he meant this in a fully comprehensive sense, and exactly what he did mean has been open to much discussion, but in his *Letter Concerning Enthusiasm*, he asked, "How comes it to pass, then, that we appear such cowards in reasoning, and are so afraid to stand the test of ridicule?"[3] What was striking in this phrase was Shaftesbury's genial willingness to submit his own thoughts, and even the most reverend and widespread cultural assumptions, to raillery, to see how they might fare. It's another question how his thoughts did fare in fact, but the notion that ridicule was an effective, perhaps the only effective, antidote to resolute nonsense and "fanaticism" became widespread in the eighteenth century. There was indeed an eighteenth-century debate over the status of ridicule, one in which English poets and theologians participated, and which concluded around mid-century with the sense that ridicule could be overdone, that this "test of truth" was too harsh to be relied upon. Despite the urgings of restraint, modesty, and caution, however, laughter was irrepressible. In German discourse of the eighteenth century, ridicule, satire, parody, and witty attack became ever more popular literary forms. Satirists now singled out not only lower-class enthusiasm and fanaticism, but almost any issue on which the writer found that he could not quite specify exactly where he disagreed with an opponent.[4] Obviously no one claims that literary ridicule was invented in the eighteenth century. Surely any acquaintance with Horace and Juvenal, to say nothing of the vulgar cartoons and scatological pamphlets of the German Reformation, would be enough to immunize us against such an oversimplification. But it does appear that writers of the eighteenth century defended the use of witty attack as a moral stance and perfected its application to serious issues in a way that marks a contrast with earlier centuries.[5] Academics remained uncomfortable, however, with the application of raillery to the sober products of their lucubrations and tried to distinguish "sociable jesting" from raillery.[6]

Laughter seemed to violate the standards of academic debate, not because it was too harsh but because it diverted attention from the matter at hand. At that time, a few basic rules structured serious controversies. Anne Goldgar has recently emphasized such rules of politeness and restraint as the bonds that tied the republic of letters together, but these rules also served to make it difficult to discuss certain matters at all.[7] This is only one part of the picture, however, for literary figures did in fact often descend into bitter personal vituperation. As Martin Gierl has described them, the rules of scholarly engagement derived from university disputations, and while they regularly allowed insult and personal invective, they tended to produce controversies that systematically strove to annihilate any opposition by syllogism.[8] Although some cautious members of the republic of letters may have discovered that it was safer elegantly to say nothing than to attack another prominent member, in fact the debates of the Enlightenment were not so vapid as the demands of politeness required. Instead many theological or legal controversies were both personal and total. And yet a properly constructed debate could proceed only if the various contestants agreed on certain ground rules: what would count as evidence, for example, or what body of texts constituted the body of acceptable evidence. Among Lutherans, for example, it was a telling conclusion if one could show that an opponent's statement did not comport well with the "symbolic books," the confessional norms and creeds of the Lutheran Church, while this would obviously be an ineffective point in argument with others. In the Gassner controversy, therefore, basic problems were bound to arise. When Lutherans, Reformed, and Catholics took part in a common controversy, it was impossible to appeal to any accepted form of evidence, and hopeless to attempt to establish a common ground of decisive, that is, authoritative, texts.

These difficulties were compounded by the dramatic rise in literacy in eighteenth-century Germany and the even more explosive growth in the publication of books, pamphlets, newspapers, and journals of all sorts. Novels, for example, rose from being no more than 2.6 percent of the Leipzig book catalogue offerings in 1740, to 4 percent in 1770, to 11.7 percent in 1800, a number that finally rivaled the percentage of religious works on sale (which had fallen to 13.5 percent of all titles by 1800).[9] At the same time, Latin was giving way to German in the vast majority of books. The percentage of Latin books listed for sale in Leipzig (a number that unfortunately does not take account of Latin Catholic publishing in the South) fell from 38 percent in 1700 to 28 percent in 1740 to 14 percent in 1770. By 1800 this percentage had fallen to only 4 percent.[10] As Rolf Engelsing has pointed out, readers also learned to read "extensively," rather than repeatedly reading the same small number of texts "intensively."[11] Book production in general expanded rapidly. In 1740 the book catalogues of Frankfurt and Leipzig allow us to reckon that about 750 new books were published annually; by 1780 the Leipzig book fair listed 2,000 German titles, and by the 1790s contemporaries estimated new book production at about 5,000 per year, a sevenfold increase in fifty years.[12] By the beginning of the nineteenth century this number had risen to about 7,000.[13]

Books were not read by only one purchaser either. The best estimates suggest that for every book one might reasonably count on twenty readers, who encountered books in taverns, reading clubs, or in lending libraries. With the lack of effective copyright protections and despite the consequent massive dangers of pirated reprints, publishers were nonetheless able to bump up print runs from several hundred in 1750 to between one and two thousand in the 1780s, according to the *Journal von und für Deutschland*.[14] Some contemporaries bemoaned the epidemic of reading, stimulated by what they called "Vielschreiberei," or "endless scribbling."[15] As more readers were reading more sorts of material in less and less structured environments, it became impossible to control the decorum of public debate. The ground rules shifted.

The subject matter of books also shifted, in certain areas decisively in just this period. In 1770 about one-quarter of all books sold at the book fairs were theological or religious in content; by 1780 their proportion had fallen to about 18 percent; and by 1800 they made up about 13.5 percent, although these numbers do not take into account the higher rates of religious publication in the South (see table 5.1).[16] Percentages do not tell the whole story, though, because

Table 5.1 New Titles Listed at the Easter Book Fair, 1740–1800

	1740		1770		1800	
	Number	Percent	Number	Percent	Number	Percent
All titles	755	100%	1,144	100%	2,569	100%
Religious literature total	291	38.5%	280	24.5%	348	13.5%
Sermons/devotional and edifying literature	144	19.1%	124	10.8%	149	5.8%
Fine arts and letters total	44	5.8%	188	16.4%	551	21.4%
Poetic works	32	4.2%	153	13.4%	424	16.5%
Poems	10	1.3%	37	3.2%	34	1.3%
Dramas	2	0.3%	42	3.7%	64	2.5%
Narrative literature and novels	20	2.6%	46	4.0%	300	11.7%

Source: Based on Erich Schön, *Der Verlust der Sinnlichkeit, oder, Die Verwandlung des Lesers: Mentalitätswandel um 1800* (Stuttgart, 1987), p. 44. Schön relies upon the data in Jentzsch, *Der deutsch-lateinische Büchermarkt*, and emphasizes that they therefore tell us only about new titles, rather than about the whole market, which obviously included reprints and books published in previous years but not yet sold out. They also pay no attention to the rapidly growing numbers of pirated editions after 1765.

religious literature did not decline in absolute numbers; it actually grew slightly, rising from 291 titles in 1740 to 348 titles in 1800.

Remarkably, the declining proportion of "sermons, devotional and edifying literature" was almost exactly replaced by the growing category of "fine arts and letters." Taken together, they continued to make up about a quarter of all books sold in Germany from 1740 to 1800. The point of relevance for the Gassner controversy is that most of the works in this struggle were both entertaining and instructive, religious but narrative as well, amusing and amazing. Those who wrote for or against the exorcist from Klösterle had learned how to reach out to a new audience of readers, who were no longer interested in sermons but wanted edification along with entertainment.

Journals and newspapers also began to take up a serious part of the publishing spectrum. Looking over the whole eighteenth century we have records of about four thousand German-language journals, some of which lived only for a few issues, but others of which had long runs. Indeed, the German Enlightenment depended overwhelmingly upon journals.[17] One of the most important of all was Friedrich Nicolai's *Allgemeine Deutsche Bibliothek* (Berlin), which he founded in 1765 and faithfully published for forty-five years (producing 264 volumes in all, and employing 433 collaborators).[18] For many North Germans this review may have been the only way they had of learning about the Gassner scandal, along with all the other literary controversies of the age. In the last decades of the eighteenth century Nicolai printed 1,800 copies of each issue of his learned journal and managed to market his journal very widely.[19] Scores of cities also enjoyed a new level of information and Enlightened opinion in a so-called *Intelligenzblatt*, but most of them included only local or regional information and could not well fill the function of a national newspaper. By the 1770s, however, political journals were also making their mark—among them Christoph Martin Wieland's *Teutscher Merkur*, with print runs of 1,500 per issue (1773–1810), August Ludwig Schlözer's *Briefwechsel meist historischen und politischen Inhalts* (later retitled the *Staatsanzeigen*) (1776–1782; 1782–1793), Heinrich Christian Boie's *Deutsches Museum* (1776–1788), with usual print runs of 1,000—but most of them, including Schlözer, Wieland, and Boie, paid no attention to the Gassner affair. The one journal that competed with the *Allgemeine Deutsche Bibliothek* in bringing Gassner to general notice was Christian Friedrich Daniel Schubart's *Deutsche Chronik* (Augsburg and Ulm, 1774–1777), to which we will turn in a moment.[20]

Despite all the recent talk about a reading explosion, however, one cannot assume that literacy spread with equal speed through all regions and social classes. Peasants were sometimes slow to see the advantages of reading, and schooling remained inaccessible for many of them. Even so, when books were aimed at such readers, remarkable successes could be registered. As far as mere publishing success went, Eberhard von Rochow's elementary reading book *Der Kinderfreund* dwarfed all other efforts, bursting forth in the years 1776–1780 in nearly two hundred editions and over 100,000 copies. Similarly

Rudolf Zacharias Becker's *Noth und Hilfsbuchlein für Bauersleut* (Help in Times of Need for Peasants) appeared in 1788 and had already sold 35,000 copies by September of that year. Down to 1798, it had been printed in 150,000 copies, most of them in pirated editions, and by 1811 fully a million copies had been distributed. Of course there is no assurance that this book, often distributed for free, was always read, but the sheer numbers are impressive all the same.[21] Such children's readers and farmer's advice books were not, however, places where one might find information about political or religious scandals. Even so, the rising tide of reading material threatened to swamp traditional styles of controversy. Contemporaries spoke of a "Lesewut," a reading frenzy.[22] Luise Mejer, for example, wrote in 1783/84 from Hamburg, "Here they stuff people with reading the way one stuffs geese with noodles."[23] Some critics thought that the new form of extensive reading was addictive and was making readers physically and psychically sick, alienating them from the world of experience and overstimulating their imaginations, fostering hypochondria, and undermining the affective bonds that held households and society together.[24] Measuring the actual impact of increased reading is, however, difficult, and scholars are only beginning to develop methods of assessing what difference it made.[25] Anyone reading through the Gassner controversy is likely to feel overwhelmed, too, by the volume and by the repetitious character of many of the journal reports and news accounts gushing out of Ellwangen and Regensburg. The "reading frenzy" and the "mania for scribbling" were clearly visible in the Gassner scandal.

This dramatic rise in reading and in publication also made it increasingly difficult to maintain the previous standards of argument by which one signaled exactly which author and which arguments one meant to answer. With the Gassner controversy, scholars, pastors, and publicists struggled with the simple flood of material to which they felt obliged to respond. Despite the continuing strength of *Streitsucht*, total victory was now all but impossible.

At this point, an ambitious scholar might engage in a detailed discussion of the roughly 150 works that make up the Gassner controversy in print, an exercise in pedantry that would, I feel sure, have its own discreet charm. Instead let's examine what the new conditions of reading and publishing did to the rules of engagement, the form or structure of debate. Some of these features represent survivals from previous decades, but often enough even familiar conventions took on a new significance in the 1770s.

Anonymity

One of the first aspects that spring out at the modern reader of these debates is the fact that a large proportion of the published works in this controversy were anonymous. We know, of course, that anonymous publication was the standard refuge of those who feared the wrath of censors and intolerant governments. The curious fact about many of the anonymous books and pamphlets about Gassner, however, is that they were often published in towns or territories where the opinions expressed were perfectly in accord with the ruling orthodoxy. In some of these cases, it may well be that authors or publishers maintained secrecy in order to forestall notoriety and ill favor of a more unpredictable sort. Other authors seem to have used pseudonyms in order to protect their reputation as sober scholars or pious clerics, whose dignity might have prohibited the language of the gutter and the coarse invectives. But since scholars were used to hurling insults at one another, this does not seem to offer a full or convincing explanation. Sophie Rosenfeld has recently suggested that anonymity could also be a cosmopolitan strategy of submerging one's individuality (one's identity and even one's locality) in the interests of a more general, a more universal argument.[26] Of the titles listed in Joseph Hanauer's bibliography, incomplete as it is, over 75 percent were lacking an author or gave only a pseudonym.

As we see in table 5.2, an author was correctly identified in only 24 of the 112 publications listed (21 percent). Pseudonyms or teasing suggestions of the author were given 25 times (22 percent), especially by the supporters of Gassner. A substantial majority (62 out of 112, or 55 percent) gave no hint of the author, although librarians and historians have been able to identify the authors for about half of these.

Table 5.2 The Gassner Controversy in Print

	Author Identified	Falsely Identified	Pseudon- ymous	No Author	Total
Pro-Gassner	3	1	15	37	56
Anti-Gassner	9	0	7	15	31
Neutral	1	0	1	0	2
Special aspects	11	0	2	10	23
Totals	24 (21% of 112)	1	25	62 (55% of 112)	112

Source: Data extracted from the incomplete but useful bibliography provided by Josef Hanauer, "Der Teufelsbanner und Wunderheiler Johann Joseph Gassner (1727–1779)," *Beiträge zur Geschichte des Bistums Regensburg* 19 (1985), pp. 306–13.

From the actual titles and the pseudonyms, moreover, one can begin to understand some of the advantages of anonymity. We find titles such as these:

- *A Question: Whether the Catechism on the Doctrine of Spirits Is a Catholic Catechism?*[27]
- *Open Letter from Hofrat von —— to Hofrat von ——, a Member of the Bavarian Academy of Sciences in Munich, Concerning certain of the Operations Undertaken during His Stay in Ellwangen by Herr Gassner, sometime priest of Klösterle*[28]
- *Sympathy: The Universal Means of Curing All Devilries, for the Use of the New Philosophy and the Old Religion*[29]

With titles like these, one could manage to sound open-minded or elevated or perhaps even witty or sarcastic without having to endure the consequences. Such titles also took the focus away from the personal bias or interest of the author in order to concentrate more effectively (less personally) on the issues under discussion. Take a look at the titles I've compiled in my own expanded list, looking only at the *A*'s and *B*'s (in the original language):

- "Francisco dell' Amavero" (pseud. = "For the Love of Truth"), *Investigation of Whether Preventive Magic Works*[30]
- *An Exposé of Gassner's Miraculous Treatments*[31]
- *An Exposé of Sterzinger's Lies, Impertinence, and Ignorance*[32]
- *An Upright Explanation by a Cleric Concerning Gassner's Treatments, Against a Pastor*[33]
- *A Thorough Description of the Remarkable Phenomenon that Occurred to a Young Nun, Maria Anna Oberhüber*[34]
- *Contributions Concerning Gassner's Sojourn and Activities in Sulzbach*[35]
- *The Deceptions of the Art of Magic and the Dreams of Witchcraft, or a Defense of the Academy Lecture Concerning the Commonplace Prejudice in Favor of Active and Effective Witchcraft*[36]
- *A Judgment Concerning Gassner's Miraculous Treatments, by a Pastor and Zealot for the Catholic Religion*[37]
- *"Blocksberg's" [the name of a mountain where witches met] Congratulations to . . . Alois Merz concerning His Defense of Witchcraft and Magic*[38]
- *Letters of a Lady to Her Friend Concerning Gassner's Miraculous Treatments*[39]

With titles like these, one could cloak one's own identity, obviously, but also present one's authorial persona in the most favorable or the most humorous light, as a lover of truth, an honorable priest, a defender of tradition, or sarcastically as a partisan of witches. One could also attack one's opponent by "exposing" him, or "doubting" him, or "querying" him, without immediately appearing to do anything more than defending oneself.

Humility

Another characteristic of many titles is the claim to humility, a claim that made better sense if the author remained anonymous. Around 1700 the rules of the Republic of Letters required a becoming modesty and humility, but by 1775 contestants had learned to play with these rules and to mock them.[40] The Gassner controversy produced works that trumpeted their own humility:

- *A Humble Request for Instruction from the Great Men Who Do not Believe in the Devil*[41]
- *A Most Humble Answer of an Unimportant Rural Pastor to the Humble Request . . .* [42]
- *Devilries of the Eighteenth Century, by the Author of the Humble Request*[43]

Meanwhile, other authors could then only respond to these "humble works" by sarcastically referring to their modest efforts, as in the *Instruction for the Author of the Humble Petition to the Great Men Who Do Not Believe in the Devil*,[44] or in titles like this: *The Answer of an Unimportant Rural Pastor to the Instruction for the Author of the Humble Request . . . .*[45] Professor Heinrich Martin Gottfried Köster even impersonated the Swedish visionary Emanuel Swedenborg with a work dealing with these questions, and proclaimed an assumed humility in his title: *Emanuel Swedenborg's Humble Thanks to the Great Man Who Has Demonstrated the Nonexistence of the Devil.*[46]

Humility could, of course, be nothing more than appearance, as Ferdinand Sterzinger sarcastically suggested. When he first met Father Gassner in Ellwangen, the priest had closed his eyes, "no doubt out of humility" ("glaublich aus Demuth").[47] Another author apologized ironically for referring to Gassner only as "Herr Gassner," without giving him all the ceremonial titles the priest had received from the Bishop of Regensburg, but he explained that "since Herr Gassner is so humble as to deny that he is a miracle worker, he will surely also be so humble that he won't insist on these high titles."[48] Modesty was so highly prized in an author that it was sometimes the only admirable quality noticed. And one of the more telling blows against Gassner was that he actually was not modest enough. A friendly but skeptical author in Prague claimed in an open letter to Gassner that Gassner's enemies would shrink back in embarrassment if only the priestly exorcist might display greater caution and modesty.[49] But the charge of immodesty could also be used against Gassner's enemies, as did one tract which accused Sterzinger of attacks on Gassner that only fed the forces of materialism and free thought. So long as the church had not declared an official position on the matter, the author conceded that the *Gassnerstreit* was a "Controversia inter eruditos" allowing both arguments pro and contra, but only so long as participants were "moderate and modest" and avoided libel and lies.[50] If one detected instead a whole structure that was un-Catholic, with thoughts that savored of materialism, and where lies and false stories festered, there one could justly condemn the immodest author. The noisy poet and chronicler Christian Friedrich Daniel Schubart used the same criterion to praise an anonymous Lutheran author whose "modest tones" were appropriate to the truth and who was therefore content merely to smile sympathetically (or ironically), while Gassner's own tracts, in contrast, seemed "shallow, miserable, simple, unphilosophical, or even blasphemous writings that contradicted both nature and Christianity."[51]

Some readers naturally found anonymity neither humble nor charming and tried what they could to unmask the secret of the author's identity. Indeed, several of the works of the Gassner controversy reveled in their "discovery" or "unmasking" of an author. Once known, an author seemed far less impartial, far more devious. The Augsburg Lutheran Georg Wilhelm Zapf compiled an annotated bibliography of the *Gassnerstreit*, and his first question, perhaps naturally enough, was who had actually written the many anonymous works. Some authors made the task easy. Bernhard Schleis lightly cloaked himself in his treatises as Doct. Schisel (an anagram of Schleis) and claimed that it was published in Schalbuz (an anagram of Sulzbach),[52] while Ferdinand Sterzinger was almost as transparently veiled as "Francone dell'Amavero."[53] One of the seductive charms of anonymity, in fact, was the game one played with one's readers, revealing a little, and perhaps a little more of one's identity, without quite giving oneself away. Many readers found the game amusing, while others sought irritatedly to unmask these nameless scribblers. The unknown author of "So Is the Devil Really Now a Nothing?" foresaw this problem and claimed, "In order that my name not hinder anyone from speaking his mind impartially, I have withheld it. I am, however, prepared to reveal it if I notice the slightest necessity, for I am not ashamed publicly to accept instruction in the eyes of the world."[54] Pastor Conrad Runge of St. Ansgar's in Bremen, however, did express his irritation that the author of "So Is the Devil Really Now a Nothing?" hid behind his anonymity.[55] Readers well beyond their youth will remember a similar puzzlement with the *Times Literary Supplement* of London, whose reviews not so long ago were unsigned and whose authors were, therefore, known to only a few but suspected by many, and constituted a regular topic for discussions in clubs and college common rooms in Britain.

From lists like these one begins to see an advantage to anonymity that was more subtle than merely the desire to escape punishment or opprobrium. But we should not underestimate the threat of punishment. In late December 1774 the Elector Maximilian III Joseph of Bavaria announced that so long as Gassner's procedures in Ellwangen were unclear, the wonderworker was to be prohibited from entering Bavaria, and no one should publish anything, for or against him. At the end of December, when Ferdinand Sterzinger published his scathing account of Gassner's operations, based on his visit earlier that month, the elector reprimanded him for what was past and strictly forbade him to publish anything else on the matter in the future.[56] The result was that Sterzinger regularly disguised his authorship and found willing publishers in Protestant cities who were willing to take the risk of displeasing the mighty lord of Bavaria. Occasionally the publishers of controversial authors hid their activities even more sedulously by listing false or vague places of publication ("in Germany"). Only rarely did this practice extend to the declaration of a false date as well, but fairly often publishers would simply omit crucial information that would permit a reader to know where a pamphlet came from.

Ridicule

One not so lucky was Christian Friedrich Daniel Schubart (1739–1791), the musician, poet, and chronicler who took up residence in Augsburg in 1774 in order to publish his new twice-weekly *Deutsche Chronik*. As a flamboyant publisher, of course, he was hardly anonymous, but he must have hoped that the fact that Augsburg was composed of two officially accepted religious groups, Lutheran and Catholic, would make it possible for his fresh, Enlightened, and rambunctious reports to make their way without trouble. He mistook the formal status of bi-confessionality for toleration, however, and found that Augsburg was actually a swarming hornets' nest of confessional rivalries, in which joking about religion was seen as disturbing the peace. As Friedrich Nicolai noticed in his famous travelogue from 1781, "The Catholics of Augsburg are doubly and triply Catholic," but the same was true of the Protestants.[57] Religious animosities, in fact, had poisoned the atmosphere of Augsburg. We can use Schubart's reports to highlight this prominent feature of the Gassner controversy. As modern readers we can't help noticing that a great deal of the struggle was carried out in terms of scorn, sarcasm, personal vituperation, ridicule, and raillery. The pretense of humility and politeness did not inhibit most writers from expressing the most blatant forms of personal attack.

Christian Friedrich Daniel Schubart has a fair claim to being the first political journalist in Germany, a fact that is all the more extraordinary because he succeeded for over three years in this role even though he lived in the German South and Southwest, where journalism even of a softly moral sort was rare, and politically critical voices were not tolerated.[58] Schubart was one of the first German observers to celebrate the American Revolution and its assault upon tyrannical authorities.[59] His warm-hearted patriotism, his enthusiastic sympathies for what became known as the *Sturm und Drang*, and his emotional, popular verses have long been the subject of scholarly analysis.

Here, however, we are more interested in Schubart's vehement opposition to the Jesuits and in his bold or frankly impertinent attacks upon Johann Joseph Gassner. He may well have placed himself and his journal in Augsburg with the hope that the more tolerant atmosphere of a city in which Protestants and Catholics had been living together for over two hundred years might offer his efforts the political space that would allow him to speak his mind. If so, he was sadly misinformed. Ever since 1686 there had been three Catholic censors who monitored Catholic writings and three Protestant censors who controlled non-Catholic writing.[60] By the mid-eighteenth century new laws sought to protect Augsburg from dangerous views of all sorts,[61] but Schubart took aim at German censorship laws in his very first issue (31 March 1774). By April the many ex-Jesuits who had gathered in Augsburg were complaining of Schubart's insulting presence, his jokes about Catholic priests, and his warm admiration of Pope Clement XIV, because of his courage in dissolving the Jesuit order just a year earlier.[62] By late spring, the *Deutsche Chronik* had been forced out of Augsburg, finding a publisher in Ulm instead, even though Schubart himself stayed on in Augsburg and kept up a steady flow of crackling anti-Jesuit invective.

Schubart's troubles were, however, only partly connected to the ex-Jesuits and to their leader Alois März (Merz), S.J., the inflammatory "Kontroversprediger" of Augsburg's cathedral. On 12 December 1774 (*Deutsche Chronik*, vol. 1, Stück 74, p. 589) he reported on Johann Joseph Gassner's healing campaign: "The pastor of Klösterle Gassner has come forth to deceive the stupid rabble of Swabia. He's healing cripples, goiters, and epilepsies—not with medicines but just by laying on his high-priesterly hand. Recently he published a glorious book on how to resist the devil if he's kicking up a rumpus in houses or in people. And there are thousands of people around me who believe this nonsense—Saint Socrates, have mercy on me! When will we ever stop falling for this folly [literally, "this Swabian nonsense": "Wann hören wir doch einmal auf, Schwabenstreiche zu machen"]?"

In fact, Gassner grew into an obsession for Schubart, who commented over twenty times in the next couple of years upon the teachings and career of the exorcist.[63] It didn't help that the ex-Jesuits, and especially Merz, were among Gassner's most fervent and frequent supporters. Schubart perfected a tone of cackling, high raillery. In the issue for 29 December 1774, for example, he claimed that someone had asked him why Berlin, Paris, and London had been spared the current wave of demonic possession; Schubart answered that evidently the devil "preferred to possess pigs," a term with which he again laughed at the to him hopeless superstitions of his region, "where to the honor of the human understanding, ghosts and witch stories, demonic possessions and exorcisms are once again all the rage" (*Deutsche Chronik*, vol. 1, Stück 79 [29 December 1774], p. 630). The flow of sarcasm and ridicule was unstoppable, even after Schubart was forced out of Augsburg at the end of 1774. By March 1775 he was invoking the spirits of Juvenal, Persius, and Lucian, along with modern satirists Butler, Swift, and Christian Ludwig Liskow (1701–1760) or Gottlieb Wilhelm Rabner (1714–1771). They would have recognized the fool who has emerged from Wolf's Augsburg publishing house "with his wooden cudgel, trying to club" his various critics "but especially me" (*Deutsche Chronik*, vol. 2, Stück 20 [9 March 1775], pp. 158–60).

Again and again Schubart expressed his embarrassment that while Berlin cultivated an air of freedom, and while the rest of Europe could take pride in their Enlightened geniuses (naming Haller, Jerusalem, Spalding, Mendelssohn, Klopstock, Home and Hume, Robertson, Rousseau, Voltaire, and a host of Enlightened physicians), the poor Swabians were now exercised by exorcists and devils. When Gassner moved from Ellwangen to Regensburg in the summer of 1775, Schubart sarcastically thanked him for "driving out of our region several thousand million devils, all according to protocols, so that we are now as clean as if we'd been swept by a broom" (*Deutsche Chronik*, vol. 2, Stück 39 [15 March 1775], p. 311). So it was with peals of malicious laughter that Schubart greeted the news that the Emperor Joseph II had ordered an end to Gassner's flamboyant exorcising (*Deutsche Chronik*, vol. 2, Stück 101 [18 December 1775], pp. 801–3).

For these joyous outbursts of ridicule, for his subversive disrespect for censorship, and for the social, political, and religious proprieties of the German Southwest, Schubart paid a high price. On 23 January 1777 he was lured from his safe haven in the imperial city of Ulm into Württemberg territory, where he was arrested on orders from Duke Karl Eugen and thrown in prison at the Hohenasperg, near Ludwigsburg, without a trial.[64] There he endured an unheated room, straw bedding, inadequate food, and solitary confinement, with only a Bible to read. When he emerged ten years later, he was a broken man, finally ready to play the subservient lapdog to his ducal lord for the four years that remained to him. When he looked back on his short career in the 1770s as a liberated political journalist, Schubart told his son that his attack on Gassner had formed the "second stone" in the vault of his prison cell.[65] It seems clear in retrospect that Duke Karl Eugen was prompted to remove the frivolous and disrespectful Schubart for holding the ruling classes of Europe, and specifically the duke of Württemberg, in total contempt.[66] *Die Deutsche Chronik* had contributed in a revolutionary way to the transformation of German journalism, but for Schubart, perhaps to our surprise, it was his religious zeal, his immoderate and satirical assault upon the ex-Jesuits and upon Gassner that had sealed his fate.

Perhaps he was right. Certainly Gassner's supporters were more incensed at Schubart's sarcastic and vehement laughter than by almost any other sort of criticism. Even Sterzinger's biting accounts failed to arouse the same level of indignation. Schubart's tone, his easy, flippant, emotional style and his overweening Protestant confidence drove Catholic traditionalists wild with rage. The anonymous author of one tract despised Schubart, the "Kronickschreiber," who dared to criticize Gassner not as a Christian but as a "Freygeist," a Freethinker, who jokes about the gospel on almost every page.[67] For the anonymous author of *A Short List of Modern Highwaymen who have dealt with the Gassner Phenomenon in Ellwangen*, Schubart was contemptible for his clownish manner, his "pickled herring" style ("Pickelheringsart"), and for his transparent envy and malice. Charging that Schubart was among the many who visited Gassner in Ellwangen, this author protested that Schubart had not understood the basis of Gassner's treatments and had suspected that the pious priest was only interested in making money, as he would have done.[68] Others objected to Schubart's shameful behavior, calling him an epicurean, a Freydenker, and an ally of Voltaire. By aiming to increase the "empire of Venus," Schubart had shown himself worse than a Protestant.[69]

The best example of how Catholic traditionalists felt about Schubart's breezy and irreligious ridicule can be found in a little-known sixty-five-page comedy entitled *Hans the Clown and Schubart* (*Hannswurst und Schubart*).[70] Anonymously written, probably by the ex-Jesuit Cathedral preacher Johann Georg Zeiler from Augsburg,[71] the play, which is actually only a few pages long, came with a lengthy preface and an afterword that cursed Schubart and laughed at him for living in exile (as a self-proclaimed German Ovid in Ulm), miserably composing lies and assailing the gods, raining insults and abuse on everyone. Zeiler took special offense at the way Schubart had mangled and misinterpreted a previous work of his entitled *Sympathy, a Universal Means of Combating All Devilries*,[72] in which the author had defended the distinction between natural and unnatural diseases. By that very distinction, there were of course natural disorders, and Schubart could hardly expect to hit his target if all he meant to show was that natural disorders existed. Over and over, in both works, Zeiler ridiculed and abused Schubart's sloppy logic, his lack of academic learning, his unchristian conclusions, and his extravagant praise for Goethe's immoral *Sorrows of Young Werther*.

Schubart's laughter failed to persuade, but perhaps that had never been his goal. Once he was jailed by the tyrannical Duke Karl Eugen, Protestant and Enlightened voices sprang belatedly to his defense (including Lavater, for example), but only a few of the Gassner controversialists publicly lamented his disappearance. The most prominent was surely Friedrich Nicolai, the remarkable publicist from Berlin, the editor and publisher of the *Allgemeine Deutsche Bibliothek*.[73] From the beginning of this venture in the 1760s, Nicolai had set himself the remarkable (and hopeless) task of reviewing every book published in Germany. He never came close to this ambitious goal with respect to most Catholic publishing, and he ignored most books from the German South, but from the very start of Gassner's exorcising career, Nicolai kept himself well informed through secret channels, using agents who sent him reports and packets of literature, which Nicolai and his contributors summarized and criticized.[74]

In this effort, Nicolai also exemplified a modern approach to the confusions generated by the Gassner affair. He tried to control or contain the turbulent debates by creating bibliographies, and it is striking how many other authors also appended shorter or longer reading lists to their pamphlets and books, lists that allowed readers to judge whether an author had "mastered" the ever-growing literature.[75] With the help of such lists, the careful historian can set many of the publications of 1775 and 1776 in a rough chronological order, creating a sort of cultural epidemiology. But these bibliographies also suggest a new approach to public controversy. We sometimes give students the same task today, when we ask them to provide annotated bibliographies or summaries of the literature on complex topics as a substitute for resolving every point in an argument. Nicolai thus provides evidence here again of how Gassner's struggle exemplified many of the major issues of his day, including the problems generated by the reading and writing frenzy of the 1770s. The annotated bibliographies provided by Nicolai suggest that the old-school efforts to comment on every argument made by an opponent collapsed under the weight of the flurry of publications from all angles and at all social levels. Other readers also came to recognize that bibliography was by no means a neutral task. Georg Wilhelm Zapf in Augsburg, for example, published his own annotated bibliography of the Gassner craze, in which he ostentatiously criticized Nicolai's efforts.[76]

Bibliographical control of the burgeoning journal literature of the late eighteenth century was so obviously necessary that in 1790 Johann Heinrich Beutler and Johann Christoph Guts-Muths published a two-volume "General Subject Index Covering the Most Important German Newspapers and Weeklies," and that was only the beginning of German efforts to register and analyze the journalistic frenzy that had broken out.[77] Of course, the Gassner affair appeared in these lists, and ambitious intellectuals could use this bibliography and the others that soon followed to familiarize themselves with a controversy that was dying away by 1790. But like most self-declared intellectuals, these lists too concentrated overwhelmingly on the Protestant North. When listing the theological writings of the 1770s, for example, Beutler and Guts-Muths publicized only one Catholic journal and then noted disparagingly that its editor, a convert from Lutheranism, was far too eager to display his "hatred against the party of the church he left behind and his vengeful sensitivity over every supposed insult, no matter how small."[78] To be fair, they also noted that an "anti-papist journal" intended for "the impartial Lutheran" was an immoderately partisan rag, "declaring war" on his "former Catholic comrades in the faith."[79] In this atmosphere Protestants had trouble learning about the Catholic South, if they ever had any desire to do so.

Even when North Germans dealt with Catholic Germany, however, there was little pretense of cool-minded objectivity. We need not again detail Friedrich Nicolai's full engagement with the Gassner affair, but merely remind ourselves that in the mid to late 1770s the exorcist confirmed all of his North German, Protestant, and Enlightened prejudices about the superstitious, backward, Catholic South, prejudices for which he became even more famous after his journey of discovery into the heart of darkness in 1781, the tour of southern Germany, Austria, and Switzerland that Nicolai memorialized at length in the 1780s. Nicolai joined Schubart in publishing scathing, scandalous, and satirical interpretations of the Catholic cultural scene. His reports echo throughout with hilarity at what he described as the ludicrous superstitions and nonsense of half-wits.

The Functions of Laughter

Contemptuous laughter was characteristic of the German Enlightenment at its coarsest and most raucous, and we can conclude this chapter by asking what such laughter actually accomplished. At first sight it might appear that Schubart, Nicolai, Sterzinger, Zeiler, Merz, and the many other satirists and participants in the Gassner controversy used their humor as a means of persuasion.[80] They seem at first glance to be seeking converts to their causes among the general reading public. But on reflection, one realizes that vengeful ridicule, harsh words and invective, biting satire and personal insults could have had little hope of winning over anyone at whom such bombards were directed, or even anyone trying to form an independent view. In fact, as we all know from personal experience, hurting someone's feelings is rarely a way of changing his or her mind. So these polemical missiles, unlike the academic discourse of disputation and response, did not actually aim to change anyone's mind. Instead, their dangerous humor aimed at solidifying the ranks of the already converted, or at excluding or warning off those who might be tempted to take up the wrong side in an argument. Indeed, as Anne Goldgar has pointed out, the fear of ridicule was a powerful disincentive to joining in certain kinds of discourse.[81] Laughter has often been understood as a triumphant expression of superiority or even of glorying dominance, but here it would appear that laugher was more a means of strengthening a party or a front when faced with opponents with whom one could not simply argue. In this way, laughter can criticize or affirm the status quo.

In a recent neo-classical account, F. H. Buckley has emphasized the ways in which adult laughter seems always directed (at least implicitly) at some butt, some target, over whom the jokester can feel justifiably superior.[82] Buckley's rather elaborate apology for laughter as a means to the good life makes larger claims than can be plausibly sustained, but he has usefully emphasized the role laughter and joking play in creating communities that feel superior to their often rigid, rule-bound, humorless, machinelike, foolish, immoral, or self-indulgent targets. Ever since Aristotle, the Western tradition has understood laughter as a sudden recognition of glorious superiority, a sense of triumph that classical rhetoricians tried to mobilize in order to make up for the recognized inadequacies of sober and reasonable discourse.[83]

Laughter firms up the boundaries of the acceptable, and may persuade some listeners or readers to move over to the laugher's side, or at least to get out of the way. Surely we all do what we can to avoid becoming the target of the spiteful humorist, even if it means no more than turning off the TV or leaving the party. This explains, I think, why we joke best in the company of those with whom we agree. The ill-advised or impolite joke is often only a joke told in the wrong company, one that wounds or silences rather than firming up the ranks of the humorful.[84] In this way, ridicule creates communities of laughter.[85] But precisely for this reason, laughter splinters the public sphere into competing groups of mutually contemptuous readers and writers.

The culture of ridicule in the Gassner controversy, the raillery of the Enlightened (including the Catholic Enlightened) and of the traditional (including both Protestant and Catholic traditionalists) could not, therefore, contribute to the creation of one conversation, one public sphere. It is true, to be sure, that the pamphlets of the 1770s aimed for a wide readership, but they did not hesitate to offend and to repel those readers who could not be expected to share the views of the writer. Without addressing them as thoughtful persons, and by generating laughter at their expense, I would suggest that these pamphlets did not actually increase conversation, dialogue, and thoughtful dissent. Instead, it would appear that there were various kinds of public formed during and by the *Gassnerstreit*. The combatants in this controversy sometimes raised this very issue to consciousness and discussed what sort of public they were addressing, what sort of public they were creating.

Nicolai, for example, often appealed to the public as a proper judge of the rank nonsense he exposed in the German South. But he too acknowledged that genuine dialogue (respectful, reciprocal conversation) with Catholics was almost impossible. In a dispute with Christian Garve concerning the general character of Catholicism, Nicolai admitted, "I know very well, that it is usually most difficult to arrive at even a modest understanding with Catholics, who from childhood on have known nothing but their religious prejudices. The more clearly and more freely a Protestant expresses himself, the stranger much of it seems to even the best Catholic."[86] With Joseph II's 1781 decree of religious toleration in Austria, Nicolai hoped that Protestants might slowly work to erase centuries of prejudice. But "even in the most Enlightened Catholic states, censorship was so strict that no one can open his mouth about the many abuses."[87] So Protestants had to do what Enlightened Catholics could not do for themselves. Others, however, could appeal to "the public," too, hoping that it would see things differently, as we see in *An Open Protest and Complaint Offered to the Public against the Frankfurt Journalist*, the Frankfurt journalist being a writer who had published a sharp critique of Gassner.[88] Another author objected to the publicity that this Frankfurt journalist had achieved and implicitly threatened a libel action against him. His fury derived in part from the very publicity that newspapers and journals afforded the most scandalous author.[89] The Ellwangen councillor Joseph Sartori complained, indeed, that various authors were appealing to different publics, making their petitions highly confusing.[90] Confronting claims that Gassner's cures were all either natural or fraudulent and that a "wise public" could be expected to recognize such frauds, Sartori objected that his opponent was asking "really what do you the public think of this episode?" And he assumed that the wise public's answer would be: "Not much!" But, Sartori countered, this public was not his, for his opponent's world was full of irreligious skeptics. "And what do you call your 'wise world'? I have no real idea of your world. Is it perhaps a landscape populated by madmen, or a well-policed society of moral egoists? Men who all think like you? . . . I appeal to another public, who will give me witnesses that there are people even among you who feel the effective force of Herr Gassner's healing power."[91] Sartori sarcastically protested that in appealing to the public, one had to distinguish the "wise" from rational fools.

From confrontations like this one, we learn that creating an Enlightened public sphere was not just a matter of carving out a realm separate from the state and from purely private interests, a realm of enlightened debate and discussion, where the rules of reason made it possible to consider issues calmly without the pressure of material interest or political intimidation. This amounts to yet another limitation on Jürgen Habermas's *Structural Transformation of the Public Sphere*, that influential effort to understand and construct the emerging conditions for truly Enlightened and useful debate.[92] The actual rules of the conversational game, what Deborah Tannen has called the conversational style, could determine whether the participants in a controversy were able to listen to each other. Genuine attempts to listen, to hear what a vehement opponent was saying remained rare in the 1770s.[93] One reason, I think, is that the raucous laughter and ridicule which each side enjoyed at the expense of the opposition made it hard if not impossible to feel willing to converse with such brutes. The Gassner controversy generated such polarized communities of laughter that each side remained unable to learn much from the other. This does not make the Gassner controversy different from other confrontations between the philosophes and the counter-Enlightenment, but it was a strikingly brilliant example of how easily debate could degenerate into a satisfied conversation of the like-minded.

This remains a continuing problem for all of our public controversies right down to today. We enjoy laughing at our political, religious, or philosophical opponents, but our very laughter can poison any genuine attempt to understand our differences. We hate it when our opponents find ways to laugh at us. Buckley may be right that laughter and good humor are necessary parts of a good life, but we must also keep our witty instincts under control or else run the risk of confining ourselves to a circle of the self-proclaimedly superior. As Cass Sunstein has recently pointed out, we need dissent and dissenters to keep the mainstream from flowing toward undesirable extremes. But nonconformists and gadflies can perform their crucial tasks only if "listeners are willing to give dissenters a respectful hearing."[94] In his criticism of Voltaire, Thomas Carlyle anticipated this point when he remarked, "All great men have been careful to subordinate this talent or habit of ridicule."[95]

In these five chapters, I have tried to show that a hitherto rather unknown German controversy raised issues far more generally important that we might have thought at first glance. I think that demonic possession actually "made sense" in the late eighteenth century, and that the conceptual framework of demons provided a way of understanding evil, sickness, and hardship in a structure which we have mostly dismantled but for which we have not really found a substitute. And those concepts made possible a series of religious experiences open only to those who truly believed in demonic possession. I have also tried to show that efforts to describe Father Gassner's healing methods probably changed what he was doing; that the rise of eyewitness protocols provided empirical evidence for the intervention of spirits in this world, evidence that Protestant and naturalist skeptics could only deny by denying the relevance of empirical evidence altogether. Protestant commentators had another problem with Gassner, of course, because the synoptic Gospels speak so frequently, and so naturally (so "geschichtsähnlich"), of demons and their damage. If one wanted to get beyond Gassner and his demons, it seemed necessary to develop a whole new style of exegesis in which Scripture came to have a metaphorical, allegorical, or spiritual significance that no longer depended upon a literal meaning. And in this chapter, I have claimed that the Gassner controversy depended so heavily upon anonymous contributions ridiculing and deriding their supposedly stupid or immoral opponents that a real or sober conversation about serious issues could not occur. Instead, an emerging modern society, one might say an emerging modern discourse, was split from the start into spheres that hardly intersected at all. The emergence of "the public" splintered almost *ab initio* into various mutually uncomprehending publics, a condition that will seem familiar to us all.

EPILOGUE

In the end it was easy enough for an emperor and a pope to stop an obedient priest from abusing or overextending his priestly powers of exorcism. It was, however, an entirely different matter to eradicate or even curtail the belief in evil spirits among a population where such ideas were deeply rooted and seemed to explain so much. Even Protestants discovered that the Gospels were resistant to Enlightened demythologizing. It slowly dawned on some advanced thinkers that just as Jesus had actually believed in an imminent apocalypse, a return to this earth that some of those who heard him would live to see (Mt 16:28; cf. Mt 10:23; Mk 9:9; Lk 9:27; Rev 3:11), so too he probably did believe that his healings had cast out demons. Efforts to interpret his utterances as accommodations to the superstitions of the Jews, as if he had merely "spoken the language" of the people among whom he lived, served rather to separate him from the culture in which he had grown up and to aggrandize the modern interpreter, who seemed to claim a unique authority to decide which of his sayings he might have meant.

When Friedrich Nicolai made his famous trip from Berlin through the Catholic lands of southern Germany and Austria, he was astonished to find that even in that self-proclaimedly Enlightened day, Catholics still enthusiastically took part in pilgrimages and processions, venerated images and relics, donned scapulars dedicated to various religious orders and saints, chastised their flesh with fasts and even with flagellation, and pinned up images of their tutelary saints. In one inn in Austria, Nicolai found a Latin exorcism posted in a room invoking all the names of God and banishing demons, which he transcribed as follows:

> Ad cognoscendum si aliquis vexetur à Spiritibus immundis.
> In Nomine Patris & Filii Spiritus † Sancti, Amen. Hel † Heloin † Sother

EPILOGUE

† Emmanuel † Sabaoth Agia † Tetragrammaton † Agyon † Otheos † Ischyros † Athanatos † Jehova † Adanay † Saday † Homnosin † Messias † Exerchye † Increatus Pater † Increatus Filius † Increatus Spiritus † Sanctus.

JEsus [sic] Christus vincit † Christus regnat † Christus imperat † Si Diabolus ligavit & tentavit te, N. suo effectu, per sua opera, Christus Filius Dei vivi, per suam misericordiam liberet te ab omnibus spiritibus immundis, qui venit de coelo, & incarnatus in utero Beatissimae Virginis Mariae, causa humanae salutis, & ejiciendi diabolum & omnem malignum spiritum at te in profundum inferni abyssi. Ecce Crucem Domini fugite partes adversae, vicit Leo de tribu Juda, Radix David Alleluja Alleluja Alleluja.[1]

To Nicolai's Prussian and Protestant amazement, faithful Austrian Catholics still wore little blessings ("Conceptions-Zettlen") with which they warded off evil spirits; even military men went into battle with little prayers and blessings in their pockets, invoking Mary and all the saints in heaven.[2] In 1784 Nicolai learned that Johanna Steinböckin, the thirty-three-year-old wife of a hatmaker from Grein, had imbibed a devil (disguised as a "Grinaigl," a green-eyed straw fly) in a mug of beer. She was sure that she had been bewitched, and indeed a priest had tried fruitlessly to exorcise the devil. The secular administrators of Upper Austria ordered her into a lazaretto, and doctors declared her a fool. But her pastor was not so easily silenced.[3] And in Munich, Nicolai learned that the ex-Jesuit Johann Nepomuk Gruber had preached so vehemently in St. Michael's against free thought, that people claimed they could hear the devils roaring, a gross trick of the ex-Jesuits that nonetheless made an impression on the "stupid masses."[4]

Echoes of Gassner could be heard in Tyrol, too. In the frescoes painted by Johann Jacob Zeiller on the church of St. Nicholas in Elbigenalp in 1776 one can make out the colorful depiction of an exorcism. Surely that was no mere coincidence. And in May of 1783 a teenage girl from the Alto Adige fell ill, experienced visions, and began to behave as if possessed. She was brought to the Augustinian monastery of Seefeld in the Tyrol, where an exorcist found that she was infested with one hundred million evil spirits; a satirical reporter feigned amazement, claiming that he thought Gassner had banished them all from the world. Here Gassner's influence extended to the use of probative exorcisms.[5] A few years later an exorcist from Seefeld composed a rhyming spoof at the expense of skeptics in Württemberg, with a view to proving the existence of the devil.[6] Clearly in Tyrol the devil had survived the death of Gassner.

At the University of Dillingen natural philosophy Professor Joseph Weber found that there were still burning coals under the ashes of the supposedly dying controversy over demons when he tried in 1787 to finish off lingering beliefs in witchcraft and demons. He wrote, he said, because to his dismay ordinary country people continued to fear "active witchcraft."[7] Just as amazing, perhaps, was the reaction of an Augsburg Catholic tobacco merchant, Franz Joseph Schmid, who immediately replied to Weber, blasting his "Witches' Reformation" and accusing him of fostering deism or even atheism. Rehashing the refutations of Semler and other Enlightenment interpreters of demons, Schmid declared that the belief in demons and witchcraft was an important pillar of Christian dogma and morals.[8] In other words, even at the level of debate over demons and witchcraft, a certain level of controversy continued to bubble beneath the notice of most self-proclaimedly Enlightened writers. Some of Gassner's followers even became imitators and carried on his method of healing in the decades after the priest from Klösterle had retired into obscurity.[9] Indeed, to the dismay of the Enlightened, "superstitious" cures and religious approaches to illness continued to characterize most parts of Germany on into the nineteenth century.[10]

It was not only the "masses," therefore, who retained their beliefs in demons and other spirits. Once the flood tide of the Enlightenment began to ebb, religious and literary figures emerged who had either never doubted or had now revived their conviction that reason and empirical science were not sufficient tools with which to interpret life in this world. Over thirty years ago Hans Grassl published a dramatic and learned book in which he argued persuasively that the Gassner controversy marked the beginning of the Bavarian Romantic movement, the moment when the forces of tradition, religion, and emotion began to mount a counteroffensive against the supposedly sterile wastes of reason.[11] He emphasized the connections between the ex-Jesuits, the Rosicrucians, the followers of Mesmer, and the opponents of the Illuminati, along with Lavater, the mystical theosophist Louis Claude de Saint-Martin, Johann Heinrich Jung-Stilling, Karl von Eckartshausen, Johann Michael Sailer, Ferdinand Maria Baader, and a host of others who worked for a revived Catholicism and a new sort of magical or romantic natural philosophy.

Although Bavaria had held firm against Gassner himself, Gassner's followers and enthusiasts worked during the 1780s and 1790s to make Bavaria a crucible for romantic philosophy and literature. In this atmosphere, full-fledged Romantics such as Adam Carl August von Eschenmeyer and Justinus Kerner rediscovered the career and writings of Gassner and celebrated his mastery of the "spiritual formative powers" (*geistige Bildungskraft*) that brought healing. For them Gassner represented one of the first who had unmasked the Enlightenment.[12] This was no longer a debate between Mesmer and Gassner, but an attempt to spiritualize and unify their divergent energies. In the 1820s or 1830s, the Swabian physician Justinus Kerner (1786–1862) even studied the manuscript *Protokolle* of Gassner's healings in Sulzbach to gain insight into the origins of a romantic medicine, seeing Gassner as the bearer of a divine power and an evangelical truth. He saw his investigations as the empirical work of a physician, carefully noting phenomena that seemed to require belief in spirits.[13] His treatment of a visionary "somnambulist," Frederike Hauffe, persuaded him that she was truly in touch with spirits of the dead, and his knowledge of Mesmer's theories only strengthened his conviction that certain afflictions were best understood as "demonic-magnetic" in nature.[14] He developed a "magical medicine" that explicitly depended upon notions of healing by use of natural, magnetic sympathy and contact with the world of spirits. So the fateful pairing of Gassner and Mesmer lived on despite their own efforts in the 1770s to distinguish themselves from each other.[15]

Among the Württemberg Protestant Pietists of the early-

EPILOGUE

nineteenth-century Awakening, moreover, the devil revived as a figure of psychological temptation and as a source of physical illness. Pastor Johann Christoph Blumhardt (1805–1880) was perhaps the crucial figure, starting in 1842, in restoring the belief in demons and in exorcism to a position of recognized and authorized practice, at least among ordinary Pietists. Over the course of the nineteenth century, numerous healers developed a ministry of healing and deliverance that fed into twentieth-century Pentecostalism.[16] Blumhardt himself learned over years of dealing with supposedly possessed patients "that everything that had hitherto been reckoned under the most ridiculous popular superstition, stepped over from the world of fairy tales into reality."[17] Although they may well have been aware of the local impact of Gassner in southern Germany, the general Pietist allergy to Catholic "superstition" insulated them from his direct influence even as they adopted many of his specific practices and beliefs.

To the north, in Berlin itself, the 1780s was a decade of increasing spiritualist enthusiasm, stimulated in part by the accession of Frederick William II to the throne of Prussia in 1786; the new ruler supported ministers and courtiers devoted to religiously conservative, mystical, visionary, and anti-Enlightenment projects.[18] Ghosts and other spiritual bodies were suddenly back on the cultural agenda, and empirical evidence, at least, seemed to support their existence. Controversies about the validity of visions even pulled in such luminaries as Goethe and Kant and shaped the growing reaction to the Enlightenment well into the early nineteenth century.

Aside from the factual or medical status of healing by exorcism, moreover, we need to remember that Gassner's rituals were also intended to bolster faith in Jesus. Even if a physical cure was unavailable or only transient, patients might credibly claim to feel better because their conditions and perhaps their lives made better sense when viewed through the lens of renewed and strengthened faith. It is in this sense that Gassner's campaign amounted to a religious revival.

The political forces mobilized during the Gassner scandal had a future as well. As we have seen, the ex-Jesuits, especially in Augsburg, organized a remarkable propaganda campaign in favor of the exorcist's healings, and many of the same persons became active in the harsh Bavarian reaction to the discovery of the obscurantist, anticlerical, and Enlightened Illuminati "conspiracy" in 1784, when the Prince Elector Karl Theodor of Bavaria cracked down on its members, jailing many and forcing others to flee.[19] Years before the French Revolution, conservative fears of a vast conspiracy to undermine both church and state fueled a theory that threw "free thinkers, free spirits, freemasons, Encyclopedists, rationalists, Jansenists, and Josephinians" into one pot.[20] In this way, reactions to the Gassner scandal helped to forge the ideology and party formations that characterized the post-Napoleonic Restoration in Germany.[21] Former Illuminati, such as Count Maximilian von Montgelas, also managed to work their way back into the Bavarian government, having given up almost all of their former conspiratorial ideals but remaining true to at least the Josephinian goal of state control of the church and the secularization of ecclesiastical properties.[22]

In these ways Gassner's healing campaign and the controversy he provoked pointed forward to political, religious, intellectual, and literary movements that erupted in the nineteenth century. His thoughts on healing survived in secular form as Mesmerism and even later as one of the remote origins of psychoanalysis. His emphasis upon teaching patients to control their own symptoms has continued to inspire modern hypnotherapists.[23] Whatever we ourselves may think of his healing practices or of his ideas about demons, Gassner was not just a figure of the pre-Enlightenment, a pious or superstitious relic of the age of the baroque. We cannot easily disentangle him and what he stood for from the many facets of the counter-Enlightenment that have troubled and enlivened our modern world. Moreover, his controversy, with its fierce publicity and contemptuous rhetoric, foreshadowed the splintered worlds of modernity and postmodernity in which our commentators only rarely step outside the comfortable assumptions of those with whom they can share a laugh in order to learn what those who radically disagree with them might be laughing about.

NOTES

Introduction

1. [Ferdinand Sterzinger], *Die aufgedeckten Gassnerischen Wunderkuren. Aus authentischen Urkunden beleuchtet und durch Augenzeugen bewiesen* (n.p., 1775), pp. 25–26. For a completely different account of these proceedings, see the sympathetic report in [Joseph Edler von Sartori], *Die aufgedeckten Sterzingerischen Lügen, Keckheit, und Unwissenheit, aus unwiderstösslichen Wahrheiten beleuchtet* (n.p., 1775).
2. The revived interest in religion in general and in the orthodox religious origins of dissent in eighteenth-century Europe is clearly visible in James E. Bradley and Dale K. Van Kley, *Religion and Politics in Enlightenment Europe* (Notre Dame, Ind.: University of Notre Dame Press, 2001). For a spectacular example, see Dale K. Van Kley, *The Religious Origins of the French Revolution: From Calvin to the Civil Constitution, 1560–1791* (New Haven: Yale University Press, 1996). For the tradition that began with Robert R. Palmer's *Catholics and Unbelievers in Eighteenth-Century France* (Princeton: Princeton University Press, 1939), see now Darrin M. McMahon, *Enemies of the Enlightenment: The French Counter-Enlightenment and the Making of Modernity* (Oxford: Oxford University Press, 2001). The speculations of John Kent are useful here: *The Unacceptable Face: The Modern Church in the Eyes of the Historian* (London: SCM Press, 1987).
3. "Critiquing prejudice was one of the central goals of the Aufklärung, but we can now see that it was not . . . a one-shot affair. It was a process, open-ended and continuous, and it embraced not only those who identified themselves with the Aufklärung but also its self-styled opponents." Jeffrey Freedman, *A Poisoned Chalice* (Princeton: Princeton University Press, 2002), p. 138.
4. Henri F. Ellenberger, *The Discovery of the Unconscious: The History and Evolution of Dynamic Psychiatry* (New York: Basic Books, 1970); among psychological studies, see also Beate Meissner, "Die Heilmethode des Exorzisten Johann Joseph Gassner. Eine Urform der Psychotherapie?" unpublished Diplomarbeit, Freiburg, 1984; Adam Crabtree, *From Mesmer to Freud: Magnetic Sleep and the Roots of Psychological Healing* (New Haven: Yale University Press, 1993). The latest student in this line of

research has reversed Ellenberger's evaluation: Burkhard Peter, "Hypnotische Selbstkontrolle. Die wirksame Psychotherapie des Teufelsbanners Johann Joseph Gassner um 1775," *Hypnose und Kognition* 17 (Doppelheft 1–2) (2000), pp. 19–34.
5. In German Gassner has been studied for more than a century. See J. A. Zimmermann, *Johann Joseph Gassner, der berühmte Exorzist* (Kempten, 1878); Georg Pfeilschifter, "Des Exorzisten Gassner Tätigkeit in der Konstanzer Diözese im Jahre 1774," *Historisches Jahrbuch* 52 (1932), pp. 401–41; Hans Grassl, *Aufbruch zur Romantik. Bayerns Beitrag zur deutschen Geistesgeschichte, 1765–1785* (Munich: Beck, 1968), esp. pp. 131–71, 424–29; Wolfgang Behringer, *Hexenverfolgung in Bayern. Volksmagie, Glaubenseifer und Staatsräson in der Frühen Neuzeit* (Munich: Oldenbourg, 1987), pp. 363, 394–97.
6. Nils Freytag, "Exorzismus und Wunderglaube im späten 18. Jahrhundert. Reaktionen auf die Teufelsbanner und Wunderheiler Johann Joseph Gassner und Adam Knoerzer," in Edwin Dillmann, ed., *Regionales Prisma der Vergangenheit. Perspektiven der modernen Regionalgeschichte (19./20. Jahrhundert)* (St. Ingbert: Röhrig, 1996) (=Saarland Bibliothek, Bd. 11), pp. 89–105, 427–34. The best example of such a regional focus on Gassner is Josef Hanauer's lengthy monograph, "Der Teufelsbanner und Wunderheiler Johann Joseph Gassner (1727–1779)," *Beiträge zur Geschichte des Bistums Regensburg* 19 (1985), pp. 303–545, an essentially unrevised version of his dissertation, Würzburg 1950. See also Manfred Tschaikner, "Von 'bösen zauberischen Leuten' in Braz um 1750. Aus der Familiengeschichte des berühmten Exorzisten Johann Joseph Gassner," *Bludenzer Geschichtsblätter* 5 (1989), pp. 15–34; Gerhard Ammerer, " 'Gegen die unbefugten Unternehmungen gewisser Exorcisten' — Der Hirtenbrief Erzbischof Colloredos gegen den Wunderheiler Johann Joseph Gassner von 1776," *Mitteilungen der Gesellschaft für Salzburger Landeskunde* (2002), pp. 141–80; Siegfried Müller, *Drei "Wunderheiler" aus dem Vorarlberger Oberland* (Feldkirch: Schriftenreihe der Rheticus Gesellschaft, no. 20, 1986).
7. Elena Brambilla, "La fine dell'esorcismo: Possessione, santità, isteria dall'età Barocca all' Illuminismo," *Quaderni Storici* 112 (2003), pp. 117–63.
8. The literature on this huge topic has exploded in recent decades. See the agenda-setting summary by Anthony La Vopa, "Conceiving a Public: Ideas and Society in Eighteenth Century Europe," *Journal of Modern*

History 64 (1992), pp. 79–116; for a succinct survey of the whole field, see James Van Horn Melton, *The Rise of the Public in Enlightenment Europe* (Cambridge: Cambridge University Press, 2001). For a useful consideration of publicity and the problem of the "Germanies," see Benjamin W. Redekop, *Enlightenment and Community: Lessing, Abbt, Herder, and the Quest for a German Public* (Montreal and Kingston: McGill-Queens University Press, 2000).

9. Behringer *Hexenverfolgung in Bayern*, p. 357; Eduard Kohl, *Maria Renata Singer von Mossau. Die Geschichte einer Zeller Ordensschwester, die als letzte fränkische Hexe verbrannt wurde* (Zell am Main, 1999).

10. See, for example, Wolfgang Wüst, "Inquisitionsprozess und Hexenverfolgung im Hochstift Augsburg im 17. und 18. Jahrhundert," *Zeitschrift für Bayerische Landesgeschichte* 50 (1987), pp. 109–26.

11. Nancy Caciola, *Discerning Spirits: Divine and Demonic Possession in the Middle Ages* (Ithaca: Cornell University Press, 2003).

Chapter 1. The Experience of Demons

1. Wolfgang Behringer, *Hexenverfolgung in Bayern. Volksmagie, Glaubenseifer, und Staatsräson in der Frühen Neuzeit* (Munich, 1987), p. 364; Wolfgang Jahn, Josef Kirmeier, Wolfgang Petz, and Evamaria Brockhoff, eds., *"Bürgerfleiss und Fürstenglanz": Reichsstadt und Fürstabtei Kempten. Katalog zur Ausstellung...* (Augsburg: Haus der Bayerischen Geschichte, 1998), pp. 225–27.

2. Gassner to Johann Christian Lentsch, 12 December 1772, Archiv der Diözese Feldkirch (ADF), Klösterle G: 1.2.3.e. I must express my deep gratitude to Dr. Elmar Schallert of the ADF for his hospitality and help with these materials.

3. Experience has become a major category of historical analysis. Philipp Sarasin, "Mapping the Body. Körpergeschichte zwischen Konstruktivismus, Politik und 'Erfahrung,'" in *Historische Anthropologie* 7 (1999), pp. 437–51; Joan Scott, "The Evidence of Experience," in James Chandler, Arnold Davidson, and Harry Harootunian, eds., *Questions of Evidence: Proof, Practice, and Persuasion across the Disciplines* (Chicago: University of Chicago Press, 1994), pp. 363–87; Martin Beutelspacher, *Kultivierung bei lebendigem Leib. Alltägliche Körpererfahrungen in der Aufklärung* (Weingarten, 1986); Michelle Z. Rosaldo, "Toward an Anthropology of Self and Feeling," in Richard Shweder and Robert LeVine,

eds., *Culture Theory: Essays on Mind, Self and Emotion* (Cambridge: Cambridge University Press, 1984), pp. 137–57; Richard A. Shweder, *Thinking through Cultures: Expeditions in Cultural Psychology* (Cambridge, Mass.: Harvard University Press, 1991); Nancy Scheper-Hughes and Margaret M. Lock, "The Mindful Body: A Prolegomenon to Future Work in Medical Anthropology," *Medical Anthropology Quarterly* 1 (1987), pp. 6–41; Margaret Lock, "Cultivating the Body: Anthropology and Epistemologies of Bodily Practice and Knowledge," *Annual Review of Anthropology* 22 (1993), pp. 133–55; Paul Münch, ed., " 'Erfahrung' als Kategorie der Frühneuzeitgeschichte," Beiheft no. 31 to the *Historische Zeitschrift* (Munich, 2001).

4. When Gassner did heal those suffering from convulsions, he did not claim that they were somehow especially demon possessed. Like almost all the others, they had diseases that looked natural. Of the 130 persons reported as cured in his diary for 1773, only six were labeled "malefaciato" (bewitched). He did not record why he thought they were so.

5. Actually, Gassner was authorized only to visit the countess of Waldburg-Zeill, but once he was there, he managed to prolong his healing tour.

6. We note that if we reckon his period of healing as three solid months during the summer of 1774, his claim that he treated over eight thousand persons would work out to almost ninety a day. This is so improbable that there must be some exaggeration, or else Gassner was counting his use of general blessings pronounced over whole groups of people.

7. Enthusiastic accounts put the total number at two hundred thousand, but there is no reason to think that anyone was counting. See the "Instruction sur les operations du Père Gassner" in the Hohenlohe Zentralarchiv Neuenstein, Bestand Gassner.

8. Susan Neiman, *Evil in Modern Thought: An Alternative History of Philosophy* (Princeton: Princeton University Press, 2002), pp. 3, 240–50.

9. Neiman, *Evil in Modern Thought*, pp. 39–47. Robert Muchembled makes a similar observation when he notes that the devil did not exactly disappear in the eighteenth century. Instead he moved to become an "inner demon," continuing to haunt the Western imagination in the nineteenth and twentieth centuries; *A History of the Devil from the Middle Ages to the Present*, trans. Jean Birrell (Cambridge, UK: Polity, 2003), pp. 167–96.

10. Neiman, *Evil in Modern Thought*, pp. 236–37: "In demystifying natural and metaphysical evils, Rousseau also decriminalized them. But the more psychology strove to become a science of nature, the more the distinction between moral and natural evils broke down. The problem was dissolved

but raised in different form: can we trust a world where human nature is subject to such despicable tendencies? The very naturalism that was the pride of those who sought to disenchant the world undermines hard distinctions they sought to establish. The more human beings become part of the natural world, the more we, like earthquakes, become one more unfortunate fact about it. The more evil itself seems explicable in terms of natural processes, the more nature itself is implicated. . . . Science may have abolished the sense that the world is inhabited by forces with wills of their own, and in this way reduced the *unheimlich*. But the price is enormous, for all nature stands condemned. Human beings themselves become walking indictments of creation."

11. Franz Anton Mesmer, *Observations sur la découverte du magnétisme animal* (1779); Ernst Benz, *Franz Anton Mesmer und die philosophischen Grundlagen des "animalischen Magnetismus"* (Wiesbaden: F. Steiner, 1977); William Hine, "Athanasius Kircher and Magnetism," in John Fletcher, ed., *Athanasius Kircher und seine Beziehungen zum gelehrten Europa seiner Zeit* (Wiesbaden: Harrassowitz, 1988), pp. 79–99; Rudolf Tischner, *Franz Anton Mesmer* (Munich, 1928), p. 71; Wolfgang Kupsch, "Bemerkungen zur wissenschaftshistorischen Einordnung F. A. Mesmers," in Heinz Schott, ed., *Franz Anton Mesmer und die Geschichte des Mesmerismus* (Wiesbaden: Steiner, 1985), pp. 44–50; Margarethe Hansmann, "Mesmer in Wien," in Schott, ed., *Mesmer und die Geschichte des Mesmerismus*, pp. 51–67; Frank A. Pattie, *Mesmer and Animal Magnetism: A Chapter in the History of Medicine* (Hamilton, N.Y.: Edmonston, 1994), pp. 13–25, 48–52; Adam Crabtree, *From Mesmer to Freud: Magnetic Sleep and the Roots of Psychological Healing* (New Haven: Yale University Press, 1993).

12. Hansmann, "Mesmer in Wien," p. 58; Pattie, *Mesmer and Animal Magnetism*, pp. 55–56. Osterwald reported dramatic improvement in walking, vision, as well as relief of a hernia and hemorrhoids. But see Hans Fieger, *P. Don Ferdinand Sterzinger. Lektor der Theatiner in München, Direktor der historischen Klasse der kurbayerischen Akademie der Wissenschaften, Bekämpfer des Aberglaubens und Hexenwahns und der Pfarrer Gassnerischen Wunderkuren. Ein Beitrag zur Geschichte der Aufklärung in Bayern unter Kurfürst Maximilian III. Joseph* (Munich: Oldenbourg, 1907), pp. 222–23, for Osterwald's conclusion that Mesmer's cures "had not the slightest effect on me." Henri F. Ellenberger, *The Discovery of the Unconscious: The History and Evolution of Dynamic Psychiatry* (New York: Basic Books, 1970), pp. 56–57; Andreas Kraus, *Die naturwissenschaftliche Forschung an der Bayerischen Akademie der Wissenschaften im Zeitalter der Aufklärung* (Munich:

Verlag der Bayerischen Akademie der Wissenschaften, 1978); Max Spindler and Andreas Kraus, eds., *Handbuch der Bayerischen Geschichte*, vol. 2: *Das alte Bayern*, 2nd ed. (Munich: Beck, 1988), p. 1155.

13. Robert Darnton traces this part of Mesmer's career and the course of the sociopolitical movement he stimulated in *Mesmerism and the End of the Enlightenment in France* (Cambridge, Mass.: Harvard University Press, 1968).

14. This is a point that modern scholars often obscure, claiming that for Gassner almost all disorders and diseases came from the devil. See, for example, Behringer, *Hexenverfolgung in Bayern*, p. 394.

15. R. Home, "Introduction," in R. Home and P. Connor, eds., *Aepinus's Essay on the Theory of Electricity and Magnetism* (Princeton: Princeton University Press, 1979), pp. 1–224; Luigi Galvani, *Commentary on the Effect of Electricity on Muscular Motion: A Translation of Luigi Galvani's "De viribus electricitatis in motu musculari commentarius,"* trans. Robert Montraville Green (Cambridge, Mass.: E. Licht, 1953); George Adams, *An Essay on Electricity . . . With an Essay on Magnetism*, 2d ed. (London: Tycho-Brahe's Head, 1785); Walter Bernardi, *I fluidi della vita: alle origini della controversia sull' elettricità animale* (Florence: Olschki, 1992); Johann August Donndorff, *Versuch eines Beweises wider die Existenz der anziehenden Kraft. Nebst einer Erklärung von der wahrscheinlichen Ursach der Wirkung des Magneten auf das Eisen, oder einen andern Magneten; Von der Beschaffenheit der Elektricität, vorzüglich in Ansehung des Anziehens electrischer Körper; Und dem leeren Raume. Mit einer Vorrede von Herrn Doctor Ziegler* (Quedlinburg: Christoph August Reussner, 1777). Patricia Fara, "An Attractive Therapy: Animal Magnetism in Eighteenth-Century England," *History of Science* 33 (1995), pp. 127–77, at pp. 133–34.

16. Patricia Fara, *An Entertainment for Angels: Electricity in the Enlightenment* (New York: Columbia University Press, 2002).

17. Alan Gauld, *A History of Hypnotism* (Cambridge, U.K.,: Cambridge University Press, 1992), pp. 25–38. For the reports see *Rapport des commissaires chargés par le Roi, de l'examen du magnétisme animal, imprimé par ordre du Roi. Sur la Copie imprimée au Louvre*, à Paris chez Moutard, 1784. A second commission, comprising members of the Royal Society of Medicine, conducted its own tests and submitted its own report: *Rapport des commissaires de la Société Royale de Médecine, nommé par le Roi, pour faire l'examen du magnétisme animal, Imprimé par ordre du roi. Sur la copie imprimée au Louvre*, à Paris, chez Moutard, 1784. It is summarized in Pattie, *Mesmer*, pp. 156–58. A minority report was also submitted by A. L. de Jussieu, *Rapport de*

l'un des commissaires chargés par le Roi, de l'examen du magnetisme animal, à Paris, chez la Vve. Hérissant et Théophile Barrois, 1784. See also C. Burdin and F. Dubois, *Histoire académique du magnétisme animal* (Paris, 1841); M. M. Tinterow, ed., *Foundations of Hypnosis: From Mesmer to Freud* (Springfield, Ill.: C. C. Thomas, 1970), who reprints the 1785 translation into English entitled *Report by Dr. Franklin, and Other Commissioners*. Denis I. Duveen and Herbert S. Klickstein provide intelligent commentary in "Benjamin Franklin (1706–1790) and Antoine Laurent Lavoisier (1743–1794)," *Annals of Science* 11 (1955), pp. 103–28, 271–308.

18. J. C. Colquhoun, *Report on the Experiments on Animal Magnetism, Made by a Committee of the Medical Section of the French Royal Academy of Sciences; Read at the Meeting of the 21st and 28th of June 1831* (Edinburgh: Robert Cadell, 1833). This report, however, also affirmed that animal magnetism allowed one to foresee the future, to achieve clairvoyance, to increase one's strength suddenly, and to "see" with one's eyes closed; pp. 154–58, 162, 164–65, 166–69, 171, 198–99. Colquhoun's introduction makes explicit comparisons with the case of Gassner, claiming that the facts of Gassner's cures "never were denied, nor attempted to be refuted," but that later some who had not witnessed his cures and could not explain them "found it convenient, as usual, to throw discredit upon the whole procedure, and ascribe it wholly to quackery and imposture" (pp. 45–46).

19. The first edition was Kempten, 1774, published while Gassner was on his first South German tour. I have used the edition published "Mit Erlaubnyss geistlicher Obrigkeit" in Augsburg and Ingolstadt in 1775 (but it is unclear what authority, if any, actually approved it; the prince abbot of Kempten?). Twelve editions appeared by 1782. Joseph Hanauer, "Der Teufelsbanner," pp. 306–13. In 1775 alone a total of sixty works appeared for and against Gassner.

20. Jeffrey Freedman provides a useful reaction to the same situation in *A Poisoned Chalice* (Princeton: Princeton University Press, 2002), pp. 34–37, 143–44; cf. Hans Erich Bödeker, "Prozesse und Strukturen politischer Bewusstseinsbildung der deutschen Aufklärung," in Hans Erich Bödeker and Ulrich Hermann, eds., *Aufklärung als Politisierung, Politisierung als Aufklärung* (Hamburg: Felix Meiner, 1987), pp. 10–31; and Bödeker, "Journals and Public Opinion: The Politicization of the German Enlightenment in the Second Half of the Eighteenth Century," in Eckhart Hellmuth, ed., *The Transformation of Political Culture: England and Germany in the Late Eighteenth Century* (Oxford: Oxford University Press, 1990), pp. 423–45.

21. Horst Weigelt has emphasized the impact of the death of Felix Hess upon the sensitive Lavater, who tried various semimagical, semireligious ways of recalling Hess to life. From 1768 onward, Lavater seemed driven to seek out wonders in the belief that "all things are possible to those who believe." He eagerly solicited accounts of modern miracles and tried to test the powers of prayer. Horst Weigelt, *Johann Kaspar Lavater. Leben, Werk und Wirkung* (Göttingen: Vandenhoeck and Ruprecht, 1991), pp. 15–19.
22. Clarke Garrett, *Respectable Folly: Millenarians and the French Revolution in France and England* (Baltimore: Johns Hopkins University Press, 1975), p. 20.
23. Philip T. Weller, trans., *The Roman Ritual in Latin and English with Rubrics and Planechant Notation* (Milwaukee: Bruce Publishing, 1952), vol. 2, pp. 172–73, paragraph 20. See Muchembled, *History of the Devil*, pp. 1, 188–90, 230–31; and the critical remarks of Henry Ansgar Kelly in "Teufel, V," *Theologische Realenzyklopädie*, vol. 33 (Berlin: de Gruyter, 2001), pp. 124–34, esp. 131.
24. Oswald Loschert, the Premonstratensian abbot of Oberzell and vehement defender of Gassner, wrote repeatedly of the need to distinguish witchcraft from possession. In his view, the devil could easily possess his victims without any human collaboration, without any *maleficium*. See, for example, [Oswald Loschert], *Zweytes Sendschreiben eines Gottesgelehrten am Tauberflusse an seinen Freund einen Weltweisen nächst dem Donaustrom; Worinn der erstere in seinen Antworten auf verschiedene an ihn gestellte Fragen, über das zeitherige Betragen des hochwürdigen Herrn Pfarrers Gassner, bey Entdeckung und Austreibung der Geistern der Finsterniss, von den geplagten Körpern der bey ihm hülfsuchenden Bedrangten, seine aufrichtige, den Grundsätzen des Christenthums und einer ächten Gottesgelahrtheit angemessene Meynung eröfnet* (n.p., 1775), pp. 15–28.
25. Stuart Clark, *Thinking with Demons: The Idea of Witchcraft in Early Modern Europe* (Oxford: Oxford University Press, 1997).
26. See the remarks of Edward Muir, "Observing Trifles," in Edward Muir and Guido Ruggiero, eds., *Microhistory and the Lost Peoples of Europe* (Baltimore: Johns Hopkins University Press, 1991), pp. vii–xxviii; Gerald Strauss, *Luther's House of Learning: Indoctrination of the Young in the German Reformation* (Baltimore: Johns Hopkins University Press, 1978); Carlo Ginzburg, *The Cheese and the Worms: The Cosmos of a Sixteenth-Century Miller*, trans. John and Anne Tedeschi (Baltimore: Johns Hopkins University Press, 1980); Wolfgang Behringer, *Shaman of Oberstdorf:*

Chonrad Stoeckhlin and the Phantoms of the Night, trans. H. C. Erik Midelfort (Charlottesville: University of Virginia Press, 1998). For popular demonology in Germany, see H. C. Erik Midelfort, *A History of Madness in Sixteenth-Century Germany* (Stanford: Stanford University Press, 1999), pp. 49–78.
27. Wolfgang Behringer, *Hexen. Glaube, Verfolgung, Vermarktung* (Munich: Beck, 1998), pp. 12–16, 70–74.
28. P. Alois Merz, *Johann Joseph Gassners, Pfarrers zu Clösterl, Antwort auf die Anmerkungen, welche in dem Münchnerischen Intelligenzblatt vom 12. Nov. wider seine Gründe und Weise zu exorcieren, wie auch von der deutschen Chronik und anderen Zeitungsschreibern gemacht worden. Mit gnädiger Erlaubniss des hochwürdig-augsburgischen Ordinariats* (Augsburg, 1774), p. 18; elsewhere Muratori's witticism was quoted slightly differently: Germans sometimes quoted him thus: "nur jene Länder mit Teufeleyen angefüllet, in welchen, und so lang sich ein berühmter Exorcist aufhält." Joseph Edler von Sartori, *Politische Gedanken über die nötige Untersuchung Gassners, und der Patienten* (Augsburg: Joh. Franz Xaver. Crätz, 1776), p. 32.
29. Hildegard Mahler, *Das Geistesleben Augsburgs im 18. Jahrhundert im Spiegel der Augsburger Zeitschriften* (Ph.D. dissertation, Munich, 1934; published Augsburg: Haas and Grabherr, 1934).
30. D. P. Walker, "The Cessation of Miracles," in Ingrid Merkel and Allen G. Debus, eds., *Hermeticism and the Renaissance: Intellectual History and the Occult in Early Modern Europe* (Washington, D.C., Folger Shakespeare Library, 1988), pp. 111–24; David D. Hall, *Worlds of Wonder, Days of Judgment: Popular Religious Belief in Early New England* (Cambridge: Harvard University Press, 1990); R. M. Burns, *The Great Debate on Miracles: From Joseph Glanvill to David Hume* (Lewisburg, Penn.: Bucknell University Press, 1981); for Calvin see the extended treatment of John Mark Ruthven, "On the Cessation of the Charismata: The Protestant Polemic of Benjamin B. Warfield" (Ph.D. dissertation, Marquette University, 1989), pp. 21–62.
31. See the brilliant discussion of these matters in Lorraine Daston and Katherine Park, *Wonders and the Order of Nature, 1150–1750* (New York: Zone Books, 1998). See also William Clark, "The Death of Metaphysics in Enlightened Prussia," in William Clark, Jan Golinski, and Simon Schaffer, eds., *The Sciences in Enlightened Europe* (Chicago: University of Chicago Press, 1999), pp. 423–73.
32. Quoted in Robert Bruce Mullin, *Miracles and the Modern Religious Imagination* (New Haven: Yale University Press, 1996), p. 12, quoting Thomas

Aquinas, *Summa Theologiae*, pt. 1, ques. 110, art. 4. Jean Céard, *La nature et les prodiges: L'insolite au XVIe siècle, en France* (Geneva: Droz, 1977).
33. My analysis here has been stimulated by Jens Ivo Engels, "Wunder im Dienste profanisierter Weltansicht? Zur Gemengelage der Weltbilder im achtzehnden Jahrhundert anhand der Debatte über jansenistische Wunder," *Historisches Jahrbuch* 117 (1997), pp. 84–110.

Chapter 2. A Niche in the Incubator

1. James A. Vann and Steven W. Rowan, *The Old Reich: Essays on German Political Institutions, 1495–1806* (Brussels: Éditions de la Librairie Encyclopédique, 1974); James Allen Vann, *The Swabian Kreis: Institutional Growth in the Holy Roman Empire, 1648–1715* (Brussels: Éditions de la Librairie Encyclopédique, 1975); Mack Walker, *Johann Jakob Moser and the Holy Roman Empire of the German Nation* (Chapel Hill: University of North Carolina Press, 1981); Karl Otmar Freiherr von Aretin, *Das Alte Reich, 1648–1806*, 4 vols. (Stuttgart: Klett-Cotta, 1993–2000); Heinz Duchhardt, *Deutsche Verfassungsgeschichte, 1495–1806* (Stuttgart: Kohlhammer, 1991); Georg Schmidt, *Geschichte des alten Reiches. Staat und Nation in der Frühen Neuzeit, 1495–1806* (Munich: Beck, 1999); Peter H. Wilson, *The Holy Roman Empire, 1495–1806* (New York: St. Martin's, 1999); Matthias Schnettger, ed., *Imperium Romanum, irregulare corpus, Teutscher Reichs-Staat: das Alte Reich im Verständnis der Zeitgenossen und der Historiographie* (Mainz: P. von Zabern, 2002).
2. Mack Walker, *German Home Towns: Community, State, and General Estate, 1648–1871* (Ithaca: Cornell University Press, 1971).
3. See Karl Otmar Freiherr von Aretin, "Die Reichskirche und die Säkularisation," in Rolf Decot, ed., *Säkularisation der Reichskirche 1803. Aspekte kirchlichen Umbruchs* (Mainz: Verlag Philipp von Zabern, 2002), pp. 13–32, for a clear and vehement statement: "Die Säkularisation war die grösste Katastrophe, die den deutschen Katholizismus je getroffen hat" (p. 30); Peter Hersche, "Intendierte Rückständigkeit: Zur Charakteristik des geistlichen Staates im alten Reich," in Georg Schmidt, ed., *Stände und Gesellschaft im alten Reich* (Stuttgart: Franz Steiner, 1989), pp. 133–49.
4. A brisk summary is available in Fritz Hartung, *Deutsche Verfassungsgeschichte vom 15. Jahrhundert bis zur Gegenwart*, 6th ed. (Stuttgart: K. F. Koehler, 1950), pp. 150–55.
5. A comparison with eighteenth-century Spain is illuminating. Although no one doubts the extraordinary wealth of the Spanish church, most of its

lands were held as an institution (*beneficial ecclesiastic*) rather than by the clergy personally (*patrimonial ecclesiastic*). The Church held about 19 percent of all cultivated lands in Castile and Aragon, but the bulk of these lands were "beneficial" rather than "patrimonial." Nothing corresponded to the wealth and splendor of princely German prelates. Maximiliano Barrio Gozalo, "The Landed Property of the Spanish Church During the Ancien Regime," *Journal of European Economic History* 31 (2002), pp. 245–72, esp. 254–60.

6. Klaus Epstein, *The Genesis of German Conservatism* (Princeton: Princeton University Press, 1966), p. 276; John G. Gagliardo, *Reich and Nation: The Holy Roman Empire as Idea and Reality, 1763–1806* (Bloomington: Indiana University Press, 1980), pp. 196–205.

7. Erwin Gatz and Stephan M. Janker, *Die Bischöfe des Heiligen Römischen Reiches 1648 bis 1803. Ein biographisches Lexikon* (Berlin: Duncker and Humblot, 1990), p. 618. The late medieval empire had also had a number of North German archiepiscopal provinces (Bremen and Magdeburg) and episcopal dioceses (Hamburg, Verden, Lübeck, Schwerin, Kammin, Lebus, Havelburg, Brandenburg, Halberstadt, Minden, Merseburg, Naumburg, and Meissen) that had been secularized and had disappeared during the Reformation. The few remaining small Catholic enclaves were under the jurisdiction of the Catholic "Apostolic Vicariate of the North." Many other West German bishops had survived but had lost major portions of their territories or of their dioceses to Protestant states.

8. Hans-Jürgen Schulz, *Kloster und Staat. Besitz und Einfluss der Reichsabtei Salem. Ausstellung zum 850. Jubiläum* (Tettnang: Markgräflich Badische Museen, Salem, 1984), pp. 15–18; Reinhard Schneider et al., *Salem. 850 Jahre Reichsabtei und Schloss* (Constance: Friedrich Stadler, 1984), pp. 37–41, 124–39; Alberich Siwek, *Die Zisterzienserabtei Salem. Der Orden, das Kloster, seine Äbte* (Sigmaringen: Thorbeke, 1984), pp. 300–304.

9. Siwek, *Salem*, pp. 300–302.

10. Konstantin Maier illuminates both the politics and the canon legal discussion surrounding the exempt imperial abbeys of southwestern Germany in *Die Diskussion um Kirche und Reform im schwäbischen Reichsprälatenkollegium zur Zeit der Aufklärung* (Wiesbaden: Franz Steiner, 1978). For enlightened writers, the attack on exempt abbeys could be extended so that the problem was no longer just that imperial prelates claimed immunity from their bishops but that the church claimed immunity from secular authority even in secular matters. A particular point of friction here was Peter von Osterwald's *Veremund von Lochsteins Gründe sowohl für*

als wider die geistliche Immunität in zeitlichen Dingen (Strasbourg: n.p., 1766); Osterwald was, we recall, the opponent of Gassner whom Mesmer successfully treated. A few Swabian monks actually agreed with Enlightened criticism, among them Ulrich Mayr, Cistercian of Kaisersheim, Jakob Danzer, Benedictine of Isny, and Benedikt Maria Werkmeister, Benedictine of Neresheim. Maier, *Die Diskussion*, pp. 58–61, 69–73, 95–102, 123.

11. Karl Otmar Freiherr von Aretin, *Das Reich* (Stuttgart: Klett-Cotta, 1986), pp. 414–18.
12. Heribert Raab, "Die 'katholische Ideenrevolution' des 18. Jahrhunderts. Der Einbruch der Geschichte in die Kanonistik und die Auswirkungen in Kirche und Reich bis zum Emser Kongress," in Harm Klueting, Norbert Hinske, and Karl Hengst, eds., *Katholische Aufklärung—Aufklärung im katholischen Deutschland* (Hamburg: Felix Meiner, 1993), pp. 104–18. The phrase "Catholic revolution of ideas" was first used in a canon-legal work by Ludwig Timotheus Spittler published in 1787.
13. Heribert Raab, *Die Concordata Nationis Germanicae in der kanonistischen Diskussion des 17. bis 19. Jahrhunderts. Ein Beitrag zur Geschichte der episkopalistischen Theorie in Deutschland* (Wiesbaden: Steiner, 1956), pp. 79, 125; Volker Pitzer, *Justinus Febronius. Das Ringen eines katholischen Irenikers um die Einheit der Kirche im Zeitalter der Aufklärung* (Göttingen: Vandenhoeck and Ruprecht, 1976). A prominent forerunner and teacher of the later generation was Zeger Bernard van Espen of the University of Louvain (1648–1728), who argued for the autonomy of local ecclesiastical provinces. See Gustave Leclerc, *Zeger Bernard van Espen (1648–1728) et l'autorité ecclésiastique. Contribution à l'histoire des théories gallicanes et du jansénisme* (Zurich: Pas Verlag, 1964).
14. Aretin, "Die Reichskirche und die Säkularisation," pp. 23–25; Karl Otmar Freiherr von Aretin, *Das Alte Reich, 1648–1806*, vol. 3: *Das Reich und der österreichisch-preussische Dualismus, 1745–1806* (Stuttgart: Klett-Cotta, 1997), pp. 237–57; Pitzer, *Justinus Febronius*; Peter Hersche, *Der Spätjansenismus in Österreich* (Vienna: Verlag der österreichischen Akademie der Wissenschaften, 1977), pp. 371–73.
15. Elisabeth Kovács, *Der Pabst in Teutschland. Die Reise Pius VI. im Jahre 1782* (Munich: Oldenbourg, 1983), pp. 42–43, 48, 105–6, 115, 153–56.
16. Aretin, *Das Alte Reich, 1648–1806*, vol. 3, pp. 257–74. By far the best account of the high politics of the Swabian imperial prelates is Konstantin Maier, *Die Diskussion um Kirche und Reform im schwäbischen Reichsprälatenkollegium zur Zeit der Aufklärung* (Wiesbaden: Franz Steiner, 1978).

17. Derek Beales, *Joseph II*, vol. 1: *In the Shadow of Maria Theresa, 1741–1780* (Cambridge: Cambridge University Press, 1987), pp. 441–79, esp. 452–55.
18. The best general introduction to the massive literature is Harm Klueting, "'Der Genius der Zeit hat sie unbrauchbar gemacht.' Zum Thema *Katholische Aufklärung* — Oder: Aufklärung und Katholizismus im Deutschland des 18. Jahrhunderts. Eine Einleitung," in Harm Klueting, ed., *Katholische Aufklärung — Aufklärung im katholischen Deutschland* (Hamburg: Felix Meiner, 1993), pp. 1–35.
19. Marc Forster, *Catholic Revival in the Age of the Baroque: Religious Identity in Southwest Germany, 1550–1750* (Cambridge: Cambridge University Press, 2001), pp. 206–7, 218–19; Eva Kimminich, *Religiöse Volksbräuche im Räderwerk der Obrigkeiten. Ein Beitrag zur Auswirkung aufklärischer Reformprogramme am Oberrhein und in Vorarlberg* (Frankfurt: Peter Lang, 1989); Leonard Swidler, *Aufklärung Catholicism 1780–1850: Liturgical and Other Reforms in the Catholic Aufklärung* (Missoula, Mont.: Scholars Press, 1978).
20. Forster, *Catholic Revival*, pp. 220–39.
21. Sterzinger's account is available in "Nachricht von Johann Joseph Gassners Teufelsbeschwörungen und den dadurch veranlassten Bewegungen, mit Beilegen," in Christian Wilhelm Franz Walch, *Neueste Religionsgeschichte*, 6 Theil (Lemgo, in der Mayerschen Buchhandlung, 1777) — section 7 (pp. 369–438; with Beylagen 439–86); section 9 = "Beytrag zu der Nachricht von den gassnerischen Teufelsbeschwörungen," pp. 539–48, here at p. 442. See also Hans Fieger, *P. Don Ferdinand Sterzinger. Lektor der Theatiner in München, Direktor der historischen Klasse der kurbayerischen Akademie der Wissenschaften, Bekämpfer des Aberglaubens und Hexenwahns und der Pfarrer Gassnerischen Wunderkuren. Ein Beitrag zur Geschichte der Aufklärung in Bayern unter Kurfürst Maximilian III. Joseph* (Munich: Oldenbourg, 1907), pp. 178–79. The semiofficial *Churbairische Intelligenzblätter* (published in Munich) criticized Gassner as early as 12 November 1774 and called attention to Gassner's dependence upon Ubald Stoiber's *Armamentarium Ecclesiasticum*, in which Stoiber outlined three kinds of possession, including the state of "circumsession," a notion that had been condemned in Rome.
22. Sterzinger in Walch, *Neueste Religionsgeschichte*, 6 Theil, p. 446. For the exempt status of certain town properties of the prince provost of Ellwangen, see Hanauer, "Teufelsbanner," pp. 475–76. Most of the town and its surrounding villages were subject to the jurisdiction of the bishops of Augsburg and Würzburg.

23. As bishop of Freising, Klemens Wenzeslaus had applauded the attack by Ferdinand Sterzinger on witchcraft beliefs in 1766, and when he took over the bishopric of Augsburg it appears that he continued to consider fear of the devil a superstition to be uprooted. He abruptly refused appeals from Gassner to be allowed into Augsburg territory. Hanauer, "Der Teufelsbanner," pp. 476–77.
24. Hanauer, "Der Teufelsbanner," pp. 479–80.
25. *Churbairische Intelligenzblätter*, 1 April 1775, p. 53. On Wolter, see Andreas Kraus, *Die naturwissenschaftliche Forschung an der Bayerischen Akademie der Wissenschaften im Zeitalter der Aufklärung* (Bayerische Akademie der Wissenschaften, Philosophisch-historische Klasse, Abhandlungen, Neue Folge, Heft 82) (Munich: Verlag der Bay. Akad. d.Wiss., 1978), pp. 41–43. On Leuthner, see Clemens Alois Baader, *Lexikon verstorbener Baierischer Schriftsteller des achtzehenten und neunzehenten Jahrhunderts* (Des Zweyten Bandes Erster Theil A-P: Augsburg and Leipzig, Jenisch und Stage, 1825), pp. 164–65.
26. Benedikt Stattler, prochancellor of the university of Ingolstadt and professor of theology, published his observations in a long Latin report, excerpts of which were quickly published in German in *Was soll man an den Kuren des Herrn geistlichen Rats Gassner die er bisher im Namen Jesu gemacht hat, noch untersuchen, so nicht schon längst hundertmal ist untersucht worden?* (Frankfurt and Berlin, 1775), pp. 89–92; cf. Hanauer, "Der Teufelsbanner," pp. 438–39; Fieger, *P. Don Ferdinand Sterzinger*, pp. 203–8. Stattler later published vehemently anti-Kantian philosophical works.
27. Hanauer, "Der Teufelsbanner," pp. 431–34.
28. Hanauer, "Der Teufelsbanner," pp. 434–36.
29. Hanauer, "Der Teufelsbanner," pp. 441–42.
30. Antonius de Haen, *De Miraculis Liber* (Frankfurt and Leipzig: Esslinger, 1776); chapter 5 is dedicated to the cures of Gassner, pp. 142–208. Gerhard van Swieten (1700–1772) had been an avid supporter of the Jansenist archbishop of Utrecht and was therefore unable to obtain a higher position in the Netherlands. When he moved to Vienna as the personal physician of the empress Maria Theresa in 1745, he became the center of a Jansenist Reform Catholic group at the Habsburg court that included Ignaz Müller, the personal confessor to Maria Theresa, and Dr. Anton de Haen. After the death of van Swieten, de Haen became the strongest voice for Jansenist reform at the Habsburg court.
31. Hanauer, "Der Teufelsbanner," p. 444.

32. This decree had its origins in a scandalous case of a possessed soldier, who had suffered *Ängste* and convulsions for the previous six years. A certain Father Eusebius OFM, claiming the permission of his ordinary, had conducted exorcisms that lasted a whole day (and would have gone on the next day as well), and crowds of curious onlookers had gathered. Maria Theresa had intervened and ordered, in her own handwritten note, that such cases be separated and sent directly to Dr. De Haen in the Bürgerspital for evaluation. Father Eusebius was not to be allowed to treat such cases anymore. In further negotiations, Maria Theresa ordered that the archbishop of Vienna should positively forbid exorcisms unless the "Politicum" (i.e., the Habsburg state) should express its approval, "because of the many deceits and abuses" of the ritual. Cölestin Wolfsgruber, *Christoph Anton Kardinal Migazzi, Fürsterzbischof von Wien. Eine Monographie und zugleich ein Beitrag zur Geshichte des Josephinismus*, 2nd ed. (Ravensburg: Hermann Kitz, 1897), pp. 201–2. See Walch, *Beytrag zu der Nachricht von den gassnerischen Teufelsbeschwörungen*, in his *Neueste Religionsgeschichte*, sechster Theil (Lemgo, 1777), p. 546.
33. Hanauer, "Teufelsbanner," p. 444, citing Walch, *Neueste Religionsgeschichte*, 6 Theil (1777), p. 477, Beilage VII.
34. Wolfsgruber, *Migazzi*, pp. 203–4. The news of Gassner's dismissal had also been published in the December 8 issue of the *Freytägige Münchner-Zeitung*. Hanauer, "Der Teufelsbanner," p. 444.
35. Hanauer speculates (p. 445, n. 65) that Bishop Fugger probably included the following bishops in his camp: Johann Baptist Anton von Federspiel, bishop of Chur; the new bishop of Constance, Maximilian Christoph von Rodt (the brother of the skeptical Franz Konrad von Rodt, who had died 15 October 1775); the suffragan bishop of Constance, Johann Nepomuk Augustin von Hornstein; and Count Ludwig Joseph von Welden, bishop of Freising. We do not know enough about their individual positions to say whether this speculation is fully justified. Behringer also counts the bishop of Eichstätt (i.e., Raymund Anton von Strasoldo), among the supporters of Gassner; Behringer, *Hexenverfolgung in Bayern. Volksmagie, Glaubenseifer und Staatsräson in der Frühen Neuzeit* (Munich: Oldenbourg, 1987), pp. 363–65, 368, 394, 468–69.
36. Wolfsgruber, *Migazzi*, p. 203; Hanauer, "Teufelsbanner," pp. 445–46.
37. Hanauer, "Der Teufelsbanner," pp. 446–48. For the Count of Hohenlohe-Schillingsfürst's unsuccessful attempts to persuade his uncle, Elector Maximilian III Joseph of Bavaria, see Fieger, *Sterzinger*, pp. 209–15. Gassner won backers even in the skeptical Austrian administration in

Freiburg: Count von Königsegg, Freiherr von Wittenbach (the vice president of the Freiburg regime), Baron von Falckenstein, the Prince of Fürstenberg, the Count of Wolfegg, as well as several princely prelates of Upper Swabia. The list could be considerably extended.

38. Hanauer, "Der Teufelsbanner," pp. 448–63. The regime in Freiburg had begun to take steps against Gassner in December of 1772, but Gassner used a combination of physical excuses and the support of the bishop of Chur to fend off these early inquiries, a support that was only strengthened after Bishop Johann Anton von Federspiel visited Vorarlberg, including a visit to Gassner in Klösterle, in May of 1774. Hanauer thinks it obvious that the bishop also witnessed Gassner's healing methods. Hanauer, "Der Teufelsbanner," pp. 460–61. Certainly the bishop was persuaded that Gassner's wondrous healings went well beyond any natural explanation.

39. Gassner's fortunes in the bishopric of Constance improved dramatically when Franz Konrad von Rodt died in October of 1775 and was succeeded by his brother Maximilian Christoph von Rodt, who had witnessed Gassner's cures in Ellwangen and had become a fervent admirer. Hanauer, "Teufelsbanner," p. 475, n. 130.

40. Hanauer, "Der Teufelsbanner," pp. 486–87. The pastoral letter was published in the *Churbairische Intelligenzblätter* no. 1 (6 January 1776), pp. 9–14, and no. 2 (13 January 1776), pp. 22–23. For an excerpt, see Hans Fieger, *P. Don Ferdinand Sterzinger*, pp. 215–18.

41. Just how many imitators Gassner inspired is an open question. With obvious exaggeration the anonymous author of one tract complained in 1777 that on a trip through Bavaria and Austria "it seemed to me that I had made a subterranean journey and come to a land where everyone was crazy. The clergy had learned their art from Gassner and ran all around curing the sick with spiritual words of power and casting out devils." *Paroli au Meme. Tisserant und Gassner. Ein Beitrag zur Geschichte des deutschen Menschenverstandes im achtzehnten Jahrhundert* ("Deutschland" ["gedruckt im lieben Deutschland"] i.e., France?, 1777), fol. b4r.

42. Erwin Gatz, ed., *Die Bischöfe der deutschsprachigen Länder, 1785/1803 bis 1945. Ein biographisches Lexikon* (Berlin: Duncker and Humblot, 1983), pp. 99–103.

43. The pastoral letter was published in the *Churbairische Intelligenzblätter* 1776, no. 10 (5 March 1776), pp. 86–90. Gerhard Ammerer, "'Gegen die unbefugten Unternehmungen gewisser Exorcisten'—Der Hirtenbrief Erzbischof Colloredos gegen den Wunderheiler Johann Joseph Gassner

von 1776," *Mitteilungen der Gesellschaft für Salzburger Landeskunde* (2002), pp. 141–80, esp. 147–56; the pastoral letter is reprinted pp. 163–67.
44. Hanauer, "Der Teufelsbanner," pp. 495–97.
45. See for example Georg Pfeilschifter, ed., *Korrespondenz des Fürstabtes Martin II. Gerbert von St. Blasien* (Karlsruhe: C. F. Müller, 1934), vol. 2 (1774–1781), pp. 403–5, 414, 416–17, 424–26, 429–30; Gerbert distributed copies of his anonymously published *Daemonurgia theologice expensa, seu de potestate daemonum in rebus humanis deque potestate in daemones a Christo ecclesiae relicta* (n.p., 1776), in an effort to gain a wider hearing for the sorts of exorcisms that Gassner performed, but he had not originally composed the work with that in mind. Georg Pfeilschifter discovered that the work was identical to Disquisitio VII of Gerbert's earlier *De energumenis eorumque exorcismis*, reprinted in volume 2 of his *Vetus Liturgia alemannica* (St. Blasien, 1776), pp. 561–792.
46. *Politische Frage, ob ein weislich regierender Landesfürst über die Gassnerischen Kuren ohne Nachteil seiner Unterthanen, noch länger gleichgültig seyn kann* (n.p., 1775). Hanauer, the Bavarian State Library in Munich, and the Leopold Sophien Bibliothek in Überlingen identify the author as a certain C. R. Reisach. Freiherr Joseph Edler von Sartori thought the author was Ferdinand Sterzinger: *Politische Gedanken über die nötige Untersuchung Gassners und der Patienten* (Augsburg: Johann Franz Xaver Crätz, 1776), p. 21.
47. *Politische Frage*, pp. 19–23.
48. *Politische Frage*, pp. 25–27, 34–37, 45–47.
49. Joseph Edler von Sartori, *Politische Gedanken über die nötige Untersuchung Gassners und der Patienten* (Augsburg: Johann Franz Xaver Crätz, 1776).
50. Epstein, *Genesis of German Conservatism*, p. 277, n. 80; Gagliardo, *Reich and Nation*, p. 199; *Allgemeine Deutsche Biographie*, vol. 30, p. 378. Sartori was later a librarian in Göttingen and Vienna. His earlier contributions to the Gassner controversy (all anonymous) include:
   (a) *Sendschreiben des Herrn H.R. von . . . an den Herrn H.R. Mitglied der churbayrischen Akademie in München. Ueber einige von dem Herr Gassner Pfarrer in Klösterle während seines Aufenthalts in Ellwangen unternommene Operationen*, 1774. (The last page is signed "Euer Wohlgebohrn, Ellwangen, den 23sten December 1774.")
   (b) *Die Aufgedeckten Sterzingerischen Lügen, Keckheit, und Unwissenheit, aus unwiderstösslichen Wahrheiten beleuchtet*, 1775.
   (c) *Merkwürdige Heilungen und Facta/welche sich zu Ellwangen bei dem hochehrwürdigen HERRN Johann Joseph Gassner, Sr. Hochfürstlichen*

Gnaden Bischoffen zu Regensburg, Fürsten und Probsten zu Ellwangen etc. geistlichen Rath und Hof-Cappellan in dem Jahr 1775. zugetragen, 1775.

(d) *Der entlarvte Lügner, Durch Anmerkungen Ueber Prüfende Anmerkungen zu dem Sendschreiben des H. Hr. von ——— an den H. Hr ——— Mitglied der Churbayerischen Akademie in München; über einige von dem Herrn Gassner, Pfarrer in Klösterle, während seines Aufenthalts in Ellwangen unternommene Operationen. Dargestellt von einem Wahrheitsfreund und Augenzeugen*, 1775.

(e) *Gassners Lehre ohne Vorurtheil: oder Beweiss, dass die Lehre Gassners der Heiligen Schrift, den Satzungen der Kirche, den Meinungen der heil. Väter — und anderer heiliger, frommer und gelehrter Männer von verschiedenem Zeit-Alter gemäss seye; mit Anmerkungen verbessert*, 1775. ("In Deutschland" [The British Library Catalog identifies the place of publication as Regensburg]).

51. Sartori, *Politische Gedanken*, pp. 7–10, 12–15, 27–29. These doubts had been stirred by a report in the *Sulzbachische Intelligenzblatt*, no. 9 (5 October 1775).

52. Sartori, *Politische Gedanken*, pp. 31–32. On the possible reasons for Sartori's change of mind in 1776, see Hanauer, "Der Teufelsbanner," pp. 391–93.

53. Sartori, *Politische Gedanken*, pp. 34–44, 50–52.

54. "Janus de St. Babilas" [pseud.], *Der entlarvte Gassner dem Salzburger Hirtenbrief entgegengesetzt* (Frankfurt and Leipzig, 1776), pp. 17, 27–28, 36–38, 40–46, 74–95.

55. "Janus de St. Babilas," *Der entlarvte Gassner*, p. 141; see Ammerer, "'Gegen die unbefugten Unternehmungen gewisser Exorcisten,'" pp. 161–62.

56. Hanauer, "Der Teufelsbanner," pp. 384–87.

57. Loschert was wrong about Candidus Brognolo, Minorite of Bergamo, whose works (both the *Manuale exorcistarum ac parochorum* [Bergamo, 1651; Venice, 1673] and the *Alexicacon, hoc est de maleficiis et morbis maleficis* [Venice, 1668 and 1714]) were placed on the *Index of Forbidden Books* in 1727. Gelasius de Cilia, OSA, was dean of SS. Andreas and Magnus in Stadt am Hof (Regensburg) and the popular author of the large compilation *Locupletissimus Thesaurus continens varias . . . Benedictiones, coniurationes, exorcismos . . .* (Augsburg, 1715, and often reprinted; the 10th ed. was Augsburg: Rieger, 1782); it was translated into German as *Geistliche Kranken-Hülff zum ewigen Leben* (Regensburg, 1743) and seems to have survived the scrutiny of the *Index of Forbidden Books*. See also Girolamo

Baruffaldi, *Ad rituale romanum commentaria* (Dillingen, 1735), which lists (at n. 107) five kinds of exorcism: praecepta communia, probativa, lenitiva, instructiva, and expulsiva. Gassner may well have learned to elevate the healing power of Jesus' name from the pastor of Scheer, Franz Anton Reichle's *Der triumphierliche Namen Jesus, das ist . . . Hilfs-Mittel, Durch welches ein jeglicher katholischer Christ . . . sich, und die Seinige von allem Unheil bewahren, allen Unfall des bösen Feinds abtreiben, alles Malefitz zernichten, ja gar den leidigen Teufel selbsten des allerheiligsten Namen Jesus verjagen und überwinden kan* (Constance: Parcus, 1753; Constance: Labhart, 1761; reprinted at the time of Gassner's visit, Sulzbach: Galwitz, 1775).

58. Nikolaus von Hontheim had studied with Zeger Bernard van Espen. See above note 13. The quotation is from [Oswald Loschert], *Altes und neues System, des geheimen Streits mit den Geistern der Finsternissen, von dem Hochwürdigen und Hochgelehrten Herrn, Johann Joseph Gassner, Seiner Hochfürstlichen Gnaden, Bischofen und Fürsten zu Regenspurg, auch Gefürsteten Probsten zu Ellwangen, geistlichen Rath und Hofkaplan, dermaligen Dechand und Pfarrer zu Pondorf etc. durch unverneinliche Thatsachen erneueret, und von einem seiner Freunden aus dem christlichen Alterthum erkläret und bestättiget. / Opera Dei revelare et confiteri honorificum est. Tobiae 12. v. 7. Die Werke Gottes offenbaren und bekennen, ist rühmlich* (n.p., 1778), p. clxxiii; this large work consists of a foreword by Loschert, pp. i–clxx, followed by an edited text of the Sulzbach protocols of Gassner's healings there, pp. 1–303. The reports from Sulzbach were also published separately as *Verzeichnis der merkwürdigsten Operationen, welche im Jahre 1775 zu Sulzbach, so wohl an dem Hofe, und in Gegenwart Ihro Hochfürstlichen Durchlaucht, der verwittibten Frauen Pfalzgräfin etc. als in der St. Leonards-Kapelle, von dem hochwürdigen und hochgelehrten Herrn Johann Joseph Gassner . . . wie auch von den von ihm vorher unterrichteten Patienten selbst, durch die wirkende Kraft des heiligsten Namens Jesus geschehen sind. . . . Nebst einem Anhang einiger wunderbaren Begebenheiten in Ellwangen den 21. Oct. 1777* (Frankfurt: Hanau and Leipzig, 1778).

59. *Instrvctionale Romano-Bambergense, sive Congeries Instrvctionvm tvm clericis, tvm laicis necessariarvm pro sacramentorvm congrva administratione, nec non pro benedictionvm, processionvm, concionvm, catechismorvm, imo et testamentorvm debita ordinatione [sic] ac praxi etc. Authorite Ordinaria ad vsvm cleri bambergensis edita* (Bamberg: Typis Ioannis Georgii Christoph. Gertner, Princ. aul. et rev'mi cap. typographi, 1773). In this *Instructionale*, exorcism is defined as the "adjurations by which demons possessing,

oppressing, or harming [obsidentes, opprimentes, vel maleficiantes] human bodies through invocation of the divine name; either the imperative adjuration when the exorcist orders the demon or the creature whom the demon inhabits, by divine mercy; that he should desist from possessing or harming; or the deprecative adjuration when the highest best God is asked through his infinite goodness to expel the demon so that the person not suffer any more harms from created things," p. 356 (my rather literal translation). Note that here too exorcisms were recommended against more than just full demonic possession. On such matters, see the learned article on "Teufel" by Henry Ansgar Kelly in *Theologische Realenzyklopädie*, vol. 33 (Berlin: de Gruyter, 2001), pp. 124–34.

Chapter 3. Healing

1. As Gassner's defenders never tired of pointing out, the reforms of 1614 did not explicitly require the exclusive use of the *Rituale Romanum* in matters of exorcism and regional, diocesan, and national variants continued to be produced well into the eighteenth century. Scholars very much need a thorough study of the publication history of the various rituals for blessing and exorcism in the early modern period.
2. Actually Gassner made a return visit to Ellwangen in October of 1777 and resumed healings and exorcisms for a brief period there, in the presence of Duke Ludwig Eugen of Württemberg and Prince Karl Albert von Hohenlohe-Schillingsfürst. Josef Hanauer, "Der Teufelsbanner und Wunderheiler Johann Joseph Gassner (1727–1779)," *Beiträge zur Geschichte des Bistums Regensburg* (ed. Georg Schwaiger and Paul Mai) 19 (1985), pp. 303–545, at p. 351.
3. I have not recovered the manuscript protocols of Gassner's healings and exorcisms in the diocese of Constance (summer of 1774) or in Ellwangen (November 1774–spring 1775), and so for these campaigns I have relied upon the dense descriptions that were published and republished during the controversies surrounding these events.
4. He explicitly said, "Als ich nun vor 2 Jahren ein Contradiction und als wan der gleichen geistliche hilff ein bure einbildung wäre von Herrn v. Sternbach hören mueste habe von selber Zeit an alle dergleichen hilff bedürfftige Persohnen mehresten theils auffgeschriben damit im fall ich sollte angefochten werden sollt Persohnen kundte vorstellen und seynd folgende. . . ." Feldkirch, Diözesanarchiv, Pfarrei Klösterle, Klösterle 1.2.2.1 ("Diarium I, 1769 mit Nachträgen seit 1759"), fol. 1r. The Baron

von Sternbach was the governor for Vorarlberg in charge of the Klostertal. On Sternbach's opposition and that of the Anterior Austrian administration in Freiburg, see Josef Hanauer, "Der Teufelsbanner," pp. 431–34; Gassner's healing methods were also criticized early on by many of his fellow priests, including especially his Klösterle fellow priest (Frühmesser) Saler and most importantly Christian Lentsch, pastor and chamberlain of St. Gallenkirch; Hanauer, "Der Teufelsbanner," pp. 449–53.

5. "letslich kombte hieher ein verheirathete weibspersohn von nassoreich aus Tyrol mit den hinfallenden sucht behaffte durch vil jahr und es hat die prob in beysein zweyer gerichtsmänner von hir es geben das sie obbemelte sucht und ist ihr auch geholffen worden." Feldkirch, Diözesanarchiv, Pfarrei Klösterle, Klösterle 1.2.2.1 ("Diarium I, 1769 mit Nachträgen seit 1759"), fol. 1v.

6. "Christian Big im Wald ware krum mit entsezlichen schmerzen ist in beysein des herrn Pauemeisters von hir durch benedictio volkomen gesundt worden als vormahlen alles mediciniren nichts genuzet." Ibid., fol 2r.

7. "Franz Riedinger zue Bludenz ist an einem aug allbereith blindt ist allhir spiritualibus vollkomen sechend worden." Ibid., fol. 3r.

8. When Gassner healed those suffering from convulsions, he did not claim that they were peculiarly demon possessed. Like almost all the others, they had diseases that looked natural. Note that of the 130 persons reported as cured in 1773, only six were labeled "malefaciato" (bewitched). He did not record why he thought they were so.

9. Adam Crabtree, *From Mesmer to Freud: Magnetic Sleep and the Roots of Psychological Healing* (New Haven: Yale University Press, 1993), pp. 8–9, 22, 86–88. Crabtree emphasizes Mesmer's contribution to the study of alternative states of consciousness and other dissociative states. In 1984 Beate Meissner submitted an M.A. thesis in psychology at the University of Freiburg i. Br., posing this question explicitly: "Die Heilmethode des Exorzisten Johann Joseph Gassner: Eine Urform der Psychotherapie?" Josef Hanauer, author of the most detailed and thorough study of Gassner's career ("Der Teufelsbanner"), concluded that the exorcist was both a "Suggestor" ("Der Pfarrer verfügte über eine Kraft, geistig auf Mitmenschen einzuwirken, wie sie nur selten einem Menschen in so enormem Masse eigen ist. Es ist die Macht der Suggestion," p. 518) and also a "Hypnotiseur" ("Heute sagt man, Mesmer habe den Triumph der Seelenheilkunde eingeleitet, die Psychotherapie. Das gleiche könnte man wohl, — der Begabung nach sogar mit noch grösserer Berechtigung —, auch von Pfarrer Gassner behaupten, — wenn er seine Praxis nicht mit

einer ausnehmend unsinnigen und abergläubischen Theorie umkleidet hätte," p. 536).

10. Ann Taves, *Fits, Trances, and Visions: Experiencing Religion and Explaining Experience from Wesley to James* (Princeton: Princeton University Press, 1999), pp. 247–49.

11. See Wayne Proudfoot, *Religious Experience* (Berkeley: University of California Press, 1985); J. Samuel Preus, *Explaining Religion: Criticism and Theory from Bodin to Freud* (New Haven: Yale University Press, 1987); David Ray Griffin, *Religion and Scientific Naturalism: Overcoming the Conflicts* (Albany: SUNY Press, 2000); David Ray Griffin, *Reenchantment without Supernaturalism: A Process Philosophy of Religion* (Ithaca: Cornell University Press, 2001); David Ray Griffin, *The Reenchantment of Science: Postmodern Proposals* (Albany: SUNY Press, 1988).

12. For these months in the summer of 1774, see Josef Hanauer, "Der Teufelsbanner," pp. 325–36. See also Georg Pfeilschifter, "Des Exorzisten Gassner Tätigkeit in der Konstanzer Diözese im Jahre 1774," *Historisches Jahrbuch* 52 (1932), 401–41.

13. Hanauer, "Teufelsbanner," p. 344, citing Zapf, *Zauberbibliothek* (Augsburg, 1776), pp. 37–38.

14. Hanauer, "Teufelsbanner," p. 374.

15. Hanauer, "Teufelsbanner," p. 375.

16. Hanauer, "Teufelsbanner," p. 377; [Ferdinand Sterzinger], *Die aufgedeckten Gassnerischen Wunderkuren. Aus authentischen Urkunden beleuchtet und durch Augenzeugen bewiesen* (n.p., 1775), pp. 27–36, 53: "dass unter den Gassnerischen Operationen eine geheimnissvolle Kraft aus dem Reiche der Natur verborgen liege. Das Reiben des Exorcisten am Cingulo, das starke Drucken auf des patienten Kopf, und zwar mit der rechten Hand and der Stirn, mit der linken am nervosen Theile des Genicks, die Betastungen an den Pulsadern, das Rütteln, die verschiedenen Stellungen, und dergleichen mehrere physikalische Vorkehrungen, wie ich alle mit Augen gesehen habe, geben mir Anlass zu glauben, dass entweder eine Magnetische, Electrische, oder Sympathetische Kraft die Wirkungen hervorbringe, und zwar um so leichter, weil die Einbildungskraft des Patienten ohnehin auf das stärkste bewegt wird, theils durch den gepredigten Glauben, theils durch das starre Ansehen, theils durch das übermässige Vertrauen auf den heiligen Mann; theils durch die ganz gewiss eingebildete Hoffnung der Genesung, und dergleichen andere reizende Vorbildungen, die fähig genug sind, die Phantasie in Verwirrung

zu setzen, und die Lebensgeister zu bewegen." To bolster this argument about the power of *Einbildung*, Sterzinger cited Muratori's *De viribus imaginationis*, and the *Tractat de l'âme sensitive* of Lamy (i.e., Guillaume Lamy, *Explication mechanique et physique des fonctions de l'âme sensitive* [Paris, 1681]), and claimed that "eveyone" knew what effects the "Electrische, Magnetische, und Sympathische Kräfte" were.

17. [D. von Schad in Wallerstein], *Prüfende Anmerkungen zu dem Sendschreiben des H. Hr. von . . . an den H. Hr., . . . Mitglied der Churbayerischen Akademie in München, über einige von dem Herrn Gassner . . . in Ellwangen unternommene Operationen. Entworfen von einem Wahrheitsfreund und Augenzeugen* (Munich and Augsburg, 1775), p. 50.
18. Hanauer, "Teufelsbanner," pp. 378–79. As Hanauer remarks, such attestations were regularly collected right after the cure, and so we cannot tell from such evidence how permanent these improvements were.
19. Hanauer, "Teufelsbanner," pp. 380–81.
20. Hanauer, "Teufelsbanner," p. 381.
21. *Unpartheyische Gedanken oder Etwas vor die Aerzte von der Kurart des Tit. Herrn Gassners in Ellwangen, herausgegeben von Doct. Schisel [Schleis] gedruckt zu Schalbuz [Sulzbach], mit Wizgallischen Schriften*, 1775, pp. 3–5, 7–16. On Schleis, see August Hirsch, ed., *Biographisches Lexikon der hervorragenden Ärzte aller Zeiten und Völker*, 6 vols. (Vienna and Leipzig: Urban and Schwarzenberg, 1884–1888).
22. Fieger, *Sterzinger*, p. 174.
23. C. A. von Eschenmayer, "Ueber Gassners Heilmethoden," *Archiv für den Thierischen Magnetismus* Bd. 8, Heft 1 (1820), pp. 86 ff, here at pp. 92–93; as cited by Burkhard Peter, "Hypnotische Selbstkontrolle. Die wirksame Psychotherapie des Teufelsbanners Johann Joseph Gassner um 1775," *Hypnose und Kognition* 17 (Doppelheft 1–2) (2000), pp. 19–34.
24. *Churbaierische Intelligenzblätter für das Jahr 1774*, no. 11 (12 November 1774), p. 167, took notice of the report or book from Kempten, *Des wohlehrwürdigen Herrn Johann Joseph Gassners . . . nützlicher Unterricht wider den Teufel zu streiten, oder Beantwortung der Fragen: I. Kann der Teufel dem Leib der Menschen schaden? II. Welchen am mehresten? III. Wie ist zu helfen?* The *Intelliganzblatt* observed that Gassner tried to make "Hexerey and Zauberkunst" an essential part of religion.
25. For Sterzinger's detailed account, see Hans Fieger, *P. Don Ferdinand Sterzinger. Lektor der Theatiner in München, Direktor der historischen Klasse der kurbayerischen Akademie der Wissenschaften, Bekämpfer des Aberglaubens und*

Hexenwahns und der Pfarrer Gassnerischen Wunderkuren. Ein Beitrag zur Geschichte der Aufklärung in Bayern unter Kurfürst Maximilian III. Joseph (Munich: Oldenbourg, 1907), pp. 179–98.

26. *Ellwangisches Protokoll vom 8. Dec. 1774, eine mit zehntausend Millionen Teufeln besessen gewesene Junge Nonne namens Maria Anna Treflerin aus München betreffend mit Anmerkungen*, 1776 (a handwritten note in the Munich copy remarks "illustravit Don Ferd. Sterzinger Theat"), Bayerische Staatsbibliothek München: Bavar, 4000–4, 18; Sterzinger quickly published an exposé of what he regarded as the fraudulent proceedings in Ellwangen: [Ferdinand Sterzinger], *Die aufgedeckten Gassnerischen Wunderkuren. Aus authentischen Urkunden beleuchtet und durch Augenzeugen bewiesen* (n.p., 1775), which appeared in a second edition that same year, and there seems to have been a third edition as well. See also Sterzinger's "Diarium über meine Reise nach Ellwangen, sammt kritischen anmerkungen und Beylagen, vom 19 bis 24 Decemb. 1774," printed in Christian Wilhelm Franz Walch, *Neueste Religionsgeschichte*, 6 Theil (Lemgo: Mayer, 1777), Beylag, pp. 441–72; Hans Fieger, *P. Don Ferdinand Sterzinger*, pp. 198–200.

27. *Unpartheyische Gedanken oder Etwas vor die Aerzte von der Kurart des Tit. Herrn Gassners in Ellwangen, herausgegeben von Doct. Schisel [Schleis] gedruckt zu Schalbuz [Sulzbach], mit Wizgallischen Schriften*, 1775, pp. 17–20, 21–38, 40; Hanauer, "Teufelsbanner," p. 339.

28. Merz noted that all remarkable events were to be recorded: "alle merkwürdige Zufälle umständlich, getreu, gesetzmässig alsogleich zu protokolliren, und die erfoderlichen [sic] Augenzeugen beyzusetzen." *Wer war Herr Johann Joseph Gassner?*, 1778, in the collection by Alois Merz of Augsburg in his *Neueste Sammlung jener Schriften . . .* , vol. 38 (Augsburg: Johann Georg Bullmann, 1788), pp. 21–22. Merz assured his readers that the full reports were still available in 1778, but I have been unable to locate them.

29. Munich, Bayerisches Hauptstaatsarchiv, GR 1210/ no. 20, case no. 56: a fifty-four-year-old man with cramps and convulsions so strong that six persons were unable to hold him still; cf. no. 58: a woman of 52 years who finally learned "ihr selbst helfen"; cf. similar remarks in nos. 59, 65, 76, 78, 79, 83, 84, 96, 111, 115, 124, 143, 147, etc.

30. Oswald Loschert specifically addressed the question of how Gassner could teach his supplicants to rid themselves of their own demons. *Zweytes Sendschreiben eines Gottesgelehrten am Tauberflusse an seinen Freund einen Weltweisen nächst dem Donaustrom; Worinn der erstere in seinen Antworten auf*

verschiedene an ihn gestelle Fragen, über das zeitherige Betragen des hochwürdigen Herrn Pfarrers Gassner, bey Entdeckung und Austreibung der Geistern der Finsterniss, von den geplagten Körpern der bey ihm hülfsuchenden Bedrangten, seine aufrichtige, den Grundsätzen des Christenthums und einer ächten Gottesgelahrtheit angemessene Meynung eröfnet (n.p., 1775), pp. 48–51.

31. Munich, Bayerisches Hauptstaatsarchiv, GR 1210/ no. 20: September 25; on September 27 another case concluded with the note that a 26-year-old widow was healed of her melancholy, sadness, and fear and of troubled visions of her dead husband by experiencing their repeated arrival and departure ("bis sie im Stand ware solche schnell selbsten zu vertreiben"). On October 4 Schleis emphasized the same process in the cure of Herr Balthasar Dillmann, a battalion surgeon from Bayreuth, whose flatulence was so loud that he could no longer serve anyone: "Nach öfters wiederhollten übungen erlente er die ihme viehmahls bekannte gewesene Heylungs arth."

32. *Altes und neues System, des geheimen Streits mit den Geistern der Finsternissen, von dem Hochwürdigen und Hochgelehrten Herrn, Johann Joseph Gassner, Seiner Hochfürstlichen Gnaden, Bischofen und Fürsten zu Regenspurg, auch Gefürsteten Probsten zu Ellwangen, geistlichen Rath und Hofkaplan, dermaligen Dechand und Pfarrer zu Pondorf etc. durch unverneinliche Thatsachen erneueret, und von einem seiner Freunden aus dem christlichen Alterthum erkläret und bestättiget. / Opera Dei revelare et confiteri honorificum est. Tobiae 12. v. 7. Die Werke Gottes offenbaren und bekennen, ist rühmlich* (n.p., 1778). This list was signed and attested on 21 October 1777, pp. clxxxi ff.

33. One year after Gassner's death Alois Merz wrote that he had been called to Ellwangen by the bishop of Regensburg (in 1777) in order to closely observe the exorcist's manner of healing. He noted that he later wrote a detailed letter to Pope Pius VI and delivered it to the bishop of Regensburg for transfer to Rome. Hanauer, "Teufelsbanner," pp. 351–52, cites this document as Alois März, "Gutachten eines grossen Theologen 1780," from the Fürstliches Hohenlohisches Archiv Neuenstein.

34. Ruth Harris, *Lourdes* (London: Penguin, 1999), pp. 331–56; Harry W. Paul, "The Debate over the Bankruptcy of Science in 1895," *French Historical Studies* 5 (1968), pp. 298–327.

35. Harris, *Lourdes*, pp. 325, 344–45, 356.

36. Harris, *Lourdes*, pp. 304–19, 344–45. This is especially evident in her treatment of the famous case of Pierre de Rudder. See also Thomas J. Csordas, *The Sacred Self: A Cultural Phenomenology of Charismatic Healing* (Berkeley: University of California Press, 1994), and Thomas A.

Kselman, *Miracles and Prophecies in Nineteenth-Century France* (New Brunswick, N.J.: Rutgers University Press, 1983), pp. 189–200.

37. The placebo has recently become controversial among the physicians who study it. See Peter Gøtsche and Asbjørn Hrobjartsson, "Is the Placebo Powerless? An Analysis of Clinical Trials Comparing Placebo with No Treatment," *New England Journal of Medicine* 344, no. 21 (24 May 2001), pp. 1594–1602; John C. Bailar III, "The Powerful Placebo and the Wizard of Oz," *New England Journal of Medicine* 344, no. 21 (24 May 2001), pp. 1630–32; Daniel Moerman, *Meaning, Medicine and the "Placebo Effect"* (Cambridge: Cambridge University Press, 2002); Anne Harrington, ed., *The Placebo Effect: An Interdisciplinary Approach* (Cambridge, Mass.: Harvard University Press, 1997). For a recent example of confident, garden-variety biophysical reductionism, see Michael Shermer, "Demon-Haunted Brain: If the Brain Mediates All Experience, Then Paranormal Phenomena Are Nothing More Than Neuronal Events," *Scientific American* 288, no. 3 (March 2003), p. 25.

38. Ed Cohen, "The Placebo Disavowed: Or the Unveiling of the Bio-Medical Imagination," *Yale Journal for Humanities in Medicine*, 26 November 2002 (http://info.med.yale.edu/intmed/hummed/yjhm/regular/ecohen1.htm).

39. Thomas J. Csordas, *Body, Meaning, Healing* (New York: Palgrave Macmillan, 2002), pp. 136–37: "To explain religious phenomena of affliction solely in medical terms is to merely put one view of the world in place of another." For a humane example of medical humility in the face of such conundra, see Howard Spiro, *The Power of Hope: A Doctor's Perspective* (New Haven: Yale University Press, 1998), esp. pp. 154–81; on the "scientific fallacy" see pp. 185–97.

40. Csordas, *Body, Meaning, Healing*, pp. 134–35.

41. Arthur Kleinman, *Patients and Healers in the Context of Culture: An Exploration of the Borderland between Anthropology, Medicine, and Psychiatry* (Berkeley: University of California Press, 1980); Arthur Kleinman, "Depression, Somatization and the 'New Cross-Cultural Psychiatry,'" *Social Science and Medicine* 11 (1997), pp. 3–10; see also Byron Good, *Medicine, Rationality, and Experience: An Anthropological Perspective* (Cambridge: Cambridge University Press, 1994).

42. This seems to be the view of Felicitas Goodman, *How About Demons? Possession and Exorcism in the Modern World* (Bloomington: Indiana University Press, 1988).

43. Anne Harrington, ed., *The Placebo Effect: An Interdisciplinary Exploration* (Cambridge: Harvard University Press, 1997).
44. See Robert A. Ader and N. Cohen, "Behaviorally Conditioned Immunosuppression," *Psychosomatic Medicine* 37 (1975), pp. 333–40; Robert A. Hahn and Arthur Kleinman, "Belief as Pathogen, Belief as Medicine: 'Voodoo Death' and the 'Placebo Phenomenon' in Anthropological Perspective," *Medical Anthropology Quarterly* 4 (1983), pp. 16–19; Irving Kirsch, *Changing Expectations: A Key to Effective Psychotherapy* (Pacific Grove, Calif.: Brooks/Cole, 1990); Donald D. Price and Howard L. Fields, "The Contribution of Desire and Expectation to Placebo Analgesia: Implications for New Research Strategies," in Harrington, *The Placebo Effect*, pp. 117–37; David B. Morris, "Placebo, Pain, and Belief: A Biocultural Model," in Harrington, *The Placebo Effect*, pp. 187–207.
45. See Anne Harrington, *Reenchanted Science: Holism in German Culture from Wilhelm II to Hitler* (Princeton: Princeton University Press, 1996); David Ray Griffin, *Reenchantment without Supernaturalism: A Process Philosophy of Religion* (Ithaca: Cornell University Press, 2001); Morris Berman, *The Reenchantment of the World* (Ithaca: Cornell University Press, 1981); Alister McGrath, *The Reenchantment of Nature: The Denial of Religion and the Ecological Crisis* (New York: Doubleday, 2002).
46. See Mark Kline Taylor, *Beyond Explanation: Religious Dimensions in Cultural Anthropology* (Macon, Ga.: Mercer University Press, 1986), pp. 68–75, for an attempt, following Paul Ricoeur, at an interpretation of the dialectical relations of explanation and understanding.

Chapter 4. Interpretation

1. See Stephan Bächter, "Aberglaube und Aufklärung im 18. Jahrhundert," *Jahrbuch des Historischen Vereins Dillingen* 103 (2002), pp. 159–80; Heinz Dieter Kittsteiner, "Die Abschaffung des Teufels im 18. Jahrhundert," in Alexander Schuller and Wollfert von Rahden, eds., *Die andere Kraft. Zur Renaissance des Bösen* (Berlin: Akademie Verlag, 1993), pp. 55–92.
2. *Gründliche Nachricht von einer begeisterten Weibsperson* (1759), as cited in Karl Aner, *Theologie der Lessingzeit* (Halle, 1929; repr. Hildesheim: Olms, 1964), p. 234. Müller was the provost and superintendent of Kemberg in the district of Wittenberg (over the border from Anhalt). Hoffmann compared Lohmann's case with the "erfurtische Liese," the "halberstadtische Kathrine," the "quedlinburgische Magdlene," and the "Baderin" of

Württemberg. Radical Pietists were attracted to those inspired with charismatic gifts. August Hermann Francke had been much influenced by three inspired girls in the Quedlinburg-Erfurt area, Gottfried Arnold had been similarly affected by Rosamunde von Asseburg, and Philipp Spener had been fascinated by Johanna Eleonore Petersen. See Jeannine Blackwell, "Controlling the Demonic: Johann Salomo Semler and the Possession of Anna Elisabeth Lohmann (1759)," in W. Daniel Wilson and Robert C. Holub, eds., *Impure Reason: Dialectic of Enlightenment in Germany* (Detroit: Wayne State University Press, 1993), pp. 425–42, at p. 427.

3. The Reformed pastor Johann Benjamin Gottlob Bobbe reported that by mid-1760 she was cured. Blackwell, "Controlling the Demonic," p. 434.
4. The debate about Lohmann included the following works:
   (a) Gottlieb Müller, *Gründliche Nachricht von einer begeisterten Weibesperson Annen Elisabeth Lohmännin von Horsdorf [sic] in Anhalt-Dessau aus eigener Erfahrung und Untersuchung mitgetheilt von Gottlieb Müllern, Probst und Superintendenten in Kemberg, auch Ehrenmitgliede der Gesellschaft der freyen Künste in Leipzig* (Wittenberg: Johann Joachim Ahlfeld, 1759; 2nd ed. with Anhang, 1760).
   (b) *Versuch einer unpartheyischen Widerlegung S. T. Sr. Hochehrwürd. Herrn Gottlieb Müllers, Probsts und Superintendentens in Kemberg Gründlichen Nachricht von einer begeisterten Weibesperson Annen Elisab. Lohmannin etc. etc. aus philosophischen und physicalischen Gründen hergeleitet, von Alethaeo Adeisidaemone* (Leipzig: Lanischens Buchhandlung, 1759).
   (c) Johann Salomo Semler, *Abfertigung der neuen Geister und alten Irrtümer in der Lohmannischen Begeisterung zu Kemberg nebst theologischem Unterricht von dem Ungrunde der gemeinen Meinung von leiblichen Besitzungen des Teufels und Bezauberung der Christen* (Halle: Johann Justinus Gebauer, 1760).
   (d) [Johann Benjamin Gottlob Bobbe], *Vermischte Anmerkungen über Sr. Hochehrwürden des Herrn Probstes und Superintendentens in Kemberg Herrn Gottlieb Müllers Gründlichen Nachricht und deren Anhang von einer begeisterten Weibesperson Annen Elisabeth Lohmännin, mitgetheilet von Antidämoniacus* (Bernberg: Christoph Gottfried Coerner, 1760).
   (e) Gotthelf Friedrich Oesfeld, *Gedanken von der Einwirkung guter und böser Geister in die Menschen. Nebst beygefügter Beurtheilung eines neuern Beyspiels einer vermeynten leiblichen Besitzung* (Wittenberg: Johann Joachim Ahlfeld, 1760).
   (f) *Das bezauberte Bauernmädgen: oder Geschichte von dem jetzt in Kemberg*

bei Wittemberg sich aufhaltenden Landmädgen Johannen [sic] Elisabethen Lohmännin. Aufgesetzt von einem vom Urtheil Befreyeten, und mit Anmerkungen eines Rechtsgelehrten versehen* (Breslau: J. E. Meyer, 1760).

 (g) Georg Friedrich Meier, *Georg Friedrich Meiers, der Weltweisheit ordentlichen Lehrers, der königlichen Academie der Wissenschaften zu Berlin Mitglieds, und d. Z. Prorectors, philosophische Gedanken von der Würkungen des Teufels auf dem Erdboden* (Halle: Carl Herman Hemmerde, 1760).

 (h) ["Christoph Matthaeus Pfaff," pseud.], *Nöthige Belehrung zweyer neuen Theologen, welche in der Geister-Lehre der Sache zu wenig und zu viel thun: oder gebührende Anrede an Hrn. Joh. Sal. Semlern u. Gottl. Müllern* (Wittenberg, 1760), with a borrowed introduction by Johann Georg Walch.

 (i) Johann Salomo Semler *Anhang zu der Abfertigung der Lohmannischen Begeisterung worin fernere historische Umstände gesamlet werden* (Halle: Gebauer, 1760).

 (j) Prof. Thomas Abbt of Frankfurt/Oder, a position paper that Johann Salomo Semler published in his *Anhang* of 1760.

5. Semler's *Abfertigung* ran to 328 pages. He rarely showed a tasteful sense of proportion in his work.
6. Semler, *Abfertigung*, pp. 20–32. Semler cited the antique work of Johann Georg Dorscheus, *Disputatio theologica de horrenda et miserabili Sataniae obsessione* (Rostock, 1656; repr. 1714) in the edition provided by Hauber's *Bibliotheca magica*, Stück 3, pp. 162 ff. Semler may also have seen Johann Friedrich Rübel's, *Systematische oder gründliche . . . Abhandlung von denen fast allgemeinen Irrthümern betreffend die Besitzung des Menschen vom Teufel* (n.p, 1758). The physician Rübel was also the author of *Physikalische Abhandlung von der Gewalt des Teufels in die Körper . . . ob er den Menschen Krankheiten zuziehen könne?* (Nuremberg: Zimmermann, 1753). Johann Heinrich Zedler, *Grosses vollständiges Universal Lexicon aller Wissenschaften und Künste, welche bisshero durch menschlichen Verstand und Witz erfunden und verbessert worden* (Halle and Leipzig: Zedler, 1732–1750), at vol. 3 (1733), s.v. "Besitzung des Teufels," cols. 1497–98.
7. Semler, *Abfertigung*, pp. 183–87, esp. p. 183 n., pp. 198 ff, where Semler notes that the devil cannot "in his substance" invade the soul or the body of human beings; at p. 249. Semler pointed out, correctly, that there is no mention of exorcism or the casting out of demons in the Old Testament, that the meaning of *daimōn* and *daimonion* had changed since antiquity,

and even claimed that there was no proof of even one truly, physically possessed person in the Epistles or Acts of the Apostles, to say nothing of the early church, into which exorcists were introduced in the third century (too late to be of any authority for Semler), pp. 209–12, 243, 250–51, 254–56. In a 112-page "Anhang" paginated and published separately, Semler listed all the relevant recent Lutheran works on demonology, including all the works on Lohmann that had come to his attention.

8. *Dissertatio theologico-hermeneutica de daemoniacis quorum in Evangeliis fit mentio* (Halle: Hendel, 1760); a second edition: Ioannis Salomonis Semleri, *Commentatio De Daemoniacis Quorum In N. T. Fit Mentio, Ed. auctior* (Halle: Hendel, 1769); an edition of 1774 is already called the fourth edition, *Commentatio de daemoniacis quorum in N.T. fit mentio, 4. ed. multo jam auctior* (Halle, 1774). An edition (it too is called the fourth) was also published in 1779: Ioannis Salomonis Semleri, *Commentatio de daemoniacis qvorvm in N. T. fit mentio* (Halle: Hendel, 1779). I cite Semler's edition of 1769, here at pp. 1–2.

9. Joseph Mede (1586–1638) was the author of *The apostasy of the latter times*, whose full title reveals the connections in his mind between the apocalypse and his notions of demons: *in which (according to divine prediction) the world should wonder after the beast, the mystery of iniquity should so farre prevaile over the mystery of godlinesse, whorish Babylon over the virgin-church of Christ, as that the visible glory of the true church should be much clouded, the true unstained Christian faith corrupted, the purity of true worship polluted: or, the gentiles theology of dæmons, i.e. inferious divine powers, supposed to be mediatours between God and man: revived in the latter times amongst Christians, in worshipping of angels, deifying and invocating of saints, adoring and templing of reliques, bowing downe to images, worshipping of crosses, etc: all which, together with a true discovery of the nature, originall, progresse of the great, fatall, and solemn apostasy are cleared / delivered in publique some years since upon I. Tim. 4. 1, 2, 3* (London: Richard Bishop for Samuel Man, 1642).

10. *Commentatio de daemoniacis*, p. 3, n. 4. Semler cited the maxim of "Beausobrius" in his Remarques on Mark 8:19: "le miracle est toujours le même, de quelque cause vienne le mal." Ibid., p. 4, n. 5.

11. Aner, *Die Theologie der Lessingzeit*, pp. 238–39.

12. Semler cited such authors as Hesiod, Homer, Thales, Pythagoras, Euripedes, Plato, Aristotle, Porphyry, and Philo; *Commentatio*, pp. 6–11; see also pp. 17, 23, n. 19, 28–29, 31–32. If demon possession was a necessary part of the faith, then why, Semler asked, are the Old Testament and the

New Testament Epistles silent on the matter? And so "profecto illae plebis opiniones nobis hodie legem non scribunt" (p. 32).

13. The anonymous author identifies himself as "T. P. A. P. O. A. B. I. T. C. O. S." (i.e., The Precentor and Prebendary of Alton Borealis in the Church of Salisbury, i.e., A. A. Sykes), *An Enquiry into the Meaning of Demoniacks in the New Testament* (London: Roberts, 1737); a second edition was published in the same year. On Sykes, see Lesley Stephen, ed., *Dictionary of National Biography*.

14. *Enquiry*, pp. 2–5, 7, 33–35, 56, citing among many other sources Hesiod, *Opera* 1; the Scholiast on Homer, *Iliad* 1.222; Justin Martyr, who declared, in *Apol.* 2, that the gods of the heathen were demons and nothing more than the *psychai apothanatōn*; and Josephus, in *De bello judaico* 7.23, who had asserted that the souls of wicked men were "*daimonia, tauta ponērōn esin anthropōn pneumata.*"

15. *Enquiry*, pp. 48–53.

16. These included:
    (a) [Leonard Twells], *An Answer to the Enquiry into the Meaning of the Demoniacks in the New Testament* (London, 1737).
    (b) [Thomas Church], *An Essay Towards Vindicating the Literal Sense of the Demoniacks in the New Testament. In Answer to a late Enquiry into the Meaning of them* (London: J. Roberts, 1737).
    (c) [Arthur Ashley Sykes], *A Further Enquiry Into the Meaning of Demoniacks in the New Testament / Wherein the Enquiry is vindicated against the objections of the Rev'd Mr. Twells, and the Author of the Essay in Answer to it* (London: J. Roberts, 1737).
    (d) William Whiston, *An Account of the Daemoniacks, and of the Power of Casting out Daemons, both in the New Testament, and in the Four First Centuries. Occasioned by a Late Pamphlet intituled,* An Enquiry into the meaning of Daemoniacks in the New Testament. *To which is added, an Appendix, concerning the Tythes and Oblations paid by Christians, during the same Four Centuries* (London: printed for John Whiston, at Mr. Boyle's Head, 1737).
    (e) [Thomas Church], *A Reply to the Farther Enquiry Into the Meaning of the Demoniacks in the New Testament* (London: J. Roberts, 1738).
    (f) Leonard Twells, *An Answer to the Further Enquiry into the Meaning of the Demoniacks in the New Testament . . . In a Second Letter to the Author* (London: R. Gosling, 1738).
    (g) S. T. P. A. P. O. A. B. I. T. C. O. [probably A. A. Sykes again], *Some Thoughts on the Miracles of Jesus; With an Introduction to that of His*

Casting out Devils, Which is particularly discuss'd. Occasion'd by Two Late Tracts, Intitled, Enquiries into the Meaning of Demoniacks in the New Testament. By an impartial Hand (London: J. Roberts, 1738).

(h) Thomas Hutchinson, *The Usual Interpretation of DAIMONES and DAIMONIA, in the New Testament, asserted in a Sermon preach'd before the University of Oxford at St. Mary's, On Sunday, March 5, 1737–8* (Oxford, 1738).

(i) "A Gentleman of Wadham College", *A Critical Dissertation Concerning the Words DAIMŌN and DAIMONION occasion'd by Two late Enquiries into the Meaning of Demoniacks in the New Testament. In a Letter to a Friend* (London: printed for J. Crockatt; sold by J. Roberts in Warwick Lane, 1738). Note that the *Dictionary of National Biography* unwittingly suggests two possible authors as the "gentleman of Wadham College": George Costard and John Swinton. See the separate entries for each of them.

(j) [Bodleian Library catalogue lists the author as Gregory Sharpe, 1713–1771], *A Review of the Controversy about the meaning of Demoniacks in the New-Testament . . . by a Lover of Truth, with an Appendix in Answer to the Critical Dissertation etc.* (London: John Roberts, 1739).

(k) Samuel Pegge, *An Examination of the Enquiry into the Meaning of Demoniacs in the New Testament* [by A. A. Sykes]. *In a Letter to the Author. Wherein it is shewn That the Word Demon does not signify a Departed Soul, either in the Classics or the Scriptures; And consequently, That the whole of the Enquiry is without Foundation* (London: Fletcher Giles, 1739).

(l) [Thomas Church], *A Short State of the Controversy about the Meaning of the Demoniacks in the New Testament: with a Vindication of the Reply to the Farther Enquiry, from all the Objections of a late Tract, intitled A Review of the Controversy, By the same Hand* (London, 1739).

(m) Thomas Hutchinson, *Remarks upon a Pamphlet, intitl'd A Review of the Controversy about the Meaning of Demoniacs, etc. Wherein the Sermon, Which asserteth the usual interpretation, etc. is vindicated from every exception of the Reviewer* (London: W. Innys and R. Manby, 1739).

17. In fact, Semler assisted in the translation or editing of several of these English works. Over his career he oversaw and introduced German translations of David Neal (1762), Samuel Clarke (1774), Hugh Farmer (1776, 1783), Arthur Ashley Sykes (1778, 1779), and Thomas Townson (1783–84). He also edited German versions of Richard Simon (1776) and Balthasar Bekker (1781–82). But see also Johann Christoph Friedrich

Schulz, *Untersuchungen über die Bedeutung des Wortes Satan und Teufel in der Bibel*, trans. Johann Christoph Friedrich Schulz (Leipzig: Weygand, 1774), a translation of Thomas Barker (1722–1809), *An inquiry into the scripture meaning of the word Satan and its synonymous terms, the devil, or the adversary, and the wicked-one: wherein also, the notions concerning devils, of demons, are brought down too the standard of scripture; the whole interspersed with remarks on various terms, passages, and phrases in the Old and New Testaments* (London: J. Wheble, 1772). Barker was also the author of *The Nature and Circumstances of the Demoniacks in the Gospels, stated and methodized and considered in the several particulars* (London: B. White, 1783).

18. Miracles attracted the attentions of many, including William Whiston, Conyers Middleton, Thomas Woolston, Bishop Richard Smalbroke, Bishop Benjamin Hoadly of Bangor, A. A. Sykes, Leonard Twells (Boyle Lecturer 1739–1741), Nathaniel Lardner, Arthur Young, William Worthington, and later Hugh Farmer, most of whom also wrote on demon possession. The English debate of 1737 actually had its origins in the scandalous writings of Thomas Woolston (*A Defense of the Miracle of the Thundering Legion* [1726] and *Discourse on the Miracles of Our Saviour* [1727–29]). See Arthur Young's attack on Woolston in *A Dissertation on the Gospel-Daemoniacks* (London: G. Woodfall, 1760) and the DNB vol. 21, pp. 908–10, on Woolston. See also John Hunt, *Religious Thought in England: From the Reformation to the End of the Last Century. A Contribution to the History of Theology*, 3 vols. (London: Strahan and Co., 1870–73), vol. 3, pp. 16–251.

19. "Die dogmatische Unterricht der Schrift betrifft niemalen leibliche Dinge." Cf. Galileo Galilei, "Letter to the Grand Duchess Christina (1615)," in Stillman Drake, trans. and ed., *Discoveries and Opinions of Galileo* (New York: Doubleday, 1957), pp. 145–216, esp. 185–86, 205–10. Galileo depended heavily upon St. Augustine's *De Genesi ad literam*, a work that Semler too could easily have known. Johann Salomo Semler, *Umständliche Untersuchung der dämonischen Leute oder so genanten Besessenen, nebst Beantwortung einiger Angriffe* (Halle: Gebauer, 1762), pp. 4–5, 24–26, 66–67, 83–86, 254.

20. Semler here repeated much that he had written in Latin two years earlier, but included specific arguments against Johann Stephen Müller's *Notionem daimoniō sive daimonos olim et inprimis Christi tempore non hoc involvisse ut anima mortui daemon esse crederetur eosque homines qui dicunt habet ille daemonem non opinatos fuisse animam mortui cuiusdam impedire et turbare animam viventis rationalem a . . . demonstrat Johann Stephan Müller*, Johann

Burckhard Caspar, respondent (Theol. diss., University of Jena, 1761)— Semler cited the published version (Frankfurt, 1762). Müller published a second comment on Semler's demonology, and they were published together as *De Daemoniacis Semlerianis: In Dvabvs Dissertationibvs Theologicis* (Frankfurt and Leipzig, 1763). Semler also attacked an "unreasonable review" ("Recension der Lohmannischen Comödie"), printed in the second and third parts of the *Neue Beyträge von alten und neuen theologischen Sachen, Büchern, Urkunden, Controversien, Anmerkungen und Vorschlägen: zum Wachsthum d. theolog. Gelehrsamkeit, wie auch d. alten u. neuen Kirchen- u. Gelehrtengeschichte etc. . . . . mitgetheilet* (Leipzig: Jacobi, 1761), which he characterized (p. 183) as nothing more than ignorant screaming at his dissertation.

In 1760 the current authority on demoniacs in Germany and Switzerland was Johann Jakob Wettstein (1693–1754), the biblical scholar of Basel, against whom many tested their learning: e.g., Johann G. Faber, *Dissertatio Academica de Daemoniacis, adversus Wetstenium*, Praeses Ioannes Gottlieb Faber, Respondens M. Carolus Fried. Renz, Kirchhemio Teccensis (Tübingen: Cotta and Reuss, [1763]).

21. Hans W. Frei, *The Eclipse of Biblical Narrative: A Study in Eighteenth and Nineteenth Century Hermeneutics* (New Haven: Yale University Press, 1974), esp. pp. 62–63, 109, 223–32.

22. A few scholars have begun to rectify the imbalance at least with respect to the debate between Enlightened theology and Protestant Orthodoxy. See Heimo Reinitzer and Walter Sparn, eds., *Verspätete Orthodoxie. Über D. Johann Melchior Goeze, 1717–1786* (Wiesbaden: Otto Harrassowitz, 1989); Gerhard Freund, *Theologie im Widerspruch. Die Lessing-Goeze-Kontroverse* (Stuttgart: Kohlhammer, 1989); Norbert Haag, *Predigt und Gesellschaft. Die lutherische Orthodoxie in Ulm, 1640–1740* (Mainz: von Zabern, 1992). The study of Catholic biblical criticism during the centuries after Trent has, however, languished, but see Gerald P. Fogarty, *American Catholic Biblical Scholarship: A History from the Early Republic to Vatican II* (San Francisco: Harper and Row, 1989); George Armstrong Kelly, *The Church's Problem with Bible Scholars* (Chicago: Franciscan Herald Press, 1985); Yvon Belaval and Dominique Bourel, eds., *Le siècle des Lumières et la Bible* (Paris: Beauchesne, 1986).

23. Notker Hammerstein, "Was heisst Aufklärung in katholischen Universitäten Deutschlands?" in Harm Klueting, Norbert Hinske, and Karl Hengst, eds., *Katholische Aufklärung — Aufklärung im katholischen Deutschland* (Hamburg: Felix Meiner, 1993), pp. 142–62, esp. 152–55. Karl Josef

Lesch, *Die Neuorientierung der Theologie im 18. Jahrhundert in Würzburg und Bamberg* (Würzburg: Echter, 1978), on the renewed importance of history and biblical exegesis based in knowledge of the ancient languages, pp. 144–45, 158, 163, 203–4, 210–11, 222–24, 237–38, 243, 267–71, 290–91.

24. Behringer, *Hexenverfolgung*, pp. 371–93, provides a circumstantial account of the Bavarian "witchcraft war" of the 1760s. The chief defenders of Sterzinger were Andreas Ulrich Mayer (writing under the humorous pseudonym F. N. Blocksberger), imperial counselor Konstantin Florian von Kautz, Heinrich Braun OSB of Tegernsee, Josef Sterzinger of Innsbruck (younger brother of Ferdinand Sterzinger), Jordan Simon OSA of Erfurt (writing under the pseudonym Arduino Ubbidiente dell'Osa), Jacob Anton Kollmann (writing under the pseudonym of an anonymous "doubting Bavarian"), and Peter von Osterwald of the Bavarian Academy of Sciences. See also Hans Fieger, *P. Don Ferdinand Sterzinger. Lektor der Theatiner in München, Direktor der historischen Klasse der kurbayerischen Akademie der Wissenschaften, Bekämpfer des Aberglaubens und Hexenwahns und der Pfarrer Gassnerischen Wunderkuren. Ein Beitrag zur Geschichte der Aufklärung in Bayern unter Kurfürst Maximilian III. Joseph* (Munich: Oldenbourg, 1907), pp. 97–150.

25. Eutychii Benjamin Transalbini [Fortunatus Durich], *Dissertatio philologica de vocibus Hhartymmim et Belahatehem. Exod. VII. 11* (Munich, 1767). Durich's pseudonym referred to his origins as a Bohemian. "Eutychius" means fortunate. Aloys von Sonnenfels, *Sendschreiben des hochedelgebohrnen Herrn Aloysius von Sonnenfels . . . an den hochgelehrten Herrn P. don Ferdinand Sterzinger, . . . über zwey Wörter Chartummim und Belahatehem: nachmals zur nothwendigen Belehrung . . . zum Drucke befördert, von einem Verehrer des Sterzingerischen Namens* (Vienna, 1768). Sonnenfels is best known perhaps as a student of alchemy, but his theological and biblical knowledge need to be better studied.

26. See Hans-Joachim Kraus, *Geschichte der historisch-kritischen Erforschung des Alten Testaments*, 3rd ed. (Neukirchen: Neukirchener Verlag, 1982), pp. 6, 40–41, 66–73, 92, 290–94; this assessment does not deny the enormous disparity in research effort between Protestants and Catholics. It is also clear that orthodox Catholic theologians reacted with fear and hostility to these early welcoming gestures toward learned biblical exegesis. By the early nineteenth century, most of these efforts had been stifled.

27. Fieger, *P. Don Ferdinand*, pp. 112–18. Sometimes we need to remind

ourselves that Salzburg, just to take one example, lies only 160 miles to the north of Venice, at least as the swallow flies. Culturally, Stuttgart was farther away.

28. In German Muratori was best known for three works: *De ingeniorum moderatione et in religionis negotio* (published under the pseudonym Lamindus Pritanius, 1714), *Della regolata divozione dei cristiani* (1723), and *Della carità cristiana in quanto essa è amore del prossimo* (1723), which were all published in frequent German translations down to the end of the eighteenth century. On the question of demons he was best known for his *De superstitione vitanda* (1742) and *Della forza della fantasia umana* (Venice: Pasquali, 1745), published in German as *Über die Einbildungskraft des Menschen*, ed. Georg Hermann Richerz (Leipzig: Weygand, 1785).

29. Behringer, *Hexenverfolgung*, pp. 369–70; Scipione Maffei, *Arte magica dileguata* (Verona, 1749), p. 17; Maffei, *Arte magica annichilata* (Verona, 1754); Gian Paolo Romagnani, ed., *Scipione Maffei nell'Europa del Settecento: Atti del convegno, Verona, 23–25 settembre 1996* (Verona: Consorzio Ed. Veneti, 1998); Gian Paolo Romagnani, *"Sotto la bandiera dell'istoria": eruditi e uomini di letterre nell'Italia del Settecento: Maffei, Muratori, Tartarotti* (Sommacampagna [Verona]: Cierre, 1999); G. P. Marchi, "Tra sofferenza psichica e modalità di comunicazione: La stregoneria nel pensiero di Scipione Maffei," in Luciano Bonuzzi and Gian Paolo Marchi, eds., *Psicopatologia e filosofia nella tradizione veronese* (Verona: AASLVR, 1994), pp. 37–49; G. Di Marco, "Oscillazioni tra razionale e irrazionale: Tartarotti, Maffei e la pollemica diabolica des XVIII secolo," in Bonuzzi and Marchi, eds., *Psicopatologia*, pp. 25–36. The influence of Muratori north of the Alps is well known; see Eleonore Zlabinger, *Lodovico Muratori und Österreich* (Veröffentlichungen der Universität Innsbruck no. 53; Innsbruck, 1970); Adam Wandruszka, "Der Reformkatholizismus des 18. Jahrhunderts in Italien und Österreich. Neue Forschungen und Fragestellungen," in Alexander Novotny and O. Pockl, eds., *Festschrift für Hermann Wiesflecker zum 60. Geburtstag* (Graz: Historisches Institut der Universität, 1973), pp. 231–40; Peter F. Barton, *Jesuiten, Jansenisten, Josephiner. Eine Fallstudie zur frühen Toleranzzeit: Der Fall Innocentius Fessler* (Vienna: Hermann Böhlaus Nachf., 1978), pp. 137–40.

30. [Ferdinand Sterzinger], *Die aufgedeckten Gassnerischen Wunderkuren* 2nd ed. (n.p., 1775), p. 46. The works upon which Gassner apparently relied were

(a) Ubald Stoiber, *Armamentarium ecclesiasticum: complectens Arma spiritualia fortissima ad insultus diabolicos elidendos, et feliciter superandos*;

ad utilitatem omnium animarum Pastorum, sedulò ex ipso S. Evangelii fonte . . . collecta (1st ed. Augsburg, 1726; 3rd ed., Editio tertia Pedeponti [= Stadt am Hof, near Regensburg]: Gastl, 1744); forbidden 1754.

(b) Candido Brognolo, *Manuale exorcistarum ac parochorum: Hoc est Tractatus de curatione, ac protectione divina* (Bergomum, 1651); forbidden 1727.

(c) Girolamo Menghi, *Compendio dell'arte essorcistica, et possibilita delle mirabili, et stupende operationi delli demoni et dei malefici* (Bologna 1586); forbidden 1709.

(d) Girolamo Menghi, *Flagellum daemonum exorcismos terribiles, potentissimos, et efficaces* (Bologna 1586; Venice, 1644; Frankfurt: Johann Adolph, 1708); forbidden 1709.

(e) Stephanus Coletus, *Energumenos dignoscendi et liberandi, tum maleficia quaelibet dissolvendi, nec non benedictiones utiliter conficiendi super aegrotos compendiaria et facillima ratio;* forbidden 1763.

(f) *Anonyma quaestiuncula ex eodem opusculo desumta de liberandis energumenis, seclusa licentia ordinarii* (Venice, 1762); forbidden 1763.

Perhaps he also knew *Manuale Benedictionum continens variarum rerum, tum benedictiones, tum exorcismos, ac coniurationes, ad pellenda maleficia, vel cavenda [et]c. Collectum: ex Romano et aliarum diversarum dioecesium ritualibus, ad usum parochorum, aliorumq[ue] sacerdotum duplici Indice, et aliquot Benedictionibus: Auctum et ad commodiorum usum, ac methodum de novo impressum MDCLXIV* (Bruntruti [= Porrentruy]: Straubhar, 1664). See Franz Heinrich Reusch, *Der Index der verbotenen Bücher. Ein Beitrag zur Kirchen- und Literaturgeschichte* 2 vols. (Bonn, 1883–1885; repr. Aalen: Scientia Verlag, 1967), vol. 2, pp. 218–23. On the Italian exorcists, orthodox and unorthodox, see Elena Brambilla, "La fine dell'esorcismo: Possessione, santità, isteria dall'età barocca all'illuminismo," *Quaderni Storici* 112 (2003), pp. 117–63, at pp. 122–25, 141–43.

31. [Sterzinger], *Die aufgedeckten Gassnerischen Wunderkuren*, 2nd ed., pp. 44–49.
32. Ibid., "Katechismus von der Geisterlehre," pp. 56–88, at pp. 59 and 84.
33. Hanauer, "Der Teufelsbanner," pp. 363–64; in 1778 Gassner had written to Oswald Loschert that he had lately discovered a universal rule, that "all conditions that do not come from a lesion [i.e., a wound or injury] come from the devil." By 1779 he had privately gone even further.
34. On the social constellation of opponents of Sterzinger and backers of Gassner, see Behringer, *Hexenverfolgung*, pp. 373–80, 391, 394–96. On

the Augsburg Jesuits, see Hildegard Mahler, *Das Geistesleben Augsburgs im 18. Jahrhundert im Spiegel der Augsburger Zeitschriften* (Ph.D. dissertation, Munich 1934; published Augsburg: Haas and Grabherr, 1934), pp. 121–36.

35. Augsburg was so favorable a city for Gassner that the publisher Stage complained to Sterzinger that he had been compelled to print Sterzinger's attack on Gassner (*Die aufgedeckten Gassnerischen Wunderkuren*) in Ulm. See Joseph Hanauer, *Der Exorzist Johann Joseph Gassner (1727–1779). Eine Monographie* (unpublished theological Dissertation, University of Würzburg, 1950), p. 81, n. 3. It was perhaps mainly his intemperate attacks on Gassner that caused Christian Friedrich Daniel Schubart to be banished from Augsburg along with his famous *Deutsche Chronik*. On the ex-Jesuits and Gassner in general, see Hanauer, *Der Exorzist*, pp. 84–85.

36. See Etienne François, *Die unsichtbare Grenze: Protestanten und Katholiken in Augsburg, 1648–1806* (Sigmaringen: Thorbecke, 1991); Alois Merz was cathedral preacher from 1763 to 1785. He was born in 1727 in Donsdorf in Swabia, joined the Society of Jesus in 1744, and died in 1792. Note that there were four Catholic writers in the second half of the eighteenth century with the names Merz or März. In addition to Alois, these were: Angelus (Agnellus) März, O. Aug., of Munich, who died 30 June 1784; Angelus März, OB of Scheyern, who died 3 February 1784; and Philipp Paul Merz, from Augsburg, who converted to Roman Catholicism in 1725 and died in Augsburg in 1754.

37. Nicolai, *Beschreibung einer Reise durch Deutschland und die Schweiz im Jahre 1781*, vol. 7 (Berlin and Stettin: Nicolai, 1786), pp. 113–20. I have used the reprint edited by Bernhard Fabian and Marie-Luise Spieckermann, *Friedrich Nicolai, Gesammelte Werke* (Hildesheim: Olms, 1994), vol. 18.

38. *Gründlicher Beweis, dass die Art, mit welcher der nun in ganz Deutschland berühmte hochw. Herr Pfarrer zu Klösterl Johann Joseph Gassner die Krankheiten zu heilen pflegt, den evangelischen Grundsätzen und den Gesinnungen der allerersten Kirche ganz gleichförmig sey. Von einem Vertheidiger der Wahrheit* (Augsburg: Joseph Wolf, 1775); reprinted in A. Merz, *Neueste Sammlung jener Schriften . . .*, vol. 40 (1787), pp. 1–80.

39. *Gründlicher Beweis*, pp. 19–20.

40. *Gründlicher Beweis* here citing the ninth edition of Gelasius de Cilia, *Locupletissimus Thesaurus Continens Varias Et Selectissimas Benedictiones, Conjurationes* (Augsburg: Rieger, 1772), p. 405.

41. *Gründlicher Beweis*, p. 33.

42. *Gründlicher Beweis*, pp. 35–37.
43. On the waning of the notion of the preternatural in the eighteenth century, see Lorraine Daston and Katharine Park, *Wonders and the Order of Nature, 1150–1750*, 2nd ed. (New York: Zone Books, 1998).
44. *Gründlicher Beweis*, pp. 62–63. Merz traveled again to Ellwangen in October of 1777 when Bishop Fugger arranged a brief revival of Gassner's healing campaign, even though by then both the pope and the emperor had forbidden any such further activity. Merz filed a report on what he had seen that was to be included in an appeal to Rome for a reversal.
45. *Gründlicher Beweis*, pp. 64n and 70n, citing Loyola, *Reg. de discret. spirituum*, and his *Sententiae asceticae* for 22 January; and Luther, *Werke*, Jena edition, vol. 5, fols. 334–35, and vol. 8, fols. 375–76.
46. It is true that Semler could appeal to various aspects of Luther's own thought, career, and exegetical practice, but there was no denying the massive shift in which Semler was involved. See Gottfried Hornig, *Die Anfänge der historisch-kritischen Theologie. Johann Salomo Semlers Schriftverständnis und seine Stellung zu Luther* (Göttingen, 1961).
47. Hanauer, "Der Teufelsbanner," pp. 388–89.
48. See the introduction herein.
49. Hanauer, "Der Teufelsbanner," pp. 384–87.
50. [Loschert], *Zweytes Sendschreiben eines Gottesgelehrten am Tauberflusse an seinen Freund einen Weltweisen nächst dem Donaustrom*, pp. 12–19, 28–30, 37–40, 48–51, 94–96. Loschert now explicitly rejected Gassner's early claims that demonic possession was often the result of witchcraft.
51. [Oswald Loschert] *Viertes Sendschreiben eines Gottesgelehrten am Tauberflusse an seinen Freund einen Weltweisen, nächst dem Donaustrome; Ueber die Frage: Ob die zeitherige Einwürfe gegen die exorcistische Handlungen des Hochwürdigen Herrn geistlichen Raths Gassner einen zureichenden Grund darbiethen, rechtglaubige Christen von der Anwendung seines Lehrsystems an ihnen selbst and undern Hilfebedürftigen abzuhalten?* (n.p., 1776), pp. 3–7, 80–87. Loschert continued this attack upon the neologists in his anonymous *Fünftes Sendschreiben eines Gottgelehrten am Tauberflusse, an seinen Freund, einen Weltweisen, nächst dem Donaustrome, oder Fortsetzung der Fragen und Antworten, deren Absicht ist, einen Freund des Herrn Gassner näher zu belehren, die Einwürfe seiner Gegner ferner zu widerlegen, und seine dadurch irregemachte Nachahmer wieder zu rechte zu weisen* (Frankfurt, Hanau, Leipzig, 1776).
52. See, for example, the voluminous collections of religious news edited

by Johann August Ernesti, *Neueste Theologische Bibliothek*, 4 vols. (Leipzig: Breitkopf, 1771–77), which displayed no interest in contemporary Catholicism.
53. From a letter dated 26 April 1775 from Hahn to Johann Kaspar Lavater, cited in Horst Weigelt, *Lavater und die Stillen im Lande: Distanz und Nähe. Die Beziehungen Lavaters zu Frömmigkeitsbewegungen im 18. Jahrhundert* (Göttingen: Vandenhoeck and Ruprecht, 1988), p. 58.
54. Horst Weigelt, *Johann Kaspar Lavater: Leben, Werk, Wirkung* (Göttingen: Vandenhoeck and Ruprecht, 1991), pp. 32–33; Klaus Martin Sauer, *Die Predigttätigkeit Johann Kaspar Lavaters, 1741–1801* (Zurich: Theologischer Verlag, 1988), pp. 98 ff, 150, 156, 178–82, 404 ff, 518 ff, and esp. pp. 501–5, for a treatment of Lavater's fifteen sermons on the temptation of Christ, delivered from 10 March 1777 through 26 October 1777. See also Jeffrey Freedman, *A Poisoned Chalice* (Princeton: Princeton University Press, 2002), pp. 129–33, 201–2.
55. Weigelt, *Lavater*, pp. 14–30.
56. Johann Georg Zimmermann (1728–1795) was a friend of Lavater and of Goethe, the royal physician to the court of Hanover, and well known for his popular works *Betrachtungen über die Einsamkeit* (1756; expanded in 4 vols. 1783–84) and *Von der Erfahrung in der Arzneikunst* (1763–64).
57. Zimmermann, *Ueber die Einsamkeit* (Leipzig: Weidmanns Erben und Reisch, 1784), vol. 1, p. 272; vol. 2, pp. 102–7n; vol. 3, p. 403; vol. 4, pp. 77–81.
58. Johann Caspar Lavater, *Auszug der Frankfurter gelehrten Anzeigen Nro 38 und 39 den 12 May 1775. Beytrag zur gelehrten Geschichte Unserer Zeit*, 4 fols. signed by JCL on 3 May 1775; see Weigelt, *Lavater*, p. 33.
59. Weigelt, *Lavater*, pp. 33–35.
60. In the years after his enthusiasm for Gassner faded, Lavater became a follower of Cagliostro and then Mesmer; see Weigelt, *Lavater*, pp. 36–37, 41–46.
61. Johann Georg Zimmermann, *Ueber die Einsamkeit*, 4 vols. (Leipzig: Weidmanns Erben und Reich, 1784), vol. 1, pp. 176–177n. On Zimmermann, see H.-P. Schramm, ed., *Johann Georg Zimmermann, königlich grossbritannischer Leibarzt*, Wolfenbütteler Forschungen, vol. 82 (Wiesbaden: Harrassowitz, 1998); Andreas Langenbacher, *Mit Skalpell und Fiederkiel: Ein Lesebuch. Johann Georg Zimmermann* (Bern: Haupt, 1995); I owe these references to the kindness of Thomas Biskup. Lavater was not entirely mistaken in writing to Zimmermann about Gassner, for later Zimmermann underwent a religious "conversion" that distanced him

from Nicolai and his other Enlightened friends. See Christoph Weiss, ed., *Von "Obscuranten" und "Eudämonisten": Gegenaufklärerische, konservative und antirevolutionäre Publizisten im späten 18. Jahrhundert, Literatur im historischen Kontext*, vol. 1 (St. Ingbert: Röhrig, 1997); on Zimmermann's relations with the Berlin Enlightenment, see Sigrid Habersaat, *Verteidigung der Aufklärung: Friedrich Nicolai in religiösen und politischen Debatten*, Epistemata: Würzburger Wissenschaftliche Schriften, Reihe Literaturwissenschaft, vol. 316 (Würzburg: Königshausen and Neumann, 2001).

62. Johann Georg Zimmermann, *Ueber die Einsamkeit*, 4 vols. (Leipzig: Weidmanns Erben und Reisch, 1784), vol. 1, pp. 176–177n, 272; vol. 2, pp. 48–51, 102–107n.; vol. 3, pp. 402–3; vol. 4, pp. 77–81.

63. Jerome McGann, *The Poetics of Sensibility* (Oxford: Oxford University Press, 1998).

64. Gottfried Hornig, *Die Anfänge der historisch-kritischen Theologie. Johann Salomo Semlers Schriftverständnis und seine Stellung zu Luther* (Göttingen, 1961); and Gottfried Hornig, *Johann Salomo Semler, Studien zu Leben und Werk des Hallenser Aufklärungstheologen* (Tübingen, 1996); Andreas Lüder, *Historie und Dogmatik. Ein Beitrag zur Genese und Entfaltung von Johann Salomo Semlers Verständnis des Alten Testaments* (Berlin: de Gruyter, 1995). These works have reoriented scholarship that was for too long bound up in the categories of Karl Aner, *Theologie der Lessingzeit*. For the best single example of Semler's theological innovation, see his *Abhandlung von freier Untersuchung des Canon*, 4 parts (Halle: Carl Hermann Hemmerde, 1771–75; repr. Gütersloh: Mohn, 1980). One can also gain a glimpse of his method in *A Christian Free Inquiry Concerning the So-Called Revelation of St. John; Published in the Year 1769, at Halle, from the posthumous Manuscript of a Learned Franconian [Georg Ludwig Oeder], with a Preface and Notes by John Solomon Semleri*, trans. A. George Moller (Cheltenham: Rowe and Norman, 1852).

65. Semler published introductions and comments to several German and foreign works on demonology in German translation: Otto Justus Basilius Hesse and Johann Salomo Semler, *Versuch einer biblischen Dämonologie, oder Untersuchung der Lehre der heiligen Schrift vom Teufel und seiner Macht* (Halle: Hemmerde, 1776; new ed. with intro. by Dirk Fleischer, Waltrop: Spenner, 1998); Hugh ["Hugo"] Farmer, *An Essay on the Demoniacs of the New Testament* (London, 1775), trans. as *Versuch über die Dämonischen des Neuen Testamentes. Aus dem Englischen von L. F. A. von Cöln. Nebst einer Vorrede D. Joh. Sal. Semlers* (Bremen and Leipzig, 1776;

repr. with intro. by Dirk Fleischer, Waltrop: Spenner, 2000); Hugh ["Hugo"] Farmer, *Letters to the Rev. Dr. Worthington, in answer to his late publication, intituled "An impartial Enquiry into the Case of the Gospel Demoniacs"* (London, 1778), trans. as *Hugo Farmers Briefe an D. Worthington über die Dämonischen in den Evangelien, mit Zusätzen und einer Vorr., den Begriff von Inspiration zu bessern, von D. Joh. Sal. Semler* (Halle: Gebauer, 1783; repr. with an intro. by Dirk Fleischer, Waltrop: Spenner, 2000); Balthasar Bekker, *De betoverde weereld*, 4 books (Amsterdam: van den Dalen, 1691–93), trans. as *D. B. Bekkers . . . bezauberte Welt. Neu übersetzt . . . Durchgesehen und vermehret von . . . J. S. Semler*, 4 vols. (Leipzig: Johann Moritz Schwager, 1781–82).

66. Hugh Farmer, *An Essay on the Demoniacs of the New Testament* (London, 1775); a second edition was published in London in 1805 by the Unitarian Society for Promoting Christian Knowledge and the Practice of Virtue. By 1805 it had obviously become easier to recognize Farmer as a Unitarian. Unfortunately, by far the best treatment of the general problem of English notions of magic, Owen Davies, *Witchcraft, Magic and Culture: 1736–1951* (Manchester: Manchester University Press, 1999), ignores these scholarly disputes while paying close attention to popular culture. The same is true of his *Cunning-folk: Popular Magic in English History* (London: Hambledon and London, 2002). After the 1730s the English dispute had calmed down a bit, but the basic issues remained unresolved; note these continuing contributions (and this list is far from complete):

(a) Richard Mead, *Medica sacra, sive de morbis insignioribus, qui in Bibliis memorantur, commentarius* (Amsterdam: Mortier, 1749); translated into English as *Medica Sacra; Or, A Commentary On the most remarkable Diseases, Mentioned in the Holy Scriptures: To which are prefixed, Memoirs of the Life and Writings of the Learned Author . . .* , trans. Thomas Stack (London: Brindley, 1755); and translated into German as *Abhandlung von den merkwürdigsten Krankheiten, deren in der heil. Schrift gedacht wird, besonders von den dämonischen Kranken, oder sogenannten Besessenen und Mondsüchtigen* (Leipzig: Böhme, 1777).

(b) Thomas Church, *A Vindication of the Miraculous Powers, which subsisted in the Three First Centuries of the Christian Church. In Answer to Dr. Middleton's Free Enquiry. By which it is Shewn, That we have no sufficient Reason to believe, from the Doctor's Reasonings and Objections, that no such Powers were contained in the Church, after the Days of the Apostles, With a Preface, Containing some Observations on Dr. Mead's Account of the De-*

moniacs, in his New Piece, intituled, Medica Sacra (London: John and James Rivington, 1750).
(c) Nathaniel Lardner, DD, *The Case of the Demoniacs Mentioned in the New Testament: Four Discourses Upon Mark v. 19: with an appendix for farther illustrating the Subject* (London: J. Buckland, 1758).
(d) Arthur Young, *A Dissertation on the Gospel-Daemoniacks* (London: G. Woodfall, 1760).
(e) [Thomas Newton], *Dissertation on the Demoniacs in the Gospels* (London: John and Francis Rivington, 1775).
(f) John Fell, *Daemoniacs. An Enquiry into the Heathen and the Scripture Doctrine of Daemons. In which the Hypotheses of the Rev. Mr. Farmer, and others on this subject, are particularly considered* (London: Charles Dilly, 1779).
(g) Thomas Barker, *The Nature and Circumstances of the Demoniacks in the Gospels, stated and methodized, and considered in the several particulars* (London: B. White, 1783).
(h) John Fell, *The Idolatry of Greece and Rome Distinguished from that of other Heathen Nations: In a Letter to the Reverend Hugh Farmer* (London: Charles Dilly, 1785).

Such a lively and continuing controversy did not go unnoticed in Germany, where England often provided the model of advanced learning and good sense. See Theodor Gerhard Timmermann (M.D. prof. at Rinteln), *Diatribe Antiqvario-Medica de Daemoniacis Evangeliorvm* (Rinteln: Ant. Henr. Boesendahl, 1786), for a good example of the effect of such a steady exchange of views between Germany and England. In his *Diatribe* Timmermann showed a heavy dependence upon English authors (especially Sykes and Mead).

The English also had their own demoniac who underwent a Methodist "exorcism" in 1788, a scandal which prompted a flurry of publications, among them: *A Narrative of the Extraordinary Case of George Lukins, of Yatton, Somersetshire. Who was possessed of EVIL SPIRITS, for near EIGHTEEN YEARS; also an account Of his remarkable Deliverance, in the Vestry Room of Temple Church, in the City of Bristol. Extracted from the Manuscripts of several Persons who attended. To which is prefixed a Letter from the Rev. W. R. W.* (n.p., n.d., but preface is signed "Bristol, June 25, 1788"); Samuel Norman, *Authentic Anecdotes of George Lukins, the Yatton Daemoniac; with a View of the Controversy and a Full Refutation of the Imposture* (Bristol: Sam. Johnson, 1788); Joseph Easterbrook, *An Appeal to the Public respecting George Lukins, (Called the Yatton Demoniac,) containing an account of his*

Affliction and Deliverance; together with a variety of circumstances which tend to exculpate him from the Charge of Imposture (Bristol: T. Mills, 1788).

67. Hugh Farmer agreed that Satan might be a fallen angel and the inspiration of sin, but he also pointed out that "satan" could also mean "adversary" and thus be applied to human beings as well. Hugh Farmer, *An Essay on the Demoniacs of the New Testament* (London: G. Robinson, 1775), pp. 16–20, 77–78, 83, 88; cf. Johann Salomo Semler, ed., *Hugo Farmer's Briefe an D. Worthington über die Dämonnischen in den Evangelien*, new ed. introduced by Dirk Fleischer (Waltrop: Hartmut Spenner, 2000), pp. 11–12.

68. On Wettstein, "a martyr to the early Enlightenment," in the polemical phrase of Hagenbach, see *Allgemeine Deutsche Biographie*, vol. 42 (published 1897), pp. 251–54. Wettstein's great New Testament edition was finally published in 1751–52, two years before his death in 1754. Semler referred often to the work, while arguing with some of Wettstein's conclusions. In 1764 Semler edited a version of Wettstein's *Prolegomena* to the study of the New Testament (which had first appeared in Amsterdam, 1730): Johann Jakob Wettstein, *Prolegomena In Novvm Testamentvm: Notas Adiecit Atqve Appendicem De Vetvstioribvs Latinis Recensionibvs Qvae In Variis Codicibvs Svpersvnt Ioh. Sal. Semler; Cvm Qvibvsdam Charactervm Graecorvm Et Latinorvm In Libris Manvscriptis Exemplis* (Halle: Renger, 1764).

69. The best study of this question is now Dirk Fleischer, in his introduction to the *Versuch einer biblischen Dämonologie, oder Untersuchung der Lehre der heiligen Schrift vom Teufel und seiner Macht* (Halle, 1776), by Otto Justus Basilius Hesse with an introduction and Anhang by Johann Salomo Semler (Waltrop: Hartmut Spenner, 1998), esp. pp. xxxiii–xxxiv, lxxiii–lxxxiii.

70. Aner, *Theologie der Lessingzeit*, pp. 239 ff, citing Ernesti's *Neue Theologische Bibliothek*, vol. 3 (1762), Stück no. 9.

71. The authorship of the *Fragments* was not finally established before 1814 when Johann Albert Hinrich Reimarus donated his father's full manuscript to the city library of Hamburg.

72. Günter Gawlick, "Reimarus und der englische Deismus," in Karlfried Gründer and Karl Heinrich Rengstorf, eds., *Religionskritik und Religiosität in der deutschen Aufklärung*, Wolfenbütteler Studien zur Aufklärung, vol. 11 (Heidelberg: Lambert Schneider, 1989), pp. 43–54; Josef Engert, *Der Deismus in der Religions- und Offenbarungskritik des Hermann Samuel Reimarus* (Vienna, 1916).

73. *Apologie oder Schutzschrift für die vernünftigen Verehrer Gottes*, ed. Gerhard

Alexander, 2 vols. (Frankfurt: Insel, 1972), pt. b (New Testament), lib. 1, cap. 2, 7–8: vol. 2, pp. 54–58; cf. pt. b, lib. 2, cap. 1, 4–5; pt. b, lib. 6, cap. 1, 8.

74. *Apologie*, pt. b, lib. 4, cap. 3, 2: vol. 2, pp. 372–75. Belief in miracles was, in Reimarus's view, always easy to propagate among simple and superstitious people: pt. b, lib. IV, cap. 3, 7: vol. 2, pp. 386–87.

75. "Auf diese Weise ward denn alles bey den damaligen Juden und Christen übernatürlich; sowohl die Krankheiten, als deren Heilung: und der Teufel konnte in den Zeiten, so wie mit dessen Hülffe auch die falschen Propheten, abenfals solche Zeichen und Wunder thun, die von den wahren nicht zu unterscheyden waren, und also auch die auserwehlten Gläubigen leichte hätten verführen mögen." *Apologie* pt. b, lib. 4, cap. 3, 2: vol. 2, p. 374.

76. Reimarus here joined the European debate on miracles and echoes several of the arguments of David Hume: "Denn wenn wir die auctores derselben, gleich, als infallibel und frey von falschen Neigungen, kurtz, als viros theopneustos annehmen wollten; so kämen wir in einen Cirkel hinein; ihre Wunder bezögen sich auf ihre Theopneustie, und ihre Theopneustie wieder auf ihre Wunder, ohne welche kein eintziger Mensch von menschlichen Fehlern und Schwachheiten frey werden kann." *Apologie*, pt. b, lib. 4, cap. 3, 3: vol. 2, p. 376. Even in Reimarus's own day, however, it was not always possible to disprove every single supposed miracle, as the well-attested Jansenist wonders at St. Medard in Paris showed. Neither the French courts nor the Jesuits had been able to disprove these miracles specifically, but that did not prove them all true. If one had to believe all the unrefuted accounts of miracles from heathen antiquity, there would be no end of contradictory nonsense. "Wenn dieses bey so aufgeklärten Zeiten noch so neuerlich geschehen ist: wie viel leichter hat ein Bericht von so entfernten Zeiten und Völkern eine Sache in dergleichen Finsterniss verhüllen können, dass man das wahre Factum, und den Ursprung der Lüge oder des Betruges nicht mehr herausfinden kann? Dies dienet überhaupt zur Antwort auf alle Wunder des A. und N. T. wie auch der Kirchen-Geschichte." *Apologie*, pt. b, lib. 4, cap. 3, 3: vol. 2, p. 377.

77. *Apologie*, pt. b, lib. 4, cap. 3, 5; vol. 2, pp. 380–83.

78. In Wilhelm Abraham Teller's *Wörterbuch des Neuen Testaments*, published in 1772, the author accepted Semler's conclusions about demons but went beyond Semler to deny the very existence of the devil. He emphasized that the Hebrew notion of Satan and the devil described an accuser, but

that supersitious Jews had extended the notion of the devil until he was the cause of all evil. In Teller's view, Jesus came to sweep away the whole doctrine, and as a result right-thinking Christians saw God as the source of all good and mankind as his own enemy. Aner, *Theologie der Lessingzeit*, p. 242. Similarly Otto Justus Basilius Hesse took off from Semler but denied the existence of the devil and even his moral influence in his *Versuch einer biblischen Dämonologie*, intro. by Dirk Fleischer. The University of Tübingen remained for decades a citadel of traditional teaching on the devil and demons. See Johann Gottlieb Faber, *Disquisitio acad.*, *an Adaemonismus cum fide et pietate Christiana conciliari possit*, praeside Jo. Gottlieb Faber, . . . Def. Mart. Schuller (Tübingen: Cotta and Reuss, 1763); Johann Gottfried Faber, *Dissertatio Academica de Daemoniacis adversus Wetstenium*, praeses Ioannes Gottfried Faber . . . Respondens M. Carolus Fried. Renz, Kirchhemio Teccensis (Tübingen: Cott and Reuss, 1763); Tobias Gottfried Hegelmaier, *Beytrag wider den einreissenden Adaemonismus in drey Predigten* (Tübingen, 1778). Hegelmaier was probably also the author of the anonymous *Sollte der Teufel Durch die Englische Schrift: Untersuchung vom Satan betitelt, Von dem Uebersetzer und seinem Notenmacher Herrn Professor Schulz aus Giesen relegirt seyn. Heil ihm!* ("Hadeln im Land Wursten," ca. 1780); I cite the copy in the Bayerische Staatsbibliothek. M. J. G. Meyer, *Historia Diaboli seu commentatio de diaboli, malorumque spirituum exsistentia, statibus, iudicis, consiliis, potestate* (Tübingen: Reuss, 1777; repr. Tübingen: Cotta, 1780). The Hauptpastor Melchior Goeze of Hamburg apparently also insisted on the "necessity of the doctrine of the devil." Aner, *Theologie der Lessingzeit*, p. 245, citing Nicolai's *Allgemeine Deutsche Bibliothek*.

79. Aner, *Theologie der Lessingzeit*, pp. 245–46.
80. I cite the third edition: [Heinrich Martin Gottfried Köster], *Demüthige Bitte um Belehrung an die grossen Männer, welche keinen Teufel glauben* ("Deutschland" [Giessen], 1775), pp. 3–4.
81. Köster, *Demüthige Bitte*, pp. 5–6, 9, 16, 18–19, 25, 30, 44–45, 51.
82. [Köster], *Die neuesten Religionsbegebenheiten mit unpartheyischen Anmerkungen* (Giessen), vol. 1 (1778): "Von den neuen Streitigkeiten über den Teufel," pp. 301–18, at pp. 309–12.
83. *Demüthigste Antwort eines geringen Landgeistlichen auf die demüthige Bitte um Belehrung and die grossen Männer, welche keinen Teufel glauben* ("In Deutschland" [Frankfurt], 1776), pp. 21, 32–35. Johann Carl Bonnet was pastor in Niederkirchen in the Ostertal of the Palatinate-Zweibrücken (1766–1777) and then in Nünschweiler.

84. *Sollte der Teufel wirklich ein Unding seyn? eine Frage und Bitte an die Theologen unserer Zeit* (n.p., 1776), pp. 4, 7–12. I cite the copy in the University of Augsburg Library.
85. [Conrad H. Runge], *Man muss auch dem Teufel nicht zu viel aufbürden. Bey Gelegenheit der Brochüre: Sollte der teufel wirklich ein Unding sein?* etc. (Bremen: Johann Heinrich Cramer, 1776), pp. xvii, xxi–xxii (Vorrede), pp. 19–21; 32–52, 75–86, 95–96. On Runge, see Meusel, *Lexikon der vom Jahr 1750 bis 1800 verstorbenen teutschen Schriftsteller* (Leipzig, 1811), p. 489. For our purposes Runge's ongoing involvement with Lavater is of interest. In 1775 he published *Des Herrn Diakonus Lavater's eigentliche Meinung von den Gaben des heiligen Geistes, oder Kraft des Gebets, geprüft und beantwortet von einem Freunde der Wahrheit* (Bremen, 1775); with a *Fortsetzung* (Bremen, 1777); and *Ende* (Bremen, 1777).
86. [Heinrich Martin Gottfried Köster], *Teufeleyen des achtzehnten Jahrhunderts von dem Verfasser der demüthigen Bitte um Belehrung an die grossen Männer, welche keinen Teufel glauben. Erste rechtmässige Auflage* (Leipzig: Karl Friedrich Schneider, 1778), pp. 21–60.
87. *Emmanuel Swedenborgs demuethiges Danksagungsschreiben ab den grossen Mann, der die Nonexistenz des Teufels demonstrirt hat* [by Heinrich Martin Gottfried Köster] (Frankfurt: Leipzig [Liegnitz: Siegert], 1778); Otto Justus Basilius Hesse, with Johann Salomo Semler, ed., *Versuch einer biblischen Dämonologie*, intro. by Dirk Fleischer; see also [Tobias Gottfried Hegelmaier], *Der Teufel unter den Bauern: der Herr sage, was er wolle von E. S. P* (n.p., 1777); [Heinrich Martin Gottfried Köster], *Die Verbindung des Teufels mit den Gespenstern* ("Teutschland" [Giessen], 1777).
88. *Die neuesten Religionsbegebenheiten*, vol. 1 (1778), pp. 612–14.
89. *Die neuesten Religionsbegebenheiten*, vol. 1 (1778), pp. 622–27.
90. [Johann Adam Brandmayer], *Theorie von den Würkungen des Teufels, und von der Gewalt der Kirche wider denselben* (Frankfurt and Mainz: Varrentrapp, 1777).
91. *Die neuesten Religionsbegebenheiten*, vol. 1 (1778), pp. 629–33 [misprinted as 625–29].
92. Christian Wilhelm Kindleben, *Der Teufeleien des achtzehnten Jahrhunderts letzter Akt. Worinn Emmanuel Schwedenborgs demüthiges Danksagungsschreiben beantwortet, der ganze bisher geführte Streit friedlich beygelegt, und in dem Büchlein über die Nonexistenz des Teufels manches zurückgenommen, ergänzt und berichtiget wird* (Leipzig: Carl Friedrich Schneider, 1779 [the preface was signed Leipzig, 30 December 1778]); the work he was correcting or retracting was his anonymous *Ueber die Non-Existenz des Teufels. Als*

eine Antwort auf die demütige Bitte um Belehrung an die grossen Männer, welche keinen Teufel glauben. "Has fabulas et errores ab imperitis parentibus discimus, et quod est gravius, ipsius studiis et disciplinis elaboramus": *Minucius Felix* (Berlin: Gottlieb August Lange, 1776). I have used the copy in the Stadtbibliothek Feldkirch.
93. Kindleben, *Der Teufeleien des achtzehnten Jahrhunderts letzter Akt*, pp. ix, 11, 19, 20–23, 35–36.
94. [Köster], *Die neuesten Religionsbegebenheiten*, vol. 2 (1779), Stück 7: pp. 557–62.

Chapter 5. Conversation and Ridicule

1. Christoph Deupmann, *"Furor satiricus": Verhandlungen über literarische Aggression im 17. und 18. Jahrhundert*, Studien zur deutschen Literatur, no. 166 (Tübingen: Max Niemeyer, 2002), pp. 227–28, in reference to Karl Wilhelm Ramler. Other figures cited by Deupmann whom time has treated badly are Johann Franz Buddeus, Johann Burkhard Mencke, Martinus Möller, Joseph a Virgine Maria, Christoph Selhamer, Johann Lorenz von Mosheim, Johann Peter Miller, Christian Weise, Georg Philipp Harsdörffer, Johann Heinrich Zedler, Johann Georg Walch, Andreas Rüdiger, Magnus Daniel Omeis, and Albrecht Christian Rotth (pp. 307–25). See also Maria Tronskaja, *Die deutsche Prosasatire der Aufklärung* (Berlin: Rütten and Loening, 1969).
2. For Shaftesbury in Germany, see Christian Friedrich Weiser, *Shaftesbury und das deutsche Geistesleben* (Leipzig and Berlin, 1916).
3. Anthony Ashley Cooper, Third Earl of Shaftesbury, *Characteristics of Men, Manners, Opinions, Times*, ed. Lawrence E. Klein (Cambridge: Cambridge University Press, 1999), "Letter Concerning Enthusiasm," pt. 1, sec. 2, pp. 8, 30. In his essay criticizing Voltaire, Thomas Carlyle claimed, "We have, oftener than once, endeavoured to attach some meaning to that aphorism, vulgarly imputed to Shaftesbury, which, however, we can find nowhere in his works, that 'ridicule is the test of truth'" (*Foreign Review* 6, 1829); see Carlyle's *Critical and Miscellaneous Essays*, in *Collected Works*, 34 vols. (London: Chapman and Hall, 1870–87), vol. 7, pp. 183–84. See R. L. Brett, *The Third Earl of Shaftesbury: A Study in Eighteenth-Century Literary Theory* (London: Hutchinson House, 1951), pp. 165–85; Stanley Grean, *Shaftesbury's Philosophy of Religion and Ethics: A Study in Enthusiasm* (Athens: Ohio University Press, 1967), pp. 120–34; Lawrence E. Klein,

Shaftesbury and the Culture of Politeness: Moral Discourse and Cultural Politics in Early Eighteenth-Century England (Cambridge: Cambridge University Press, 1994).

4. After long being a topic among students of literature, laughter has recently become a center of scholarly attention in philosophy, theology, anthropology, and history. See the bibliography provided by Jan Bremmer and Herman Roodenburg, eds., *A Cultural History of Humour: From Antiquity to the Present Day* (Malden, Mass.: Polity Press, 1997), pp. 247–49. For the literary history, see for example Manfred Pfister, *A History of English Laughter: Laughter from Beowulf to Beckett and Beyond* (Amsterdam: Rodopi, 2002); Robert Favre, *Le rire dans tous ses éclats* (Lyon: Presses universitaires de Lyon, 1995); Anne Richardot, *Le rire des Lumières* (Paris: Honoré Champion, 2002), esp. pp. 83–126.

5. Brett, *The Third Earl of Shaftesbury*, pp. 174–75.

6. See for example Georg Friedrich Meier, *Gedanken von Schertzen* (1744), ed. Klaus Bohnen (Kopenhagen: Text und Kontext, 1977), esp. pp. x, xvi, xxviii. Maier (1718–1777) was a professor at the University of Halle. Bohnen usefully lists works printed between 1706 and 1789 on the topic of laughter and jokes (pp. 145–48).

7. Anne Goldgar, *Impolite Learning: Conduct and Community in the Republic of Letters, 1680–1750* (New Haven: Yale University Press, 1995).

8. Martin Gierl, "'The Triumph of Truth and Innocence': The Rules and Practice of Theological Polemics," in Peter Becker and William Clark, eds., *Little Tools of Knowledge: Historical Essays on Academic and Bureaucratic Practices* (Ann Arbor: University of Michigan Press, 2001), pp. 35–66.

9. James Van Horn Melton, *The Rise of the Public in Enlightenment Europe* (Cambridge: Cambridge University Press, 2001), p. 94, citing Rudolf Jentzsch, *Der deutsch-lateinische Büchermarkt nach den Leipziger Ostermesse-Katalogen von 1740, 1770, und 1800 in seiner Gliederung und Wandlung* (Leipzig, 1912), table 2. Erich Schön, *Der Verlust der Sinnlichkeit oder Die Verwandlung des Lesens: Mentalitätswandel um 1800* (Stuttgart, 1987), p. 44.

10. Jentzsch, *Der deutsch-lateinische Büchermarkt*, p. 333; Engelsing, *Analphabetentum und Lektüre. Zur Sozialgeschichte des Lesens in Deutschland zwischen feudaler und industrieller Gesellschaft* (Stuttgart, 1973), p. 53. As Erich Schön points out, the numbers of titles listed in the Frankfurt and Leipzig fair catalogues do not correspond perfectly to the books actually published, and not even to the books produced by the publishers who listed their books there. Many, perhaps half, of the books advertised in the

seventeenth century were merely proposed and never published. Erich Schön, *Der Verlust der Sinnlichkeit, Oder Die Verwandlungen des Lesers. Mentalitätswandel um 1800* (Stuttgart: Klett-Cotta, 1987), p. 38.

11. Rolf Engelsing, "Die Perioden der Lesergeschichte in der Neuzeit," *Archiv für Geschichte des Buchwesens* 10 (1970), p. 966; Engelsing, *Analphabetentum und Lektüre*; Melton, *The Rise of the Public in Enlightenment Europe*, pp. 89–92.

12. Richard van Dülmen, *Kultur und Alltag in der Frühen Neuzeit*, vol. 3: *Religion, Magie, Aufklärung 16.–18. Jahrhundert* (Munich: Beck, 1994), p. 242, citing Reinhard Wittmann, *Geschichte des deutschen Buchhandels. Ein Überblick* (Munich, 1991), p. 111. See also Albert Ward, *Book Production, Fiction, and the German Reading Public, 1740–1800* (Oxford: Oxford University Press, 1974).

13. Helmuth Kiesel and Paul Münch, *Gesellschaft und Literatur im 18. Jahrhundert: Voraussetzungen und Entstehung des literarischen Markts in Deutschland* (Munich: Beck, 1977); Ernst Fischer, *Der Buchmarkt der Goethezeit. Eine Dokumentation*, 2 vols. (Hildesheim: Gerstenberg, 1986), vol. 2, p. 428.

14. Engelsing, *Analphabetentum und Lektüre*, p. 57; "Über den schlechten Bücherdruck in Deutschland," in *Journal von und für Deutschland* (1785), St. 2, p. 546.

15. "Ueber die Ursachen der jetzigen Vielschreiberey in Deutschland," in *Journal von und für Deutschland* (1790), St. 4, pp. 324–26; reprinted in Fischer, *Der Buchmarkt der Goethezeit*, vol. 2, pp. 99–101. Cf. "Schreiben an einen Freund über die Ursachen der jetzigen Vielschreiberey in Deutschland," in *Journal von und für Deutschland* (1789), St. 2, pp. 139–43; reprinted in Fischer, *Der Buchmarkt der Goethezeit*, vol. 2, pp. 93–98.

16. Van Dülmen, *Kultur und Alltag in der Frühen Neuzeit*, vol. 3, p. 242.

17. Paul Raabe, "Die Zeitschrift als Medium der Aufklärung," in *Bücherlust und Lesefreuden. Beiträge zur Geschichte des Buchwesens im 18. und frühen 19. Jahrhundert* (Stuttgart: J. B. Metzler, 1984), pp. 105–16, 293–94.

18. Van Dülmen, *Kultur und Alltag in der Frühen Neuzeit*, vol. 3, p. 245.

19. Engelsing, *Analphabetentum und Lektüre*, p. 61.

20. Van Dülmen, *Kultur und Alltag in der Frühen Neuzeit*, vol. 3, p. 245, citing Joachim Kirchner, *Die Grundlagen des deutschen Zeitschriftenwesens. Mit einer Gesamtbibliographie der deutschen Zeitschriften bis zum Jahre 1790*, 2 vols. (Leipzig: Hiersemann, 1928–31).

21. Engelsing, *Analphabetentum und Lektüre*, pp. 59–60.

22. Jörn Göres and Hartmut Schmidt, eds., *Lesewuth, Raubdruck und Bücher-*

luxus: Das Buch in der Goethe-Zeit (Düsseldorf: Goethe Museum, 1977); D. von König, "Lesesucht und Lesewut," in Herbert G. Göpfert, ed., *Buch und Leser: Vorträge des. 1. Jahrestreffens des Wolfenbütteler Arbeitskreises für Geschichte des Buchwesens, 13. u. 14. Mai 1976* (Hamburg: Hauswedell, 1977), pp. 89–124; Hermann Bausinger, "Aufklärung und Lesewut," in *Württembergisch Franken* 64 (1980), 178–95; Günter Erning, *Das Lesen und die Lesewut. Beiträge zu Fragen der Lesergeschichte dargestellt am Beispiel der schwäbischen Provinz* (Bad Heilbrunn: Julius Klinkhardt, 1974); Helmut Kreuzer, "Gefährliche Lesesucht: Bemerkungen zu politischer Lektürekritik im ausgehenden 18. Jahrhundert," in *Leser und Lesen im 18. Jahrhundert. Colloquium der Arbeitsstelle Achtzehntes Jahrhundert, Gesamthochschule Wuppertal* (Heidelberg: Carl Winter, 1977), pp. 62–75.
23. Van Dülmen, *Kultur und Alltag in der Frühen Neuzeit*, vol. 3, p. 247.
24. Alberto Martino, *Die deutsche Leihbibliothek. Geschichte einer literarischen Institution, 1756–1914* (Wiesbaden: Otto Harrassowitz, 1990), pp. 14–29.
25. See for example Martin Neubauer, *Indikation and Katalyse. Funktionsanalytische Studien zum Lesen in der deutschen Literatur des ausgehenden 18. Jahrhunderts* (Stuttgart: Hans-Dieter Heinz, 1991).
26. Sophia Rosenfeld, "Citizens of Nowhere in Particular: Cosmopolitanism, Writing, and Political Engagement in Eighteenth-Century Europe," *National Identities* 4 (2002), pp. 25–43.
27. *Frage, ob der Katechismus von der Geisterlehre ein katholischer Kathechismus sey?*
28. *Sendschreiben des HR von . . . an den Herrn HR von . . . Mitglied der Churbayerischen Akademie in München über einige von dem Herrn Gasner, gewessten Pfarrer in Clösterle, während seines Aufenthalts in Ellwangen unternommene Operationen.*
29. *Die Sympathie, ein Universalmittel wider alle Teufeleyen, zum Behufe der neuen Philosophie und der alten Religion.*
30. Francisco dell'Amavero, *Untersuchung, ob es eine Vestigkeit gebe.*
31. *Die aufgedeckten Gassnerischen Wunderkuren.*
32. *Die Aufgedeckten Sterzingerischen Lügen, Keckheit, und Unwissenheit.*
33. *Aufrichtige Erklärung eines Geistlichen gegen einen Seelsorger über die gassnerischen Kuren.*
34. *Ausführliche Beschreibung jener merkwürdigen Begebenheit, die sich mit einer gewissen jungen Klosterfrau Maria Anna Oberhueberin.*
35. *Beyträge zu Gassners Aufenthalt und Weesen in Sulzbach. Allda gedruckt mit Galwitzischen Schriften.*

36. *Betrügende Zauberkunst und träumende Hexerey oder Vertheidigung der akademischen Rede von dem gemeinen Vorurtheile der wirkenden und thätigen Hexerei.*
37. *Beurtheilung der Gassnerischen Wunderkuren, von einem Seelsorger und Eiferer für die Catholische Religion.*
38. *Blocksberger, Glückwünschungsschreibung an . . . A. März, über seine Vertheidigung der Hex- und Zauberey.*
39. *Briefe eines Frauenzimmers an einen ihrer Freunde, die gassnerischen Wunderkuren betreffend.*
40. For the rules of modesty, see Anne Goldgar, *Impolite Learning: Conduct and Community in the Republic of Letters, 1680–1750* (New Haven: Yale University Press, 1995), pp. 158–63.
41. *Demütige Bitte um Belehrung an die grossen Männer, welche keinen Teufel glauben.*
42. *Demüthigste Antwort eines geringen Landgeistlichen Auf die demüthige Bitte u.s.f. Mit Anmerkungen.*
43. *Teufeleyen des achtzehnten Jahrhunderts, von dem Verfasser der demüthigen Bitte* (Leipzig, 1778).
44. *Belehrung des Verfassers der demütigen Bitte an die grossen Männer, welche keinen Teufel glauben.*
45. *Des geringen Landgeistlichen Antwort auf die Belehrung des Verfassers der demüthigen Bitte an die grossen Männer, welche keinen Teufel glauben* (au. = J. Bonnet, Frankfurt a.M., 1777).
46. *Demüthiges Danksagungsschreiben an den grossen Mann, der die Nonexistenz des Teufels demonstrirt hat* (Frankfurt and Leipzig, actually Liegnitz: Siegert, 1778).
47. *Die aufgedeckten Gassnerischen Wunderkuren. Aus authentischen Urkunden beleuchtet und durch Augenzeugen bewiesen* (n.p., 1775), pp. 21–22.
48. "Aber weil Herr Gassner aus Demuth kein Wundermann seyn will: so wird er auch aus Demuth von Titulaturen kein Freund seyn." *Beurtheilung der Gassnerischen Wunderkuren, von einem Seelsorger und Eiferer für die Catholische Religion* (n.p., 1775) (from the "Avertissement" at the end).
49. *Sendschreiben des Wohlehrwürdigen F. Don Placidus Suadens, Theatiner Ordens in Prag, an den Hochwürdigen Herrn Gassner, Bischöflich-Regensburgischen geistlichen Rath und Hof-Caplan* (Prague, 1775), p. 15.
50. *An den unglücklichen Aufdecker der gassnerischen Wunderkuren* (n.p., 1775), p. 8.
51. *Deutsche Chronik*, Bd. 2, St. 37 (8 May 1775), pp. 291–94. Schubart was commenting on Memmingen Pastor Johann G. Schelhorn's anonymous

tract *Von des Wunderthäter Gassners. . . . Unterricht wider den Teufel zu streiten. Auszug aus einem Brief eines Schwaben an einen Niedersächsischen Gelehrten. Dem scharfsinnigen . . . Sterzinger gewiedmet* (Frankfurt, 1775). Schubart noted approvingly the modest tones that seemed appropriate to the truth, and set them in contrast to one of Gassner's own tracts, which was "eine seichte, elende, einfältige, unphilosophische, der Naturlehre und dem Christenthum widersprechende, ja gar gotteslästerliche Schrift" (p. 292).

52. *Unpartheyische Gedanken oder Etwas vor die Aerzte von der Kurart des Tit. Herrn Gassners in Ellwangen, herausgegeben von Doct. Schisel, gedruckt zu Schalbuz, mit Wizgallischen Schriften*, 1775.

53. Friedrich Nicolai's *Allgemeine Deutsche Bibliothek*, vol. 24 (1775), p. 619, noted that "Francisco dell'Amavero's" *Untersuchung, ob es eine Vestigkeit gebe . . . 1774* was either by Sterzinger or by someone who wrote as he did.

54. *Sollte der Teufel wirklich ein Unding seyn? eine Frage und Bitte an die Theologen unserer Zeit* (n.p., 1776), p. 24.

55. [Conrad H. Runge], *Man muss auch dem Teufel nicht zu viel aufbürden. Bey Gelegenheit der Brochüre: Sollte der teufel wirklich ein Unding sein?* (Bremen, bey Johann Heinrich Cramer, 1776), Vorrede.

56. "diese Ungebühr pro praeterito ernstlich zu verweisen, pro futuro aber scharf zu verbieten und das gänzliche Stillschweigen aufzutragen." Cited in Hanauer, "Der Teufelsbanner und wunderheiler Johann Joseph Gassner," p. 437. The *Churbaierische Intelligenzblätter für das Jahr 1775*, Blatt for 1 April 1775 (no. 5 for the year) announced that the elector of Bavaria had proclaimed a "Verordnung" against forbidden and nasty religious discussions, dated 13 February 1775. The Obrigkeiten everywhere are to punish without respect of persons any ridicule of the Catholic faith or personnel, whether in fun or in earnest (p. 53).

57. Friedrich Nicolai, *Beschreibung einer Reise durch Deutschland und die Schweiz im Jahre 1781*, vol. 7 (Berlin and Stettin: Nicolai, 1786), p. 101. I have used the photo-mechanical reproduction edited by Bernhard Fabian and Marie-Luise Spieckermann, *Friedrich Nicolai, Gesammelte Werke* (Hildesheim: Olms, 1994), vol. 18.

58. Hans Krauss, ed., *Deutsche Chronik, herausgegeben von Christian Friedrich Daniel Schubart, Jahrgang 1774–Jahrgang 1777* (Heidelberg: Lambert Schneider, 1975). Krauss provides a most informative Nachwort in vol. 4, Anhang, pp. l–lxviii. See also Michael Myers, *"Für den Bürger." The Role of Christian Schubart's "Deutsche Chronik" in the Development of a Political Public Sphere* (New York: Peter Lang, 1990); and Stadtbibliothek Ulm,

ed., *Christian Friedrich Daniel Schubart bis zu seiner Gefangensetzung 1777. Ausstellung aus Anlass seines 250. Geburtstages* (Ulm: Stadtbibliothek, 1989), pp. 112–27, 137–46.
59. North German journalists tended to side with England when they took notice of the American rebellion at all.
60. On censorship in Augsburg after the Reformation see Allyson Creasman, "Policing the Word: The Control of Print and Public Expression in Early Modern Augsburg, 1520–1648," Ph.D. Dissertation, University of Virginia, 2002; Myers, *"Für den Bürger,"* p. 219; Etienne François, *Die unsichtbare Grenze: Protestanten und Katholiken in Augsburg, 1648 - 1806* (Sigmaringen: Thorbecke, 1991).
61. G. Costa, *Die Rechtseinrichtung der Zensur in der Reichsstadt Augsburg* (Augsburg, 1916), pp. 37–38; Hans-Jörg Künast, *"Getruckt zu Augspurg": Buchdruck und Buchhandel in Augsburg zwischen 1468 und 1555* (Tübingen: Niemeyer, 1997). The dissolution of the Jesuits was so recent that by the spring of 1774 the authorities in Augsburg had not yet decided to publish or implement the papal order (Myers, *"Für den Bürger,"* p. 223).
62. Myers, *"Für den Bürger,"* p. 222.
63. Konrad Gaiser, "Schubart im Exorzistenstreit," *Euphorion. Zeitschrift für Literaturgeschichte*, ed. Josef Nadler, August Sauer, and Georg Stefansky, vol. 29, no. 1 (Stuttgart, 1927), pp. 564–95. Schubart read and distributed as many of the works of the Gassner controversy as he could. On 18 May 1775, for example, he sent his brother Conrad a packet of "Gassnerian writings, pro and contra." Christian Friedrich Daniel Schubart, *Briefe*, ed. Ursula Wertheim and Hans Böhm (Munich: Beck, 1984), p. 147.
64. The circumstances and reasons for his arrest have remained somewhat murky. Myers summarizes the evidence in *"Für den Bürger,"* pp. 248–55, 265–68. It does appear clear enough that Duke Karl Eugen could not stand Schubart's irreverance and insolent attitude toward all princes. For the brutal letter from the duke ordering Schubart's arrest, see Christian Friedrich Daniel Schubart, *Briefe*, ed. Ursula Wertheim and Hans Böhm (Munich: Beck, 1984), pp. 339–40. The outraged duke claimed that imprisoning Schubart would "purify human society of this unworthy and infective member." See also the documents dated 24 January–27 March 1777 reprinted in ibid., pp. 341–48.
65. Christian Friedrich Daniel Schubart, *Leben und Gesinnung (von ihm selbst im Kerker aufgesetzt)*, 2 vols. (Stuttgart: Mäntlern, 1791–93), ed. Ludwig Schubart, pp. 48–49. "Ich beging gleich Anfangs die Unvorsichtigkeit (eine Furie, die mich immer geisselte) den gefallenen Jesuiten-Orden

anzugreifen [. . .] Ein Stein zu meinen Kerkergewölbe! — Gleich darauf mischte ich mich in Gassners Sache; der zweite Stein zu meinen Kerkergewölbe!" Schubart had already connected these two "stones" in his mind while he was in prison. See, for example, the rather hopeless letter he composed to the Emperor Joseph II (to be sent by his mother, impersonating her voice) asking for his release: "To be sure, his fire sometimes overcame him, so that he struck a string too harshly, so that it resounded roughly in many an ear. Gassner's well-known exorcisms and the suspended Jesuit Order that defended them brought him many a hot persecution." Draft of a petition to Emperor Joseph II, 5 October 1783, Schubart, *Briefe*, p. 195.

66. Myers, *"Für den Bürger,"* pp. 117–23, 250–54. Myers points out, for example that Schubart had ridiculed the duke for being the "father of his country in the literal sense," in view of Karl Eugen's huge number of illegitimate children (p. 118).

67. *Antwort auf den aus einem Brief eines Schwaben an einen Niedersächsischen Gelehrten gemachten Auszug von des Hrn. Gassners, Pfarrers in dem Klösterle, Unterricht wieder den Teufel zu streiten.* CUM LICENTIA SUPERIORUM (Kempten: Aloys Galler, 1775), p. 18.

68. *Kurze Verzeichniss einiger Schnapphanen jetziger Zeit bei den Gassnerischen Begebenheiten zu Ellwangen; nebst einer Sammlung deren sowohl für, als wider Herrn Gassner herausgekommenen Schriften,* 1775. Gedruckt in eben diesem Jahr.

69. *Der nach aller Möglichkeit entschuldigte Herr P. Don Ferdinand Sterzinger in Betreff der aufgedeckten gassnerischen Wunderkuren. Von einem Freunde sowohl des Hrn. geistlichen Raths Gassner als des Hrn. P. Sterzingers, in den Druck gegeben* ("Sterzing," 1775), pp. 37–39, 45–50n. Hanauer identifies the author as Alois Merz.

70. *Hannswurst und Schubart. Ein Lustspiel, aufgeführt von dem Verfasser der Sympathie, zum Vergnügen der Schwaben./ Wann hören wir doch einmal auf Schwabenstreiche zu machen? Schubarts Chronik* 74. Stück, vorigen Jahrs, 1775, 65 pages. The title page has a comical printer's device with a man beset by two satyrs, while a third sits and reads. Hanauer lists the "Exjesuit Zeiler von Augsburg" as the author. Michael Myers (*"Für den Bürger,"* p. 228) reports that no copies of this comedy survive, but I have found copies listed in the library catalogues of the University of Tübingen, the University of Augsburg, the Leopold-Sophien-Bibliothek Überlingen, the Evangelisches Stift Tübingen, the Württembergische Landesbibliothek, the Staatliche Bibliothek Regensburg, the Nieder-

sächsische Staats- und Universitätsbibliothek Göttingen, the Universitäts- und Landesbibliothek Sachsen-Anhalt in Halle, the Bayerische Staatsbibliothek in Munich, the Staatsbibliothek zu Berlin, and in the Staats- und Stadtbibliothek of Augsburg.

71. Most libraries with this title attribute it to Zeiler, but some catalogue entries found in the online Karlsruhe Virtueller Katalog (www.ubka.uni-karlsruhe.de/kvk.html) suggest that the author was the well-known Bavarian intellectual Ferdinand Maria Baader.

72. *Die Sympathie, ein Universalmittel wider alle Teufeleyen, zum Behufe der neuen Philosophie und der alten Religion*, 1. u. 2. Aufl. ("Sterzingen in Tyrol," 1775), "Verlegens Niemand und Fragenicht." University of Tübingen, 2nd ed., "vermehrte." A manuscript note in the Munich exemplar attributes this book thus: "Zeiller, Exjesuita, alli Savonarollam Exjesuitam esse credunt." Other librarians and bibliographers have supposed that Gassner himself was the author.

73. In *Allgemeine Deutsche Bibliothek*, vol. 27 (1776), pp. 594–95, Nicolai specifically praised Schubart's amusing writing and unusually good German style, especially considering its origins. He was less impressed with Schubart's poetry, however, and rejected his epigrams as coarse ("gar plump").

74. We now know that in the case of Gassner, his informant was Johann Heinrich Braun, a journalist and former Benedictine monk living in Munich. Michael Schaich, *Staat und Öffentlichkeit im Kurfürstentum Bayern der Spätaufklärung* (Munich: Beck, 2001), pp. 17–18, citing letters from Braun to Nicolai on 30 December 1774, 6 May 1775, 12 October 1775, and 20 January 1776 in the Staatsbibliothek Preussischer Kulturbesitz, Nachlass Nicolai, Bd. 8.

75. See, for example, the thoughtful revision by Paul Raabe of the value of such works in "Johann Georg Meusels Schriftstellerlexikon," in his *Bücherlust und Lesefreuden. Beiträge zur Geschichte des Buchwesens im 18. und frühen 19. Jahrhundert* (Stuttgart: J. B. Metzler, 1984), pp. 117–39, 294–300; and more generally his chapter "Gelehrte Nachschlagewerke im 18. Jahrhundert," pp. 89–105, 291–93.

76. Zapf, *Zauberbibliothek*.

77. Johann Heinrich Beutler and Johann Christoph Guts-Muths, *Allgemeines Sachregister über die wichtigsten deutschen Zeit- und Wochenschriften*, 2 vols. (Leipzig: Weygand, 1790; repr. Hildesheim: Olms, 1976). It was quickly followed by Johann Samuel Ersch, *Repertorium über die allgemeinern [sic] deutschen Journale und andere periodische Sammlungen für Erdbeschreibung, Geschichte, und die damit verwandten Wissenschaften*, 3 vols. (Lemgo:

Meyer, 1790–92), and by Johann Georg Meusel, *Leitfaden zur Geschichte der Gelehrsamkeit* (Leipzig: Fleischer, 1799–1800). The modern successor is the massive index by Klaus Schmidt et al., eds., *Index deutschsprachiger Zeitschriften 1750–1815*, 10 vols. (Hildesheim: Olms, 1997).

78. Beutler and Guts-Muths, *Allgemeines Sachregister*, vol. 1, p. 114, criticizing the *Journal für Freunde der Religion und Litteratur*, vol. 1 (Augsburg: [Bartl,] 1779).
79. Beutler and Guts-Muths, *Allgemeines Sachregister*, vol. 1, pp. 104–5, criticizing the *Antipapistisches Journal, oder der unpartheyische Lutheraner. Herausgegeben von M. Fer. Amb. Fidler*, vol. 1 (Leipzig, 1770).
80. One can follow other contours of the discussion through the work of the Göttinger Arbeitsstelle, Klaus Schmidt et al., eds., *Index deutschsprachiger Zeitschriften 1750–1815* (Hildesheim: Olms, 1997).
81. Goldgar, *Impolite Learning*, pp. 205, 236, 240, 250.
82. F. H. Buckley, *The Morality of Laughter* (Ann Arbor: University of Michigan, 2003).
83. Quentin Skinner explains the classical and Renaissance tradition of using laughter as a means of moving audiences when mere reason might adduce good reasons on both sides of a controverted issue; see "Why Does Laughter Matter to Philosophy," *The Passmore Lecture*, Australian National University (Canberra), December 2000, pp. 4–13. Available at http://socpol.anu.edu.au/pdf-files/passmorelect2000.pdf.
84. Indeed, the dangers of laughter as impolite or uncivil led to early modern attacks upon laughter as boorish, gross, and disagreeable. By 1748 Lord Chesterfield could admonish his son to avoid even giggles as "low and unbecoming." There was "nothing so illiberal and so ill bred, as audible laughter." Quoted in Skinner, "Why Does Laughter Matter to Philosophy?" p. 17. See also Michael A. Screech, *Laughter at the Foot of the Cross* (New York: Penguin, 1997); Daniel Ménager, *La renaissance et le rire* (Paris: Presses universitaires de France, 1995); and Keith Thomas, "The Place of Laughter in Tudor and Stuart England," *Times Literary Supplement*, 21 January 1977, pp. 77–81.
85. Buckley, *Morality of Laughter*, pp. 186–90.
86. Friedrich Nicolai, *Beschreibung einer Reise*, vol. 7, Anhang, p. 130. Nicolai argued that Protestants grew up with fewer prejudices.
87. Nicolai, *Beschreibung einer Reise*, vol. 7, Anhang, p. 131.
88. *Oeffentliche Anzeige und Beschwerde an das Publicum gegen den Frankfurter Journalisten* (Mannheim, 1775). The Frankfurter journalist was attacked as a denier of religion, a fool, an insulter of the human race. Really, the

anonymous complaint continued, we expected better from Mannheim in the year 1775.
89. *Ehrenrettung des S. T. wohlehrwürdigen Herrn Johann Joseph Gassners und seiner in Teutschland soviel Aufsehens machenden Teufelsbeschwörungen und geistlichen Kuren zu Ellwangen wider die unverschämte Lästerungen eines ehrlosen Zeitungsschreibers, und seiner Helfershelfer.* / *[small print:] Diese aber lästern alles, was sie nicht verstehen. Im Briefe Judas, Vers 10* (n.p., 1775).
90. [Joseph Edler von Sartori], *Der entlarvte Lügner, Durch Anmerkungen Ueber Prüfende Anmerkungen zu dem Sendschreiben des H. Hr. von —— an den H. Hr—— Mitglied der Churbayerischen Akademie in München; über einige von dem Herrn Gassner, Pfarrer in Klösterle, während seines Aufenthalts in Ellwangen unternommene Operationen. Dargestellt von einem Wahrheitsfreund und Augenzeugen*, 1775.
91. [Sartori], *Der entlarvte Lügner*, pp. 43–45.
92. Jürgen Habermas, *The Structural Transformation of the Public Sphere: An Inquiry into a Category of Bourgeois Society*, trans. Thomas Burger and Frederick Lawrence (Cambridge: MIT Press, 1989). See also the able discussion and interpretation of James Van Horn Melton, *The Rise of the Public in Enlightenment Europe* (Cambridge: Cambridge University Press, 2001).
93. Friedrich Nicolai noticed the rage of Catholic imperial officials when Pastor Melchior Goeze of Hamburg undertook to castigate Catholic prayer as useless; *Beschreibung einer Reise*, vol. 7, pp. 115–17.
94. Cass R. Sunstein, *Why Societies Need Dissent* (Cambridge: Harvard University Press, 2003), p. 212. I owe this reference to Sophie Rosenfeld.
95. Carlyle, "Voltaire," *Collected Works*, 34 vols. (London: Chapman and Hall, 1870–87), vol. 7, p. 184.

Epilogue

1. Friedrich Nicolai, *Beschreibung einer Reise durch Deutschland und die Schweiz im Jahre 1781*, vol. 5 (Berlin and Stettin: Friedrich Nicolai, 1785), Beylag no. 13.4a, pp. 19–22, at p. 22. I have used the reprint edited by Bernhard Fabian and Marie-Luise Spieckermann, *Gesammelte Werke* (Hildesheim: Olms, 1994), in which the *Beschreibung* is vols. 15–20, here vol. 17. This blessing could be translated roughly as follows: "In order to discern if someone is tormented by unclean spirits. In the name of the Father, and the Son, & the Holy † Ghost. Amen. . . . [here follow twenty-one names for and attributes of the Lord]. Jesus Christ conquers † Christ

rules † Christ commands † If the Devil has bound and attacked you, [Name], in his performance, through his works, Christ the Son of the living God, who came from heaven and was made flesh in the womb of the Blessed Virgin Mary, the cause of human salvation, will free you through His mercy from all unclean spirits. May He cast the devil and every evil spirit out into the depths of hell and into the abyss. Behold the Cross of the Lord and flee to another place. The Lion of the tribe of Judah, the root of David, has conquered. Hallelujah, Hallelujah, Hallelujah."

2. Nicolai, *Beschreibung einer Reise*, vol. 5, p. 65, and Beylage 13.4b., pp. 23–25; Beylage 13.13, pp. 57–59.
3. Nicolai, *Beschreibung einer Reise*, vol. 6, Beylage 1.3, pp. 63–75. For the identification of "Grinaigl" as a green-eyed straw fly, I am much indebted to Professor Heide Dienst of Vienna. See also Grimm, *Deutsches Wörterbuch*, vol. 9 (1935), col. 665.
4. Nicolai, *Beschreibung einer Reise*, vol. 6, pp. 733–34n.
5. *Anmerkungen über den Teufel zu Seefeld in Tirol verfasst von einem geistlichen Ganser* [Gassner] *der Ex-Klarisserinnen* (auf Unkosten der St. Monicabruderschaft in Seefeld, 1783), pp. 5, 32–33, 48, 77–79.
6. Willibald Gross [pseud.], *Sonder- und wunderbare, doch wahre Geschichte, wie der Teufel ††† sich einmal in der leiblichen Gestalt eines Esels auf dem Rathhause zu B——r [= Bottwar?] im W—b—g—schen* [Württembergischen] *sehen liess; Zu Frommen und Besserung der izigen, höchst unglaubigen Welt, auch zum Beweiss des, in unsern Tagen so sehr geläugneten Daseyns eines Teufels ††† in Reimen, nach der bekannten Melodie: Ein Ritter, wie die Chronik sagt*, ed. Paul Weisshammer [pseud.] (Seefeld, 1786).
7. Joseph Weber, *Ungrund des Hexen- und Gespenster-glaubens, in ökonomischen Lehrstunden dargestellt* (Dillingen: Bernhard Kälin, 1787), pp. v–vii.
8. [Franz Joseph Schmid], *Ueber die Hexenreformation des Herrn Professor Weber in Dillingen* (Augsburg, 1787), pp. 3, 9, 16–19. He explicitly invoked the memory of Gassner in his defense and contemptuously rejected the laughter of the Enlightened (p. 48n). Weber replied with *Die Nichtigkeit der Zauberey, eine Vorlesung*, ed. Hübner (Salzburg, 1787); and Schmid returned fire with a second expanded edition of his *Ueber die Hexenreformation*, with a *Nachschrift des katholischen Weltmannes zur zwoten Auflage seiner Piece. über die Hexenreformation des Herrn Professor Weber zu Dilingen* (Augsburg, 1787), and with *Des katholischen Weltmanns Erörterung der Professor Weberschen Erklärung ans Publikum, die Hexenreformation betreffend* (Augsburg, 1788), along with a more massive declaration, *Und der Satz: Teuflische Magie existirt, bestehet noch: In einer Antwort des*

katholischen Weltmannes auf die von einem Herrn Landpfarrer herausgegebene Apologie der ProfessorWeberschen Hexenreformation (Augsburg: Styx, 1791). By then the self-proclaimedly Enlightened had moved on beyond the specific Scriptural and demonological issues surrounding Gassner and were ducking charges that they had provoked the French Revolution.

9. Manfred Eder, "Teufelsglaube, 'Besessenheit' und Exorzismus in Deggendorf, 1785–1791," *Beiträge zur Geschichte des Bistums Regensburg* 26 (1992), pp. 295–321; Nils Freytag, "Exorzismus und Wunderglaube im späten 18. Jahrhundert. Reaktionen auf die Teufelsbanner und Wunderheiler J. J. Gassner und A. Knoerzer," in Edwin Dillmann, ed., *Regionales Prisma der Vergangenheit* (St. Ingbert: Röhrig Universitätsverlag, 1996), pp. 89–105; Dominik Burkard, "Die Prophetin von Weissenau und die 'andere Revolution.' Milieus und Mentalitäten im katholischen Oberland um 1848. Zugleich ein Beitrag zur Klärung des Verhältnisses von Religion und Revolution," *Rottenburger Jahrbuch für Kirchengeschichte* 20 (2001), pp. 211–37, for the case of a woman in 1848 from whom Father Patriz Seibold cast out demons publicly.

10. Nils Freytag, "Aberglauben, Krankheit und das Böse. Exorzismus und Teufelsglaube im 18. und 19. Jahrhundert," *Rheinisch-Westfälische Zeitschrift für Volkskunde* 44 (1999), pp. 67–93; Freytag, *Aberglauben im 19. Jahrhundert. Preussen und seine Rheinprovinz zwischen Tradition und Moderne, 1815–1918* (Berlin: Duncker and Humblot, 2003); Freytag, "Wunderglauben und Aberglauben. Wallfahrten und Prozessionen im Bistum Trier im 18. und 19. Jahrhundert," in Martin Persch, Michael Embach, and Peter Dohms, eds., *500 Jahre Wallfahrtskirche Klausen* (Mainz: Gesellschaft für mittelrheinische Kirchengeschichte, 2003), pp. 261–82.

11. Hans Grassl, *Aufbruch zur Romantik. Bayerns Beitrag zur deutschen Geistesgeschichte, 1765–1785* (Munich: Beck, 1968).

12. Grassl, *Aufbruch*, p. 424.

13. Otto-Joachim Grüsser, *Justinus Kerner, 1786–1862: Arzt, Poet, Geisterseher: nebst Anmerkungen zum Uhland-Kerner-Kreis und zur Medizin- und Geistesgeschichte im Zeitalter der Romantik* (Berlin: Springer, 1987), pp. 201–44; Uwe Henrik Peters, *Studies in German Romantic Psychiatry: Justinus Kerner as a Psychiatric Practitioner, E. T. A. Hoffmann as a Psychiatric Theorist* (London: Institute of Germanic Studies, University of London, 1990).

14. Kerner published often on these themes. See his *Die Seherin von Prevorst* (1829; translated into English as *The Seeress of Prevorst*, 1845); *Geschichten Besessener neuerer Zeit. Beobachtungen aus dem Gebiete kakodämonisch-*

magnetischer Erscheinungen (1834); *Nachricht von dem Vorkommen des Besessenseyns, eines dämonisch-magnetischen Leidens und seiner schon im Altertum bakannten Heilung durch magisch-magnetisches Einwirken, in einem Sendschreiben an den Herrn Obermedizinalrath Dr. Schelling in Stuttgart* (1836); *Die somnambülen Tische: Zur Geschichte und Erklärung dieser Erscheinung* (1853); and his editorial work on *Blätter aus Prevorst*, 12 vols. (1831–39); *Magikon: Archiv für Beobachtungen aus dem Gebiete der Geisterkunde und des magnetischen und magischen Lebens*, 5 vols. (1840–53); and *Franz Anton Mesmer aus Schwaben* (1856).

15. Grassl, *Aufbruch*, pp. 425–29.
16. Hartmut Lehmann, "Neupietismus und Säkularisierung: Beobachtungen zum sozialen Umfeld und politischen Hintergrund von Erweckungsbewegung und Gemeinschaftsbewegung," *Pietismus und Neuzeit. Ein Jahrbuch zur Geschichte des neueren Protestantismus*, vol. 15 (Göttingen: Vandenhoek and Ruprecht, 1989), pp. 40–58; Dieter Lange, *Eine Bewegung bricht sich Bahn. Die deutschen Gemeinschaften im ausgehenden 19. und beginnenden 20. Jahrhundert und ihre Stellung zu Kirche, Theologie und Pfingstbewegung* (Giessen: Brunnen, 1979); Birgit Meyer, *Translating the Devil: Religion and Modernity among the Ewe in Ghana* (Trenton, N.J.: Africa World Press, 1999), pp. 44–53.
17. Johann Christoph Blumhardt, *Die Krankheitsgeschichte der Gottliebin Dittus* (1850; ed. Gerhard Schäfer, Göttingen: Vandenhoek and Ruprecht, 1978), p. 58, as quoted in Meyer, *Translating the Devil*, p. 48; see also Michael Schulz, *Johann Christoph Blumhardt: Leben-Theologie-Verkündigung* (Göttingen: Vandenhoek and Ruprecht, 1984); Frank D. Macchia, *Spirituality and Social Liberation: The Message of the Blumharts in the Light of Wuerttemberg Pietism* (Metuchen, N.J.: Scarecrow Press, 1993).
18. Henri Brunschwig, *Enlightenment and Romanticism in Eighteenth-Century Prussia*, trans. Frank Jellinek (Chicago: University of Chicago Press, 1974). This spiritualist enthusiasm is the current research project of Yvonne Wübben ("Geisterseherei in Berlin in der Regierungszeit Friedrich Wilhelm II.") as part of AG [Arbeitsgruppe] "Berliner Klassik. Eine Grossstadtkultur um 1800," a project of the Berlin-Brandenburgische Akademie der Wissenschaften; see her "Von 'Geistersehern und Proselyten.' Zum politischen Kontext einer Kontroverse in der Berlinischen Monatsschrift, 1783–1788," in Ursula Goldenbaum and Alexander Kosenina, eds., *Berliner Aufklärung. Kulturwissenschaftliche Studien*, vol. 2 (Hannover-Latzen: Wehrhahn, 2003), pp. 189–220.
19. Klaus Epstein, *The Genesis of German Conservatism* (Princeton: Princeton

University Press, 1966), pp. 87–104; Grassl, *Aufbruch zur Romantik*, pp. 173–292.
20. Grassl, *Aufbruch zur Romantik*, p. 265; Fritz Valjavec, *Die Entstehung der politischen Strömungen in Deutschland* (Munich: Oldenbourg, 1951), p. 292.
21. Grassl, *Aufbruch zur Romantik*, pp. 432–40; Epstein, *Genesis*, pp. 674–75; Behringer, *Hexenverfolgung in Bayern: Volksmagie, Glaubenseifer und Staatsräson in der frühen Neuzeit* (Munich: Oldenbourg, 1987), p. 396. Darrin M. McMahon goes further, arguing that the Counter-Enlightenment itself embodied elements of modernity; see *Enemies of the Enlightenment: The French Counter-Enlightenment and the Making of Modernity* (Oxford: Oxford University Press, 2001), pp. 197–203.
22. Grassl, *Aufbruch zur Romantik*, p. 287; Epstein, *Genesis*, p. 607.
23. Burkhard Peter, "Hypnotische Selbstkontrolle: Die wirksame Psychotherapie des Teufelsbanners Johann Joseph Gassner um 1775," *Hypnose und Kognition* 17 (2000), pp. 19–34.

INDEX

abbeys, exempt, 159 n. 10
Aepinus, Franz Ulrich Theodosius, 19
Alberti, Alessandro, a Rocha, 56
Alto Adige, 144
Altona, 88
Amberg, 15
Anhalt-Dessau, 88
animal magnetism, 2, 59, 146
  revival of, 155 n. 18
anonymity, 125–27
Anterior Austria (Vorderösterreich), 39, 45, 49
Aquinas, Thomas, 29
Aretin, Karl Otmar von, 40
Augsburg, 28, 98–100, 123, 131–33, 135, 145, 147, 186 n. 35
Augsburg, bishop of, 1, 38, 43–44, 49
  see also Klemens Wenzeslaus, duke of Saxony
Austria, 5, 33, 143–44
  see also Anterior Austria; Joseph II, Holy Roman Emperor; Maria Theresa, empress of Austria; Vienna; Vorarlberg

Baader, Ferdinand Maria, 146
Bamberg, 61
Bamberg, bishop of, 37–38, 57
Bamberg, University of, 94
Baruffaldi, Girolamo, 56
Basel, 107

Basel, Council of (1438), 40
Bavaria, electorate of, 39, 43–44, 49
  Romanticism and, 146
  see also Karl Theodor, elector of Bavaria; Maximilian III Joseph, elector of Bavaria
Bavarian Academy of Sciences, 15, 18–19, 69, 94–95
Bavarian "witchcraft war" (1760s), 6–7, 15, 73, 94–95, 100, 183 n. 24
Bayle, Pierre, 16
Beales, Derek, 42
Becker, Rudolf Zacharias, 124
Behringer, Wolfgang, 6, 95
Bekker, Balthasar, 107, 110, 114
Benedictine Order, 9
Berlin, 88, 123, 133, 143, 147
Beutler, Johann Heinrich, 136–37
Biblical criticism, 92–94
  Catholic, 94–98, 100–102
  deist, 108–11
  neologist, 105–8
  Protestant Orthodox, 111–12
bibliography, history of, 136–38
bishoprics, effect of Reformation on, 159 n. 7
bishops, Gassner's support among, 163 n. 35
Bludenz, 61
Boie, Heinrich Christian, 123
Bonnet, Johann Carl, 113

INDEX

Blumhardt, Johann Christoph, 147
book publishing, history, 120–24, 197 n. 10, 202 n. 60
Bourgeois, Abbot, 71–72
Bourges, Pragmatic Sanction of (1438), 40
Braunschweig, duchy of, 33
Braz, 12
Bremen, 130
Brixen (Bressanone), bishop of, 38
Brognolo, Candidus, 56, 96, 166 n. 57
Buckley, F. H., 138, 141
Butler, Samuel, 133

Capuchins, 43
Carlyle, Thomas, 141
Catholic ecclesiastical administration, 34–42
 maps of, 34–37
Catholic ecclesiastical principalities, 34, 36–37
charismatic healing, 7, 105
Chur, bishop of, 14, 38, 45, 48, 57
Cilia, Gelasius de, 56, 166 n. 57
circumsession, 13–14, 50, 57, 62, 67–68, 71–72, 81, 96–97, 161 n. 21
Clement XIV, pope, 53, 132
Cohen, Ed, 84
Coletus, Stephen, 96
Colloredo, Hieronymus Joseph Franz de Paula von, archbishop of Salzburg, 42, 50, 55–57
Cologne, archbishops of, 37–38
Constance, bishop of, 38–39
 see also Rodt, Franz Konrad von
convulsions, 152 n. 4, 172 n. 29

counter-Enlightenment, 2, 4, 19, 31, 83–85, 111–17, 145–48
Csordas, Thomas, 84–85

daimōn, meaning of, 90–92, 107
Dalaas, 12
debate, rules for, 119–20, 125–30, 141–42
deists, 108–11
Delrio, Martin, S. J., 99
demonic possession
 Biblical examples of, 89, 92–93, 99, 106–16
 canonical signs of, 89
 celebrated cases of, 175 n. 2
 English debate on, 106–7
 fraud and, 97
 natural explanations of, 50, 55, 90, 93, 106–12
 proofs of, 85
 symptoms of, 1, 4, 11, 13–14, 54–55, 61–64, 70–81
 types of, 96, 166–67 n. 57
demonology, English debate on, 91–92, 179–80 n. 16, 190–92 n. 66
demons
 disputes about, 24–25, 31
 evil and, 17
 image of, 20–21
 as tool for thought, 3, 12–13, 24
demythologizing, 90, 106–11
 see also Biblical criticism; demonic possession, natural explanations of; neologists
Dessau, 88
devil
 development of idea of, 114

INDEX

as distinct from demon, 107
doctrine of, 193 n. 78
Gassner's idea of, 13, 20, 61–65
see also *daimōn;* demonic possession; demons
Diderot, Denis, 30
Dillingen, University of, 145
dismissals, of those deemed naturally ill, 75–81
Dorothea Francisca, countess of Upper Palatinate-Sulzbach, 70, 78
Dresden, 88
Durich, Fortunat, O. F. M. de Paula, 95

Ecclesiatical states of Holy Roman Empire, 33–39, 51
Eckartshausen, Karl von, 146
Eichstätt, bishopric of, 41, 49
Einbildung, 105, 170 n. 16
Elbigenalp, 144
Ellenberger, Henri, 6, 19
Ellwangen, 1–2, 27, 43–44, 73
Ellwangen, princely provostry of, 14, 38, 41, 49, 53
empirical evidence, doubts concerning, 89
English demonology, 106–7
Enlightenment, 4–8
  Catholic, 23, 30–31, 39–44, 69, 95–96
  German, 22–24, 104–11, 123,
  impact of, 5, 9, 14, 64–65
enthusiasm, 7
epilepsy, 1, 62–64, 74
Erdt, Baroness von, 44, 73
Ernesti, Johann August, 108, 187–88 n. 52

Eschenmeyer, Adam Carl August von, 146
evil, 16–17, 142
exorcism
  canonical, 2
  expulsive (*expulsivus*), 67
  as fraud, 132–33
  Gassner's use of, 1–3, 12, 21, 59
  Jesus' use of, 3, 28, 76–77
  light (*lenitivus*), 67
  manuals of, 166 n. 57, 167 n. 59
  physical explanations of, 67–70
  Protestant use of, 88
  success of, 4
  test (*exorcismus probativus*), 12, 50, 61, 67–68, 99
  see also demonic possession; Roman Ritual
experience, history of, 12–13, 24–27, 30–31, 142, 151 n. 3
eyewitness reports, 3, 72–75, 77, 89, 98, 100

Farmer, Hugh, 106–7, 114–15
Febronius, Justinus (Johann Nikolaus von Hontheim), 39–42, 57
forerunners of, 160 n. 13
Feldkirch, 61
Forster, Marc, 43
Foucault, Michel, 25
Frankfurt a. M., 140
Franklin, Benjamin, 20
fraud, possession as, 65
Frederick William II, king of Prussia, 147
Freedman, Jeffrey, 3
Frei, Hans, 93
Freiburg, Habsburg administration in, 164 n. 38

Freiburg i. Br., 49
Freising, bishop of, 38, 41, 49
Fugger, Anton Ignaz von, bishop of Regensburg, 14–15, 32, 45, 47–49

Galvani, Luigi, 19
Garve, Christian, 139
Gassner, Johann Joseph
   appearance of, 59–60
   controversy over, 22, 31, 73–75, 120–22, 124–26, 130–37, 139, 141
   exile, 56
   exorcisms of, compared to those of gospels, 99
   exorcisms of, exploited by others, 52
   exorcizing in Ellwangen, 1–2, 73–75, 81–82
   life of, 11–16, 45–51
   imitators of, 165 n. 41
   method of, 66–82
   political objections to, 52
   Protestant reactions to, 102–16
   Regensburg healings of, 75–78
   sources of ideas of, 184 n. 30
   Sulzbach healings of, 78–81
   writings of, 22, 73
Gerbert, Martin, prince abbot of St. Blasien, 51
Gierl, Martin, 120
Goethe, Johann Wolfgang, 5, 135, 147
Goldgar, Anne, 120, 138
Grassl, Hans, 145–46
Gravamina of the German nation, 40
Grein, 144

Gruber, Johann Nepomuk, S. J., 144
Guillotin, Joseph Ignace, 20
Guts-Muths, Johann Christoph, 136–37

Habermas, Jürgen, 141
Haen, Anton de, 45–46
Hahn, Philipp Matthäus, 102
Halle, 15, 88
Hamburg, 88
Hanauer, Joseph, 51, 125
Hanover, 104
Harris, Ruth, 83
Hauffe, Frederike, 146
healing, 59–86
   exorcism and, 104–5
   explanations of, 83–86
   metaphors and, 84–85
Heiligenberg, counts of, 39
Hell, Maximilian, S. J., 17–18
Hersche, Peter, 40
Hesse, Otto Justus Basilius, 115
historical understanding, 90, 93
   see also neologists
Hohenlohe, 81–82
Hohenlohe-Schillingsfürst, Karl Albert von, count of, 48, 51, 82, 163 n. 37
Holy Roman Empire, 15, 32–41, 45, 51–52
   ecclesiastical components of, 33–39
Hontheim, Nikolaus von, *see* Febronius, Justinus
Horace, 118–19
Hume, David, 30, 193 n. 76
humility, as posture, 127–30
hysteria, 7, 65

INDEX

illness, mental, 50
  natural and unnatural, 49, 71–72
Illuminati, 146, 148
imagination, body and, 105
  power of, 26, 74
  see also *Einbildung*
Ingolstadt, University of, 20, 44, 162 n. 26
Innsbruck, 12

James, William, 65
Jansenists, 7, 40, 42, 46, 50, 148, 162 n. 30, 193 n. 76
Jesuits (Society of Jesus), 42–43, 96, 100, 132
  former members of, 1, 15, 28, 46, 98–100, 134, 146–48
  suppression of, 5, 15, 53
Jesus, beliefs of, 143
Jesus, power of name of, 70, 72
Jews, 90–92, 95, 107, 109–13
Joseph II, Holy Roman Emperor, 15, 17, 30, 32, 41–43, 46–49, 133, 139–40
journalism, Gassner and, 131–33
journals, rise of, 122–23
Jung-Stilling, Johann Heinrich, 146

Kant, Immanuel, 147
Karl Eugen, duke of Württemberg, 32, 134, 135
Karl Theodor, elector of Bavaria, 41, 148
Kaunitz, Wenzel Anton von, 45
Kautz, C. F., 73
Kemberg, 88
Kempten, imperial abbey of, 11, 41

Kerner, Justinus, 146
Kindleben, Christian Wilhelm, 116
Kircher, Athanasius, S. J., 18
Kleinman, Arthur, 85
Klemens Wenzeslaus, duke of Saxony, archbishop of Trier and bishop of Augsburg, 44
Klösterle, 12, 14, 27, 49, 61
Kollmann, Jacob Anton, 73
Korn, Christoph Heinrich, 11
Köster, Heinrich Martin Gottfried, 111–16, 128

Langenegg, 11, 23
language, persuasion and, 83
Lardner, Nathaniel, 110
Latin, use of, 1, 12, 67–68
laughter
  function of, 137–42
  objections to, 205 n. 84
  tradition of, 205 n. 83
Lavater, Johann Kaspar, 5, 15, 23, 31, 103–4, 116, 118, 135, 146
  correspondence with Semler, 87, 105–6
  religious evolution of, 156 n. 21
Lavoisier, Antoine de, 20
Leipzig, 88
Lessing, Gotthold Ephraim, 6, 108–9
Leuthner, Johann Nepomuk Anton, 44
Linz, bishopric of, 41
Liskow, Christian Ludwig, 133
literacy, German, 120
Lohmann, Anna Elisabeth, 88–89, 91, 106

Loschert, Oswald, abbot of Oberzell, 56–57, 101–2
Lourdes, 83
Loyola, Ignatius of, 100
Ludwig Eugen, duke of Württemberg, 32, 51, 82
Lutherans, 23, 68, 87, 89, 100, 102, 111, 120, 137

McGann, Jerome, 105
Maffei, Scipione, 96
magnetism, 19–20, 68, 74, 100
Mainz, archbishop of, 38
maleficium (harmful magic), 98, 101
Maria Bernardina, countess (Truchsess von Wolfegg and Friedberg), 14, 41
Maria Renata Singer, 8–9, 56, 101
Maria Theresa, empress of Austria, 5, 42, 45, 47–49, 53–56, 163 n. 32
Maximilian III Joseph, elector of Bavaria, 17–18, 32, 44, 73, 130
Mayer, Andreas Ulrich ("Blocksberger"), 73
Mede, Joseph, 90
Mejer, Luise, 124
melancholy, cure of, 173 n. 31
Memmingen, 11
Menghi, Girolamo, 56, 96
mental illness, Gassner's inability to heal, 75
Merz (März), Alois, S. J., 74–75, 81, 98–100, 132, 186 n. 36
Mesmer, Franz Anton, 2, 6, 17–20, 23, 53, 59, 105, 146
mesmerism, 146, 148

Middleton, Conyers, 110
Migazzi, Christoph Anton, cardinal archbishop of Vienna, 46–48
miracles, 28–31, 46–47, 49–50, 83–86, 90, 99, 105–11
 debate on, 181 n. 18, 193 n. 76
 Jesus', 90–93, 96–99, 106, 109–10
Montafon, 61
Montgelas, Maximilian von, count, 148
Mozart, Wolfgang Amadeus, 18
Müller, Gottlieb, 88–89
Munich, 2, 41, 44, 61, 73
Muratori, Ludovico Antonio, 26, 54, 96

Neiman, Susan, 16–17
neologists, 3, 87, 93, 100, 106–8, 117
Neuenstein, 61
Nicolai, Friedrich, 113, 123, 131, 135–37, 139–40, 143–44
 informants of, 204 n. 74
Niederkirchen, 113
nobility, as supporters of Gassner, 14–15, 48, 70, 81–82
nunciatures, papal, 39–41

Oberzell, 56, 101
Oetinger, Freidrich Christoph, 102–3
Offenburg, 45
Old Testament, exorcism and, 177 n. 7
Osterwald, Peter von, 18
Öttingen-Wallerstein, princes of, 53

Palatinate, electorate of, 113
Passau, bishop of, 38
Pentecostalism, 147
persuasion, 66–67, 72, 86
physicians, consultation of, 63
Pietism, 102–4, 146–47
Pitzer, Volker, 40
Pius VI, pope, 16, 32, 41, 51, 57, 81
placebo response, 3, 84–86, 174 n. 37, 175 n. 44
Poland, 5, 33
Pondorf, 16
possession, *see* demonic possession
postmodernism, 25
praecepta (lessons or admonitions), 13, 57, 67
Prague, 12, 128
Prague, archbishop of, 16, 32, 38, 55
Premonstratensians, 8–9
Prichovic, Antonín Petr, archbishop of Prague, 42, 49–50, 56
Protestants, pilgrims to Gassner, 23, 55–56, 68, 99
Prussia, 5, 33, 144
pseudonyms, *see* anonymity
psychotherapy, exorcism and, 169 n. 9
public, appeals to, 140
public sphere, history of, 8, 140–42, 150–51 n. 8

Rabner, Gottlieb Wilhelm, 133
reading, history of, 124
Reform, Catholic, 40–43, 46–47, 50, 95–96
  see also Enlightenment, Catholic

Regensburg, 15, 18, 27, 44–45
  reports of Gassner's cures in, 75–78
Regensburg, bishop of, 37, 41, 49, 57
  see also Fugger, Anton Ignaz von
Reichle, Anton, 56
Reichskirche (imperial church), 37–42
  compared with Spanish church, 158 n. 5
Reimarus, Hermann Samuel, 6, 108–11
revival, religious, 2, 7, 31, 48, 51
ridicule, 118–42
Ried, Freiherr von, 45
Rochow, Eberhard von, 123
Rodt, Franz Konrad von, cardinal prince bishop of Constance, 32, 39, 41, 43, 49, 66
Roman Ritual (Rituale Romanum)
  of 1614, 23–24, 29, 49–50, 57, 59, 83, 89, 96–97, 168 n. 1
Romanticism, 145–46
Rosenfeld, Sophie, 125
Rousseau, Jean-Jacques, 16, 133
Royal Academy of Sciences, French, 20
Runge, Conrad H., 114, 130

Sailer, Johann Michael, S. J., 146
St. Anthony, 105
St. John, knights of, 38
Saint-Martin, Louis Claude de, 146
St. Pölten, bishopric of, 41
St. Vitus' dance, 1
Salem (Upper Swabia), 14, 39, 41

INDEX

Salzburg, archbishop of, 16, 32, 38, 55–56
  see also Colloredo, Hieronymus Joseph Franz de Paula von
Sartori, Joseph Edler von, 53–55, 140, 165 n. 50
satire, German, 196 n. 1
Saxony, 33
Schleis, Bernhard Joseph, von Löwenfeld, 70–71, 78, 129
Schlözer, August Ludwig, 123
Schmid, Franz Joseph, 145
Schönborn dynasty, 37
Schubart, Christian Friedrich Daniel, 123, 129, 131–36, 202 n. 64
Schwab, Anselm, prince abbot of Salem, 39
Schwägelin, Maria Anna, 8, 11, 23
Scripture, historical understanding of, 92–94, 100, 106–8
  see also historical understanding; neologists
Seefeld, 144–45
Seiler, Georg Friedrich, 87
Semler, Johann Salomo, 15, 117
  on demonic possession, 87, 89–91
  and Lavater, 105–6
  and Lohmann, Anna Elisabeth, 106
  on Scripture, 92–94, 100–101
sensibility, cult of, 105
Shaftesbury, Anthony Ashley Cooper, Third Earl of, 118–19
Simon, Jordan, O. S. A., 73, 96
Singer, Maria Renata, 8–9, 56, 101
Sonnenfels, Aloys Wiener von, 95

Sprezzi (Spretti), count von, 43
Steinböckin, Johanna, 144
Sternbach, baron von, governor of Vorarlberg, 45, 49
Sterzinger, Don Ferdinand, O. Theat., 2, 15, 43, 49, 53, 73, 96–97, 128–30, 134
  on demonic possession, 100
  image of, 69
  on witchcraft, 94–95
Stoiber, Ubaldus, 56, 96
Strasbourg, bishop of, 38
suggestion, healing and, 85
  see also persuasion; placebo response
Sulzbach, 15, 27, 54, 146
Sunstein, Cass, 141
superstitions, 31, 41, 45, 47, 55, 66, 90–91, 93–94, 96, 107–17, 145
Swabia, ecclesiastical organization of, 36–37
Swabian-Franconian Circle, 45
Swedenborg, Emmanuel, 115
Swieten, Gerhard van, 46
Swieten, Gottfried van, 45
Swift, Jonathan, 133
Switzerland, 61
Sykes, Arthur Ashley, 91, 107, 110
sympathy, 3, 126, 135, 146

Tannen, Deborah, 141
Tartarotti, Girolamo, 95–96
Taves, Ann, 65
Teller, Wilhelm Abraham, 113
Teutonic knights, 38
Thyraeus, Petrus, S. J., 99
Trier, archbishop of, 38
  see also Febronius, Justinus;

Klemens Wenzeslaus, duke of Saxony
Tyrol, 61, 144–45

Überlingen, 39
Ulm, 123
Unterzell, 56
Upper Palatinate, 15
Upper Swabia, 14, 43, 49

Vienna, 17–18, 45–48, 95
 Concordat of (1448), 40
 demon posssession in, 163 n. 32
Vienna, archbishop of, 38, 46–48
Voltaire, François-Marie Arouet de, 16, 30, 133, 135, 141
Vorarlberg, 2, 12, 14, 45, 49

Wagstaff, John, 114
Walker, Mack, 32–33
Warburton, William, bishop of Gloucester, 114
Weber, Joseph, 145
Weber, Max, 27
Wettstein, Johann Jacob, 107–8
Wieland, Christoph Martin, 123
witchcraft
 ideas of, 9, 69, 73
 suspicions of, 8, 24
 trials, 1, 11, 13, 23, 26, 53, 56, 87–88, 97–98, 100
 "witchcraft war," Bavarian, 6–7, 15, 73, 94–95, 100, 183 n. 24
Wittelsbach dynasty, 37
Wittenberg, 88
Wolfegg, 14
 see also Maria Bernardina, countess
Wolfenbüttel, 109
Wolff, Christian, 95
Wolter, Johann Anton von, 44, 73
Württemberg, 145
Würzburg, 8
Würzburg, bishop of, 9, 37–38
Würzburg, university of, 94

Zapf, Georg Wilhelm, 66, 129, 136
Zedler, Johann Heinrich, 89
Zeiler, Johann Georg, 135
Zeiller, Johann Jacob, 144
Zimmermann, Johann Georg, 103–4, 188 n. 61
Zurich, 103